BYRON THE MAKER

By the same author

The Myth of the Bad Lord Byron (Old Forge Press, 1998)

Bright Darkness: The Poetry of Lord Byron Presented in the Context of his Life and Times (Nottingham Court Press, 1984)

In Search of Byron in England and Scotland (Old Forge Press, 1988)

This Means Mischief (Robert Hale, 1996)

Death and Deconstruction (Robert Hale, 1995)

The Desert and the Marketplace: Writings, Letters, Journals of Ursula Fleming, ed. A Fleming (Gracewing, 1995)

Sophie is Gone (Robert Hale, 1994)

There Goes Charlie: A Rural Murder (Collins Crime Club, 1990)

BYRON THE MAKER

Truth or Masquerade – An Exploration

Volume One: Byron in England

Anne Fleming

Book Guild Publishing
Sussex, England

First published in Great Britain in 2006 by
The Book Guild Ltd
25 High Street
Lewes, East Sussex
BN7 2LU

Typesetting in Times by
Keyboard Services, Luton, Bedfordshire

Printed in Great Britain by
Antony Rowe Ltd, Chippenham, Wiltshire

A catalogue record for this book is available from
The British Library

ISBN 1 84624 006 9

BYRON THE MAKER

Maker – one that makes; (archaic) – a poet

If the essence of poetry must be a *Lie* – throw it to the dogs – or banish it from your republic – as Plato would have done – he who can reconcile Poetry with truth and wisdom – is the one true '*Poet*' in its real sense – '*the Maker*' '*the Creator*'.

(Byron's Letter to John Murray Esqre, 1821)[1]

In one of the plates of *Los Caprichos*, originally intended as a frontispiece, Goya shows the artist asleep over his drawing-board, while nightmarish bats, owls and huge cats swarm up behind him. It is captioned *El sucho de la razón produce monstruos*. Byron has not a little in common with his great elder contemporary. They recall each other in their real feeling for gaiety and innocence; in their savage indignation against war and tyranny; in their honesty, more shattering than mere contempt, towards little men in great places; in their rejoicing in the sensuous beauty of women. Not least, both were sons of the Enlightenment, who, without denying the claims of the heart, believed passionately that 'the sleep of reason breeds monsters'.

M.K. Joseph, *Byron the Poet*[2]

Byron's years of sexual and geographic exploration made him the great and sympathetic reader of human motives that he was.

Jonathan David Gross, *Byron the Erotic Liberal*[3]

To my grandson, Oliver Sutton,
who has shown unflagging interest
in the production of this book.

CONTENTS

INTRODUCTION

This book is, I believe, at a rough guess, the 204th biography of Byron since his death. I have called it *Byron the Maker* because writing the life of a great poet requires a treatment which regards the works as not wholly other than the life. No-one could write a satisfactory life of Beethoven without understanding, and even perhaps foregrounding, the music.

Professor John Clubbe has asked for such a biography 'so that Byron's words may be as compelling for our time as Beethoven's music and for comparable reasons – because they exalt and challenge the human spirit.'[1]

I do not believe that *Byron the Maker* will achieve what Professor Clubbe is looking for, but it is written in answer to his request and I hope it is a step in the right direction. To those familiar with William Anderson's *Dante the Maker* I should make it clear that in echoing his title I am naturally making no comparison of *Byron the Maker* with that brilliant work, but I do invite comparison of Byron with Dante and this should raise no eyebrows.

Byron the Maker will work from the evidence in order to build (so far as possible) a true image of Byron the Poet just as a forensic scientist builds up the simulacrum of a living face from the bare bones of the skull when the flesh and skin and features have been obliterated. The forensic scientist neither wants, nor expects, a certain sort of face – a beautiful face or an ugly face. He wants the real face. So do I. This requires the reader to expunge all preconceived notions about the subject and be willing to start afresh.

In his book, *Gorky Park*, Martin Cruz Smith describes how the scientist builds the face and arrives at a mid-point which might have been the building of the features by a sculptor or a dissection of them by an anatomist.[2]

The biographer working on his subject may be either, or both, sculptor (artist) or anatomist (scientist) but, more important, he must be passionate in pursuit of the truth we owe the dead, whether the biographer and his readers find it palatable or not.

The story of Byron as man and poet is startling enough. It requires no suppression of evidence, no exaggeration, no distortion, no unfounded speculation, no unnecessary and definitive judgements, no overarching psychological or theoretical explanations. It does, however, need extensive and representative quotations.

Byron's character cannot easily be pinned down, studied and explained. His great friend (and biographer) Thomas Moore judged that his poetry and his life were so intermingled that it was not easy to distinguish the real from the fanciful in either.

It was unfortunate that the young woman Byron chose as his bride was wholly unable to distinguish between the fanciful and the real in Byron's discourse. It is not easy for the biographer. Byron is as changeable as our images of the moon. If he says something outrageous at one time he may say the opposite at another. And both may be true. His comprehension and grasp of a reality as protean as himself is all-encompassing. We should expect a biography to explore as far as possible the bewildering totality of Byron's character and life rather than abide by some master interpretation of it.

In 1822 he listed some comparisons made by his contemporaries:

> I have seen myself compared personally or poetically – in English, French, *German* (as interpreted to me), Italian and Portuguese within these nine years – to Rousseau – Goethe – Young – Aretine – Timon of Athens – 'An Alabaster Vase lighted up within', Satan – Shakespeare – Buonaparte – Tiberius – Aeschylus – Sophocles – Euripides – Harlequin – The Clown – Sternhold and Hopkins – to the Phantasmagoria – to Henry the 8th, to Chenier – to Mirabeau – to young R. Dallas (the school boy) to Michael Angelo – to Raphael – to a petit mâitre – to Diogenes, to Childe Harold – to Lara – to the Count in *Beppo* – to Milton – to Pope – to Dryden – to Burns – to Savage – to Chatterton – to 'Oft have I heard of thee my Lord Biron' in Shakespeare, to Churchill the poet – to Kean the Actor – to Alfieri etc. etc.[3]
>
> (*Detached Thoughts*, 1821)

To produce a clear-cut image of so many-faceted a character may prove impossible. It may be necessary to admit to being completely baffled by the complex nature of the poet who was acclaimed a genius at the age of twenty-four. We may have to settle for no more than a shimmering reflection of the clear-cut image we are trying to build,

This will be something, but it will not be enough. We can hope that the 205th biography will go a little further in pursuit of what Professor Clubbe and all his colleagues in the world of Byron studies require, but which is needed, not by professional Byronists, but by the informed general public to whom, unlike many of his contemporaries, Byron addressed his writing and the judgement on his life.

PREFACE

In telling the story of Byron's life and work my aim is to rely on nothing which is not supported by what appears to be reliable evidence. The sources I have used are the works of writers and scholars of integrity both familiar and recent who have researched Byron's life; of literary critics whose explanations of the poetry and the literary traditions surrounding Byron, have proved most useful to me; of those historians and letter-writers who have cast useful light on the time in which Byron lived; and, above all, the letters and journals, the poetry and the prose of Byron himself.

Where I provide insufficient detail for some readers the best bet remains the three-volume *Byron a Biography* by Leslie A. Marchand (1957), bearing in mind, however, that Professor Marchand was obliged by the rigid decorum of that period to censor his own work. By 1971 when he published the shorter version, *Byron a Portrait* he was able to speak freely on matters which were unmentionable in print in 1957. Marchand's work has the great advantage of scrupulous reliance on declared sources.

By far the most valuable source on Byron is his own words. To paraphrase them would be absurd. But there are pitfalls of which the reader should be made aware throughout. Particularly in his early days Byron is apt to strike dramatic attitudes which did not necessarily represent his true feelings but, confusingly, sometimes do; in common with many other young men in Regency society he often went in for 'bamming and humming', that is, talking nonsense so earnestly as to hoodwink the onlooker into taking seriously what was meant in jest. Another Byronic trait to look out for is his habit of boasting of his own transgressions in such exaggerated language as to constitute a *fanfaron des vices*. His friends and his half-sister knew him well enough to judge how much of this trumpeting to believe. Others, including Lady Byron, did not.

M.K. Joseph starts his book on *Byron the Poet* with a quotation from William J. Calvert – a watchword for the wary biographer:

> It is impossible not to take Byron seriously, and it is disastrous to take him literally.[1]

ACKNOWLEDGEMENTS

I am particularly indebted to one of Britain's most generous, brilliant and well-loved Byronists, Bernard Beatty of the University of Liverpool, Academic Editor of *The Byron Journal*, who kindly found time to read an early draft of *Byron the Maker*, advised, rebuked and made suggestions, thereby re-shaping and honing the text. His encouragement and praise were invaluable. He is, of course, in no way responsible for any shortcomings which may have arisen since then.

I am most grateful to that most amiable and clubbable of bookmen, Derek Wise, for his generosity in opening his collection to me, ferrying books to and fro, drawing my attention to some obscure nineteenth-century publications and tracking down books on the internet.

My thanks go to the staff of the Public Library in Haywards Heath who gave me the impression that I had both an English and an American University Library on my doorstep which could produce recent publications from both sides of the Atlantic at great speed.

I must thank Deborah Fletcher who typed the text from my handwriting, dealt patiently with second thoughts, alterations and lost pages, and said she couldn't wait to turn the page.

I am grateful to Christine Padmore who kindly took over when Deborah had to withdraw, and brought her splendid efficiency and understanding into play.

My thanks go to all the writers and scholars whose works on Byron I have enjoyed and learned from over the years, in particular, to Leslie Marchand and Doris Langley Moore, and to those from whom I have quoted in this volume. Among these are Jerome J. McGann, Michael Cooke, M.K. Joseph, Paul Elledge, G. Wilson

Knight, Jeffery Vail, Jonathan David Gross, Louis Crompton, William St Clair, David Erdman, Ian Gilmour, Peter Gunn, Michael and Melissa Bakewell.

I would like to thank the editors of *The Byron Journal*, Liverpool University Press, and the writers of articles in the *Journal* from whom I have quoted, namely William St Clair, C.J. Tyerman, David Woodhouse, Graham Pont and Philip Shaw. The *Journal* is an invaluable resource for Byronists.

My thanks go to several people who have encouraged me over the years; Michael Foot, Doris Langley Moore, Elizabeth Longford, Peter W. Graham, Vincent Newey, William St Clair, Mrs Elma Dangerfield, Michael Rees, J. Drummond Bone and Vivian, Maureen O'Connor, Therèse Tessier, Malcolm and Mary Kelsall, Barbara and Jim Jackson, Peter Cochran, Val Doulton, Maureen Crisp and Ken Purslow, Ridley Burnett and Michael Sidney (who published my first book on Byron).

Every book ever published on Byron owes a debt to the firm of John Murray, beginning with the original John Murray, who not only allowed the young Byron to criticise important and influential people and institutions in *Childe Harold's Pilgrimage*, but stood by him for most of *Don Juan* and, on learning that the bailiffs had moved in and that Byron was preparing to sell his books, sent him a large cheque and offered to sell the copyrights of the poems for his benefit. Byron refused to accept such generosity, but he never forgot it.

Finally, I am grateful to Isabel Quigly for many kindnesses and for recommending The Book Guild to me. In this independent publisher I have met with unequalled enthusiasm, energy, efficiency and patience, and the employment of discrimination and good judgement on every issue; qualities certainly displayed by Joanna Bentley, the Managing Editor, who dealt with the unexpected external tribulations which beset the preparation of the typescript, and Gareth Vaughan, my dauntless copy-editor. I am most grateful to Carol Biss, the Managing Director, who took on *Byron the Maker* and offered the author both encouragement and guidance.

1

SCOTLAND

... my heart flies to my head, –
As 'Auld Lang Syne' brings Scotland, one and all,
Scotch plaids, Scotch snoods, the blue hills and clear streams,
All my boy feelings, all my gentler dreams.[1]

Byron is not usually counted among the Scottish poets although he himself claimed to be 'half a Scot by birth and bred/A whole one'.[2] Nor is he thought of as anything but an English poet in England although he was born a Gordon and spent the first ten years of his life in Scotland.

On his father's side Byron was descended from the Norman Byrons or Buruns who came over from France with William the Conqueror and received Newstead Abbey and its lands from Henry VIII some centuries later, after the dissolution of the monasteries. At the Restoration of Charles II Sir John Byron of Newstead was granted the Barony of Rochdale as his reward for commanding a cavalry regiment during the Civil War (with marked lack of success) and loyally accompanying his King into exile.

It was said that the family which accepted the Abbey taken from the monks would suffer only misfortune as a result. The Third Baron lost most of his fortune and the Fifth Baron was tried before his peers for killing a neighbour in a duel. The legend which has been widely accepted until recently is that the fifth Lord Byron, henceforth known as 'The Wicked Lord', became a recluse after the duel and began to lay waste his estate to spite his son and heir, cutting down great oak trees and slaughtering two thousand head of deer. His motives, it appears, were not inimical to his son but the result was the same. His son died young and his grandson was killed at Calvi and when the Wicked Lord died the ten-year-old George Gordon Byron, who was living in Aberdeen, succeeded to the Barony and the despoiled estates.

Colourful as the history of the Byrons might be it could not compare with the goings on of the poet's maternal ancestors, the Gordons of Gight, lairds of Gight Castle which stands in the valley of the River Ythan thirty miles north of Aberdeen.

> My mother was precise on points of genealogy like all the Aristocratical Scots. She had a long list of ancestors – like Sir Lucius O'Trigger – most of them to be found in the old Scottish Chronicles – in arms and doing mischief.[3]
>
> (Byron to John Murray, 25 October 1820)

The first Laird of Gight was the third son of the Earl of Huntley and his second wife, Arabella Stuart, daughter of James I of Scotland. He swapped his lands at Aboyne with his elder brother in return for Gight in 1490. He fell at Flodden. One of his sons and a son-in-law fell at Pinkie. His grandson took part in the murder of Wallenstein and was executed. In 1592 John Gordon of Gight was hanged at Edinburgh for the murder of Lord Moray. The carnage went on – foray, poison, siege and murder – till one Laird drowned in the River Ythan and his son drowned himself in the Bath Canal. In the (unsurprising) absence of a male heir, his daughter, Catherine Gordon, became mistress of Gight. In 1785 she went to Bath to find herself a husband. There she met Captain John Byron, a charming, handsome, French-educated, Guards officer who had recently sold out, had lost his first wife (also an heiress) and who married Catherine Gordon six weeks later.

Catherine Gordon was a lively young woman with a tendency to corpulence (a characteristic inherited by her son), a warm heart and an unbridled temper. She gave her feckless husband unconditional love. All he wanted from her was access to her fortune. Scottish pipers were soon playing this ballad about the heiress of Gight and her Sassenach fortune-hunter:

> Oh whaur are ye ga'en, bonny Miss Gordon?
> Oh whaur are ye ga'en, sae bonny and braw?
> Ye've married, ye've married wi' Johnny Byron
> To squander the lands o' Gight awa'.

At the time of her marriage Catherine Gordon owned salmon fisheries, timber and a small fortune in the Bank at Aberdeen as well as the lands and Castle of Gight. Her husband owned nothing but debts and a monumental facility for amassing more and more of them. Catherine's friends and kinsmen and advisors, Captain William Abercromby of Glassaugh, Colonel Duff of Fetteresso, Mr John Leslie, Captain Alexander Davidson, Mr Russell of Aden, were not present in Bath to see that proper marriage settlements were made. The result was that Catherine's fortune was at the mercy of every one of her husband's creditors. It was somewhat ironic that Catherine's kinsmen had plotted to get her to Bath to protect her from possible Scottish fortune hunters.

The young couple came to live at Gight in the summer of 1785. Soon uneasy rumours were circulating as far as Aberdeen. Gight was said to be the scene of wild extravagance: guests every night for the reels and they never left off at midnight even on the eve of the Sabbath; quantities of brandy and wine brought up from the cellars; foreign kickshaws served at table; a French novel (*La Nouvelle Héloise*) lying about for all to see and the needy husband out and about using his wife's funds to buy horses and hounds. Worst of all, Jack Byron was selling off his wife's lands. Advertisements went up: 'To be Sett. The Mains of Gight. Enquiries of Mr John Byron Gordon of Gight.'

On the banks of the River Ythan was the Gight Heronry where herons had nested for hundreds of years in the reeds. An old Gordon saying ran:

> When the herons leave the tree
> The Lairds of Gight will landless be.

The third Earl of Aberdeen was walking with his factor when they saw the herons from Gight come flying in. A year later the earl bought Gight Castle and its lands for the sum of £17,850 most of which went straight to John Byron's creditors.

The adult Byron wrote to his friend and banker, Douglas Kinnaird, before setting off on his last journey to Greece:

> My Dear Kinnaird
> My mother's estate of Gight was sold to the former Lord Aberdeen many years ago – before I was born I believe – I have always preferred

> my mother's family – for its royalty – and if I could buy it back – I would consent even at a reduction of income. – It is in Scotland.[4]
>
> (To Douglas Kinnaird, R[avenn]a, 2 February 1821)

Looking back, Byron must have forgotten that he often took issue with his mother over which of the two families was the grander:

> My Mother, who was as haughty as Lucifer with her descent from the Stuarts, and her right line, from the *old Gordons*, *not the Seton Gordons*, as she disdainfully termed the Ducal branch always reminding me how superior *her* Gordons were to the southern Byrons ... notwithstanding our Norman, and always masculine descent.[5]

In 1787 Captain William Abercromby wrote from Hampshire to his kinsmen in Scotland that John Byron had hired a vessel and fled to France for debt. Mrs Byron, 'poor unhappy woman', was 'big with bairn' and must soon follow him. For a time the Byrons lived at Chantilly, the town near Paris dominated by the Château of the Condé. There Mrs Byron nursed her little step daughter, Augusta, through a serious illness. Then, knowing that John Byron was unfit to have the care of a child, she took Augusta back with her to England to her maternal grandmother, Lady Holderness, and set to work to find lodgings for herself in London in preparation for her confinement.

George Gordon Byron was born in a back room on 22 January 1788 at no. 16 Holles Street. He was baptised at St Marylebone Church and his kinsmen, Colonel Duff of Fetteresso and the Duke of Gordon, stood sponsors. Within two years Mrs Byron had moved to Scotland. Byron spent most of his first ten years in Aberdeen with forays to Banff and Deeside. John Byron, who had continued sponging on his wife in London, followed her to Scotland to get more money from her. They quarrelled violently and took separate lodgings, meeting only to drink tea with each other. The child was three years old when his father went back to France where he died at Valenciennes in 1791.

The little boy who might have been brought up in feudal grandeur at Gight Castle, neighbour to Lord Aberdeen, served by his own people and pipers, presiding over the yearly Gight Games when the prettiest girl was dubbed the Rose of Gight, lived instead with his mother (her income now reduced to £150 a year) in a flat on Broad Street, Aberdeen. This may have been no bad thing, for Aberdeen provided him with influences which affected his whole life. Aberdeen first formed his ideas on books, politics, war, and love and instilled into him a certain superstition that he never quite lost, a love of the sea, scepticism about medical men, a love of the theatre, a love-hate relationship with religion, and the common touch – an ability to get on with people of all sorts.

Aberdeen was no provincial backwater. It boasted two colleges, one of which, the Marischal, though rebuilt since Byron's day, still stands in the same place, a little further down Broad Street than the house, long gone, where Mrs Byron lived with her 'wee cruikit deevil' Geordie Byron. The boy had been born with a deformed foot which gave him pain when he walked so that he was never easily able to walk far. Efforts were made to cure it by bandaging, special boots, and a wooden contraption which hurt abominably and did no good. He was lame all his life and suffered much anguish over his deformity.

The Professors from the Marischal gave public lectures. There were three circulating libraries and several bookshops, among them Brown at the sign of the Homer's head, and Angus, whose catalogue may still be seen at Aberdeen Central Library. As a small boy Byron was sent to Bodsy Bowers' little school where he had to repeat his lessons by rote. He failed to learn to read by this method. Mrs Byron then put him in the hands of two excellent teachers from the Marischal. Mr Ross, a gentle scholarly clergyman, inspired Byron with a passion for Roman history. Somewhere he acquired an equal passion for the history of Turkey. Once he had learned to read he read voraciously but he was more interested in proving his prowess at sports than in study.

A comment on his education (or lack of it) was confided to his *Journal*:

> I acquired this handwriting, which I can hardly read myself, under the fair copies of Mr Duncan of the same city (Aberdeen); I don't think he could plume himself much upon my progress.[6]

Aberdeen formed his views on politics. *The Aberdeen Journal* was positively cosmopolitan. Local events got scant coverage. Aberdonians were glued to accounts of the stirring happenings in France: first the Revolution and later the rise of Napoleon. Mrs

Byron was brought up by her grandmother, Mrs Duff, cousin to the Earl of Fife, who was known as Lady Gight and was of the Whig persuasion. Mrs Byron read the papers intelligently, thought herself quite a Democrat (a term of opprobrium in that period) and held that the French king would have behaved as cruelly as the Jacobins if he had succeeded in crushing the Revolution.

Something of the commonsense spirit of this verdict was later echoed by her son in *Don Juan* though he was never 'quite a Democrat' like his mother:

> I wish men to be free
> As much from mobs as kings – from you as me.[7]

Byron attended the Grammar School which was founded before 1256 and was the oldest in the British Isles. When they were not involved in the daily grind of Latin, Latin and then more Latin, the boys romped in the playground, playing marbles, hand ball and peg tops, fighting and racing each other. This happy rough and tumble may have given Byron that common touch that made him so beloved of his friends from all walks of life, especially at Cambridge:

> This evening a large assortment of *Jockies*, *Gamblers*, *Boxers*, *Authors*, *Parsons* and *Poets* sup with me.[8]

From the grammar school yard the boys used to watch the volunteers marching by in their brave, brightly-coloured uniforms with drums and trumpets. This may have contributed to Byron's enthusiasm for military glory which he never lost, though he later confined it to wars of liberation and, inconsistently, grew to abhor the horrors of war and to blame those who caused others to engage in it, for their stupidity and indifference. Looking back on his childhood he remembered 'My earliest dreams were all martial.' The young Byron told his friends:

> I will, some day or other raise a troop of men which shall be dressed all in black and ride on black horses! They shall be called 'Byron's Blacks' and you will hear of their performing prodigies of valour![9]

Having learned to 'hate licensed murder' the adult Byron would have smiled at the naïvete of his younger self:

[There are] ways to benefit mankind as true
Perhaps as shooting them at Waterloo.[10]

Even as a child Byron valued courage highly, but he was not immune from fear. The verse on the Brig o' Balgounie by Thomas the Rhymer is said to have inspired superstitious terror in the boy as he rode over the bridge:

Brig o' Balgounie
Wight is thy wa'
Wi' a wife's ae son
And a mare's ae foal
Down shalt thou fa'

Byron was the only son of his mother and he knew by heart this verse. He was afraid that he and his pony would fall down into the deep pools below the bridge and be drowned. Byron dreaded his thirty sixth year as he had been told that the years 1816 and 1824 would be dangerous for him. The Brig o' Balgounie may still be standing but 1816 was the year of Byron's downfall and 1824 the year of his death. We may smile at these correspondences but Byron would not have done.

It was perhaps at Banff that Byron conceived his distrust of the doctors of his day, later to be increased by the quack in Nottingham who made him suffer by ignorant attempts to cure his lameness. His doctor at Aberdeen, however, was perfectly sensible about the case and corresponded with the famous surgeon Dr John Hunter, who had special boots made for the child. He remained lame.

While staying with the minister and his wife at the manse in Banff Byron climbed a tree in the garden and, reaching for some fine pears hanging over the wall, tumbled to the ground. His mother called in 'the old red-nosed doctor' as Byron described him, and the child was told he was to be bled. Byron had seen the doctor bleed his nurse and he was determined not to submit to the procedure. Scoldings from Mrs Byron had no effect. Kicking and screaming, he told the old man, 'I'll pull your nose.' The doctor departed in high dudgeon, first instructing Mrs Byron to put the boy to bed, give him nothing but water and gruel and administer drops twice a day. Byron threw the medicine out of the window, and his mother (who alternately spoiled and ranted at him, but always adored him) let him get up and gave him a whole plate of bread and butter instead of *brochan*.

Mrs Byron sent her lame son to the dancing class in Peacock Close where, every week, he saw his cousin Mary Duff. He was seven, she eight. Byron fell desperately in love with the little girl and wrote later of his restlessness and sleeplessness and how he tormented his mother's maid into writing to her for him as he was unable to write himself. 'How the deuce could this occur so early? Where could it originate? I certainly had no sexual feelings for years afterwards'.[11] Thomas Moore regards this episode as significant for Byron's development as a poet. In a note he writes, 'Dante we know was but nine years old when, at the May Festival, he saw and fell in love with Beatrice, and Alfieri, himself a precocious lover, considers such early sensibility to be an unerring sign of a soul formed for the fine arts.'[12]

Moore does not consider the scenes of wildness and grandeur (Lachin-y-Gair, Morven, Deeside – where Byron had wandered in his early years) were in any way an influence on his poetry. Experiences such as these 'no more *make* the poet than – to apply an illustration of Byron's own, – the honey can be said to make the bee.'[13] Taken literally, this judgement cannot be denied, but one has only to bear in mind Byron's reaction to similar scenes in Switzerland and even at Malvern to conclude that wandering in the Highlands as a boy must have contributed to the development of the poetic imagination which imbued both *Manfred* and parts of the third Canto of *Childe Harold's Pilgrimage* with the majesty and horror of high mountains.

The husband of Byron's former nurse, Agnes Gray, told Moore, after Byron's death, that the small boy was always inquisitive and puzzling about religion. Byron himself claimed to have been cudgelled to church for the first ten years of his life. Agnes Gray made him recite the psalms and so did her sister May. But May crept into his bed and sexually abused him before he was ten and this gave him a somewhat jaundiced view of both women and religion. He always respected those who were sincerely religious but he loathed hypocrisy. As a child he experienced Calvinistic gloom and this perhaps explains his later preference for Catholicism and his decision to make his illegitimate daughter, Allegra, a Roman Catholic. But he had no patience with squabbling clergymen of any persuasion, deploring the behaviour of 'seventy-two villainous sects tearing each other to pieces for the love of the Lord and hatred of each other'.[14]

His characteristic attitude to religion was:

> I deny nothing but doubt everything.[15]

Wandering round the harbour and along the shores of Aberdeen Bay Byron grew to love the sea. He swam in the Don and found that he was equal to boys with two perfect feet. He learned not to fear the water and this early familiarity with it explains his calmness when in peril at sea. Imagery and descriptions of the sea are to be found throughout the poetry:

> In the wind's eye I have sailed and sail; but for
> The stars I own my telescope is dim.
> But at the least I have shunned the common shore,
> And leaving land far out of sight, would skim
> The Ocean of Eternity.[16]

At the age of nine Byron was taken to the play, the beginning of a long association with the theatre. We know of Byron attending plays and operas in London, Nottingham, Brighton and Venice, where he loved the Fenice Theatre. He joined the management of Drury Lane. He was often moved to tears and sometimes taken ill by a particularly moving or dramatic performance. In Aberdeen he threw himself rather too literally into a performance of *The Taming of the Shrew*:

PETRUCCHIO: Good Lord, how bright and goodly shines the moon!
KATHERINE: The moon! The sun: it is not moonlight now.
PETRUCCHIO: I say it is the moon that shines so bright!
KATHERINE: I know it is the sun that shines so bright!
PETRUCCHIO: Now by my mother's son, and that's myself,
It shall be moon, or star, or what I list,
Or ere I journey to your father's house
HORATIO: Say as he says, or we shall never go.
KATHERINE: Forward, I pray, since we have come so far,
And be it moon, or sun, or what you please,
And if you please to call it a rush-candle,
Henceforth I vow it shall be so for me.
PETRUCCHIO: I say it is the moon!
KATHERINE: I know it is the moon!

PETRUCCHIO:	Nay then, you lie, it is the blessed sun.
KATHERINE:	Then, God be praised, it is the blessed sun.

Here the young Byron jumped up from his place crying out in a fury, 'But *I* say it is the *moon*, sir', which caused consternation on stage and in the audience.

Life was to change for Byron. It was only by chance that Mrs Byron learned in 1794 that her son's cousin, heir to the Wicked Lord, had been killed at Calvi. No-one had taken the trouble to inform her that her small boy was now heir to the Barony, to Newstead Abbey and all its lands. Four years later the Wicked Lord was dead.

When the Headmaster of the Grammar School broke the news to him that he was now Sixth Baron Byron of Rochdale, the boy's reaction was 'Must the other boys know?', and when his name was read out at Assembly next morning as Georgius Dominus de Byron he burst into tears. But he was not so upset as to be unable to deal intelligently with the change in his circumstances, agreeing with his mother that although neither of them could see any change in him since he became a Lord everybody behaved very differently to him now, even the Headmaster, who offered him wine and cakes to celebrate his accession to the peerage. For Mrs Byron it was more honourable to be descended from the kings of Scotland than to be an English Lord and own wide lands. All the same, she proceeded to deal briskly with her son's new situation, packing up their belongings and organizing a 'Sale of Furniture Belonging to Genteel Persons who are leaving the Country'. The sale fetched no more than £74 17s 7d and with this, and little more, in her pocket Mrs Byron set out for Nottingham with the ten-year-old Peer of the Realm and his nurse.

Notes

1. *Letters and Journals of Lord Byron with Notices of his Life* by Thomas Moore is the chief source for Byron's early years. Much as he loved Byron, Moore does not hesitate to offer criticism where criticism is due. His biography is no work of hagiography. It is judged by William St Clair 'one of the great biographies of the nineteenth century'.[1] He adds that its success was well deserved: 'He was a careful and thorough researcher – he took the trouble to interview Byron's friends and to borrow and copy as many original documents as he could find.'

Jeffery Vail agrees with St Clair, defending Moore's biography from criticism by Joseph W. Reed for being insufficiently theoretical. Vail demurs: '... the lack of an "organising structure" of the kind Reed expects in a biography is really a triumph of Moore's realism and his respect for the disorderliness of human life, especially in the case of Byron.'[2]

Moore refrained from imposing his own theoretical explanations and patterns on a life as lacking in any imposed structure as *Don Juan.*

2. Until the publication of the researches of John Beckett in his interesting and useful book, *Byron and Newstead Abbey. The Aristocrat and the Abbey*, which treats Byron not as poet but as custodian of Newstead Abbey, it was believed that the fifth Lord Byron stripped his estates of timber and deer to spite his son because the young man had ruined his plans for retrieving his fortunes by refusing to marry the heiress picked out for him by his father. The legend of the so-called 'Wicked Lord' also had him so vilified and traumatised over the unorthodox duel in the course of which he killed his neighbour, William Chaworth, in a dark room at the Star and Garter Inn in London, that he became a recluse, hiding himself away at Newstead.

   Beckett shows that if the fifth baron became a recluse it was only in the final years of his life. Until then he continued to plan for his estates, dividing part of his lands into new farms and employing as steward a sensible man called Daws who managed the land efficiently and was on good terms with the tenants, from whom he regularly collected the rents.

   When his son left the chosen bride at the altar and ran off to Gretna Green to marry his cousin Juliana, daughter of the John Byron who won fame in the navy as 'Foulweather Jack', and became an admiral, Lord Byron was angry but John Beckett shows that he was reconciled with his son within a few years.

   The fifth baron's financial arrangements appear to have vied with those of his successor for recklessness, extravagance and muddle. The result was an estate stripped of many of its assets. This was the condition of Newstead Abbey on his death when, the heir having died in London, his son having been killed at Calvi, the house and lands went to the little boy from Aberdeen.

2

NEWSTEAD ABBEY

'Before the mansion lay a lucid Lake.'[1]

Moore spoke to many who knew and remembered the young Byron in Scotland and from these researches we have some idea of the character of the child who arrived at Newstead Abbey in 1798:

> That as a child his temper was violent, or rather sullenly passionate, is certain. Even when in petticoats, he showed the same uncontrollable spirit with his nurse, which he afterwards exhibited when an author, with his critics. Being angrily reprimanded by her, one day, for having soiled or torn a new frock in which he had just been dressed, he got into one of his 'silent rages' (as he himself has described them) seized the frock in both hands, rent it from top to bottom, and stood in sullen stillness, setting his censurer and her wrath at defiance.

Moore points out that such tantrums were encouraged by the example of his mother 'who frequently, it is said, proceeded to the same extremities with her cap gowns etc.' (Mrs Byron was volatile, noisy and, on occasion, violent, but Moore ignores her tragic situation and the courage with which she endured it.) Moore goes on: '... There was in his disposition, as appears from the concurrent testimony of nurses, tutors and all who were employed about him, a mixture of affectionate sweetness and playfulness, by which it was impossible not to be attached; and which rendered him then, as in his riper years, easily manageable by those who loved and understood him sufficiently to be at once gentle and firm enough for the task.'[2] From Byron's former schoolfellows in Aberdeen Moore learned that he was:

> a lively, warm-hearted, high-spirited boy – passionate and resentful, but affectionate and companionable with his schoolfellows – to a remarkable degree adventurous and fearless and, as one of them significantly expressed it, 'always more ready to give a blow than to take one.'[3]

Moore felt that the boy came into his inheritance too early:

> Had he been left to struggle on for 10 years longer, as plain George Byron, there can be little doubt that his character would have been, in many respects, the better for it.[4]

Byron spent his early years not in aristocratic but in middle class circles. This gave rise to anxiety about his status exemplified by his reply to an Aberdonian who told him she looked forward to hearing his future speeches in the House of Commons. The child showed that he had thought about his future inheritance and was fully aware of its significance. 'I hope not', he told the lady. 'If you read any speeches of mine, it will be in the House of Lords.'[5]

The sudden acquisition of wealth (as he supposed), status, ownership of a great mansion and some of the servants of the fifth baron, the lands and all that went with them, was confusing enough for a boy of ten with an exalted notion of the dignity and honour pertaining to his new rank. The disappointment which followed was heart-rending. It was not long before he would have to reconcile himself to spending the next few years away from his magically beautiful new possession with its lakes and monastic ruins, vast overgrown gardens and pleasure grounds, the two forts built by the Wicked Lord for fake naval manoeuvres on the lakes, and the kindly old servant, Joe Murray, who showed him round his new domain and was dearly loved by Byron for the rest of Joe's life.

The fifth baron had taken no notice of his heir. Mrs Byron received no advice from the Byron family about the future of her son. She dealt with this situation by hiring a London lawyer, John Hanson, to manage the financial affairs and other arrangements which must now be made for the boy. Everything she did was for the future welfare of her son. Without friends, without family, without funds, she gave little or no thought to her own status and welfare and was always ready to sacrifice provision for herself to that of her son.

Mr and Mrs John Hanson travelled from London to meet the new arrivals at Newstead Abbey, treating them with the utmost kindness. Hanson had familiarised himself with the situation of the estate. He explained that repairs were urgently needed (which they could see for themselves, since parts of the roof had collapsed, cattle were stabled in the hall and hay was stored in the monks' refectory) and little money was available to pay for them. The rents had not been raised for years in spite of the marked increase in prosperity of the tenant farmers. This had to be put in hand and as soon as possible. The Abbey and its lands would be let until Byron reached his majority. For the time being Mrs Byron and her son could move into a few rooms, using what sticks of furniture remained.

Byron's lameness prevented him from exploring his new domain on foot so a pony was borrowed from the Parkyns family in Nottingham who were related to the widow of the brother of the fifth Baron. Mrs Parkyns lived with her sister, Byron's great aunt the Hon. Frances Byron, and her own two daughters. Mrs Byron was able to indulge in quiet visits to these ladies – not the most exciting of social lives but probably more congenial than she had expected.

When the weather became colder and the roofs let in the autumn rain Byron and his mother moved to Nottingham where Byron was often left in the care of May Gray while his mother did what she could to deal with the disorder of Newstead. During this time Byron's deformed foot was subjected to unavailing but extremely painful treatment by an unskilled practitioner in Nottingham.

It was at this early age that the boy began to try to take control (as far as was possible for a young child) of his own destiny. He insisted on being allowed to go to lessons with the tutor of the Misses Parkyns, Dummer Rogers. He wrote to his mother:

> I am astonished that you do not acquiesce in this scheme... I recommend this to you because if some plan of this kind is not adopted I shall be called or rather branded with the name of dunce, which you know I could never bear, I beg you will consider this plan seriously and I will lend it all the assistance in my power...[6]
>
> (Nottingham, 13 March 1799)

This new tendency of Byron to think and plan for himself would cause violent disputes with his mother who was often in the right of it but tactless in making her will felt.

In these early days of their long relationship Hanson exerted himself energetically in the management of the affairs of the Byrons and became very fond of the boy. Later he was to become almost criminally negligent and both Catherine Byron and her son were exasperated, tormented and finally deprived of funds as a result of his dilatory handling of their affairs.

Now Hanson went back to London to search for necessary papers connected with Byron's inheritance and, calling on the Earl of Carlisle (who was a kinsman of Byron through the marriage of Isabella, the wayward sister of the fifth baron, to the fourth Earl of Carlisle), he persuaded the somewhat reluctant nobleman to act as joint guardian to the young peer together with himself and Catherine Byron. Lord Carlisle was already playing the part of kindly and hospitable guardian to Byron's half-sister, Augusta Byron, daughter of John Byron by his first wife. Later Hanson took the boy to London to meet his guardian and arrange what was to be done about the deformed foot and whether the boy should be sent to school to prepare him for entrance to Harrow. The Earl was persuaded to agree to a course of treatment for the foot by a distinguished London practitioner, Dr Baillie, and to the plan of sending Byron to Dr Glennie's Academy in Dulwich.

Now the unfortunate effect of Byron's early enoblement became apparent. Moore remarks that 'Lord Byron's high notions of rank were, in his boyish days, so little disguised or softened down as to draw upon him at times the ridicule of his companions.' He was not unpopular at Dr Glennie's but was sometimes mockingly referred to as 'the old English baron.'[7] Mrs Byron took lodgings in London to be near her boy and often insisted on taking him home for visits, interrupting his studies, which were somewhat half-hearted, though he read widely among many of the books in Dr Glennie's study. Remonstrance by Dr Glennie, who disapproved of Mrs Byron's Scottish accent and untidy appearance, brought noisy outbursts of wrath from her which were commented on by Byron's schoolfellows, much to his humiliation.

Mr Hanson invited the boy to spend part of his holidays at his home, a practice that was repeated on several occasions while Byron was at Harrow, and introduced the boy to his four children thus providing him with his first experience of family life. On leaving Harrow Byron wrote a poem entitled 'Childish Recollections' some lines of which express movingly the pleasure the lonely child must have experienced in joining the Hanson household. It is, however, likely that the young poet was thinking not of the Hansons who welcomed him into their family, but of the Howards, who did not:

> friendship will be doubly dear
> To one, who thus for kindred hearts must roam,
> And seek abroad, the love denied at home...
> Stern Death forbade my orphan youth to share
> The tender guidance of a Father's care;
> Can Rank or e'en a Guardian's name supply
> The love, which glistens in a Father's eye?
> For this, can Wealth, or Title's sound atone,
> Made, by a Parent's early loss, my own?
> What Brother springs a Brother's love to seek?
> What Sister's gentle kiss has prest my cheek?[8]
> (From 'Childish Recollections', 1807)

Mrs Byron could have instructed her son in how much 'tender guidance' he might have received from John Byron had 'Stern Death' spared him. Soon after Byron's arrival in London a 'father's tender care' was in fact extended to him by John Hanson. Byron asked Hanson to tell his mother to send May Gray away. She had taken to beating him till his bones ached and bringing undesirable drinking companions into his room in Nottingham and at Newstead. He also told the kindly lawyer (but this was never repeated to Mrs Byron) that May Gray used to get into bed with him and, as Hanson described it, 'play tricks with his person'. Hanson advised Mrs Byron that so able and honourable a boy as her son, should not be allowed to suffer ill-treatment from a servant.

Mrs Byron reluctantly dismissed May Gray before Byron came home for the Christmas holidays. Later Byron wrote of this episode:

> My passions were developed very early – so early – that few would believe me – if I were to state the period – and the facts which accompanied it.'[9]
>
> (*Detached Thoughts*, 1821)

Little account has been taken by biographers of this plain statement of Byron's. Yet nowadays the sexual abuse of a boy of nine would result in counselling, psychotherapy, and possibly the intervention of the police. Recent biographers have been more diligent in uncovering charges against Byron than emphasising actions perpetrated against him for which formidable evidence exists.

It was soon decided by Lord Carlisle in consultation with Mr Hanson that, as he was not making satisfactory progress at Dr Glennie's establishment, Byron's going to Harrow should no longer be delayed and, at the age of thirteen and a half, he was delivered by Mr Hanson in the spring of 1801 to the care of Dr Joseph Dury who had been a most successful Headmaster there for the last 16 years.

3

HARROW

I have been idle *and I certainly ought not to talk in Church. But I have never done a mean action at this school to him or any one.*[1]

The boy who rode up Harrow Hill with Mr Hanson to join his new schoolfellows was described to Thomas Moore by Dr Drury after his death: 'I found that a wild mountain colt had been submitted to my management... But there was mind in his eye ... he might be led by a silken string ... rather than by a cable.'[2] In his extremely useful paper on 'Byron's Harrow' (later developed into a book), C.J. Tyerman (who, as a master at Harrow for many years is steeped in the history of the school) invites his readers to compare what Joseph Drury told Thomas Moore with what he wrote about Byron privately when Byron was at the school. Moore heard nothing of the boy's 'negligence', 'childish pranks', 'idleness and indifference', 'animal spirits' and 'want of judgement'.[3] Nevertheless, Drury was kind to the boy, putting him into the care of his son, Henry, so that he need not go straight into a form where his backwardness would be apparent to his schoolmates.

After various arguments with Henry Drury, Byron wrote to his mother in great distress refusing to have anything more to do with him. (It is typical of Byron that Henry Drury later became a friend he kept up with long after Harrow.)

Had I *stole* ... his language could not have been more outrageous, what must the boys think of me? ... better let him take away my Life than ruin my *character* – I have been *idle* and I certainly ought not to talk

> in church, But I have never done a mean action at this school to him or any*one*... If you love me you will now show it.[4]
>
> (Harrow on the Hill, Sunday, 1 May 1803)

Instead of punishing the boy Dr Drury sensibly dealt with the problem by transferring him to the care of another master.

Henry Drury, we are told by Paul Elledge, was a big man and a fierce, intimidating figure. It took courage for Byron to oppose him. Elledge points out that Byron felt that the masters, including Henry Drury, and some of the boys, despised him for his lameness and his poverty. This may have been his motivation for attempting to shine at the Speech Day recitals in his later years at Harrow. His success in his first appearance at the event, playing the part of King Latinus in the *Aeneid*, was, according to Elledge, a pivotal occasion. Dr Drury's praise delighted Byron and seemed to give his approval to the prospect of a parliamentary career for his turbulent pupil. Byron had come to regard Dr Drury as a father figure by this time. But to begin with Byron was bored and rebellious and was regarded as a difficult and unruly boy.

Tyerman gives an account of:

> ...formal teaching of the classics at Harrow (about all that was taught), which was 'monotonous and endlessly repetitive'... Learning was something that largely occurred outside the form room. It was as social figures, models of behaviour and tone, rather than as pedagogues that masters were respected or not... The syllabus was exclusively classical and based heavily on the Eton system. Founded on Latin, in particular Latin verse, the curriculum, apart from the customary obeisance to Virgil, displayed a typically eighteenth-century preference for the convivial, speculative and satirical Horace, a preference that, for all his later disdain, may be thought to have left a profound influence on Byron's poetic style and tone. Harrow was unusual in the prominence it gave to Greek... So Byron read Greek tragedies as well as Homer. Throughout, the emphasis lay on verse, as an exemplar of grammar and vocabulary and a model of how to express thoughts in a disciplined style.[5]

Byron's first year at Harrow was turbulent. He wrote in 1820, 'I always hated Harrow until the last year and a half.'[6] He fought those who mocked him for his deformity. He fought to protect younger or weaker boys. He fought later on to protect his bust of Napoleon. The explanation of this exaggerated pugnacity which best fits the facts is that boys tend to torment those who suffer from infirmity and resent those who refuse to conform. Byron's reaction was to fight them. When he came south from Scotland, the English were to him a strange, almost a foreign, race. He was precocious in many ways. An intelligent 13 year old who had been brought up in Aberdeen by a mother who was interested in politics, read the papers and called herself almost a Democrat, was likely to question much that English boys would take for granted. Political discussion in Aberdeen was European in outlook and certainly not prejudiced in favour of the English Establishment. The *Aberdeen Journal* was enthusiastic for the French Revolution; and France, the traditional enemy of England, was the traditional ally of Scotland.

Byron distanced himself from his schoolfellows in other ways. Tyerman has pointed out that Dr Drury had succeeded in more than doubling the size of the school since 1797. Byron felt the need to escape from the crowded buildings. He took to lying for hours on end on the Peachey tomb in the churchyard on Harrow Hill, looking out over the wide countryside below.

Tyerman points out that the real importance of Harrow was that, as a schoolboy, Byron began to write poetry:

> Byron the schoolboy was by no means unique, Byron the poet, it could be argued, was ... Perhaps of more importance than his brawls and pranks, his attempts to prove himself an athlete and a cricketer [he became a fairly competent cricketer and was inordinately proud of having played against Eton] his quicksilver skill at doing the minimum of preparation for form work, or even his famed friendships with glittering young aristocrats, was the present he received, not from a peer or a peer's son, but from the son of a banker, Henry Boldero, who in 1803 gave his friend Byron, then fifteen, a copy of the works of Alexander Pope.[7]

Tyerman believes that the contrast between the frenzied world of school rivalries, arguments, games and friendships, and the tranquillity of the churchyard and the surrounding countryside lent piquancy to some of Byron's early school verse. So did his friendships. His early verse includes poems addressed to the Duke of Dorset, the Earl of Clare, to George, Earl Delawarr and to Edward Noel Long. Another of Byron's young favourites was William Harness who had been lamed in an accident and whom Byron tried to protect. His strong relationship with these boys developed after his passionate love for his pretty neighbour at Newstead was frustrated.

When Byron first arrived at Newstead Hanson took him to be introduced to the Clarks of Annesley Hall and Mrs Clark's daughter by a previous marriage, Mary Chaworth. Byron knew the story of the duel in which William Chaworth had been killed by The Wicked Lord in dubious circumstances. He told Mr Hanson that, for him, meeting the Chaworths seemed like Montagues meeting Capulets.

Byron took to riding over to Annesley to visit Mary. The orderly beauty of Mary's home and the care with which she was looked after by her parents, her old nurse and the groom who followed her whenever she rode out was a painful contrast to his own circumstances at Newstead. Washington Irving describes Annesley Hall. 'You enter a paved court – shrubs and antique flower pots – ruined stone fountain in the centre. It is like the approach to a French chateau.'[8] Under the window of Mary's sitting room was a flower garden; below the house a long terraced walk, heavy stone balustrade, sculpted urns with ivy and evergreens, great flights of steps down to the flower gardens which were laid out in formal plots, unlike the neglected gardens at Newstead.

By the age of fifteen Byron was desperately in love. Mary teased him, flirted with him and treated him as the schoolboy he was. She was already in love with Jack Musters, a handsome young neighbour whose chief pleasure was riding to hounds.

Years later, Mary's old nurse gossiped with Irving about the young poet who had become so notorious and the subject of such hideous rumours that he had to leave the country:

> Like him? Bless him that I did. He used to ride over here and stay three days at a time and sleep in the blue room. Ah! poor fellow, he was very much taken with my young mistress. He used to walk about the terrace and gardens with her and seemed to love the very ground she trod on. Ah, sir, and why should I not like him? He was always main good to me when he came over. Well well they say it is a pity he and my young lady did not make a match of it, but it was not to be. He went away to school and then Mr Musters saw her and so things took their course.[9]

By March 1803 Hanson had managed to find a tenant for Newstead, the 23-year-old Lord Grey de Ruthyn. Mrs Byron moved into a house standing on the Green near the edge of the pleasant village of Southwell. Byron later wrote of life in Southwell:

> There are very few books of any Kind that are either instructive or amusing, no society but old parsons and old Maids; I shoot a Good deal, but thank God I have not so far lost my reason as to make shooting my only amusement. There are indeed some of my neighbours whose only pleasures consist in field sports, but in other respects they are only one degree removed from the brute creation...[10]
>
> (Burgage Manor, 2 April 1804)

Hanson had engaged a steward for the Newstead estate who had moved into the lodge near the Pilgrim's Oak. This man, Owen Mealey, was a surly unpleasant fellow who tried to make trouble by complaining to Hanson of both Byron and his mother. Byron now insisted on spending the summer holidays in the lodge, waited upon by Mealey. He had the grace to write to his mother 'You know as well as I do that it is not your Company I dislike but the place you reside in.'[11] A more pressing reason was his passion for Mary. When the time came to return to Harrow he wrote his mother an impassioned plea for one day's grace:

> I was not wishing to resist your commands and really seriously intended coming over tomorrow ... I know it is time to go to Harrow. It will make me unhappy but I will obey; I only *desire*, *entreat*, this one day and on my *honour* I will be over tomorrow, in the evening or afternoon. I am Sorry you disapprove my Companions, who however are the first this county affords, and my equals in most respects, But I will be permitted to Chuse for myself, I shall never interfere in yours and I desire you will not molest me in mine; If you Grant me this favour and allow me this one day unmolested you will eternally oblige your unhappy son, Byron...[12]
>
> (To Mrs Catherine Gordon Byron [15 September 1803])

Mrs Byron could no more resist her son in this vein than she had been able to resist her rapacious husband in another. It was not until the beginning of the next term that he returned to Harrow. She wrote an explanation to Hanson to be passed on to Dr Drury admitting that young Byron was headstrong and was refusing to return to Harrow because he was desperately in love, a condition, in her view, worse than any sickness.

Byron returned to school disillusioned and deeply wounded. He had overheard Mary telling her maid that she could never love that lame boy. His reaction was to lavish affection on his young friends at Harrow. He was quite open about his love for these boys and this is borne out by a letter to his half-sister, Augusta Byron, with whom he developed, while at Harrow, a loving and protective relationship:

> You, Augusta, are the only relation I have who treats me as a friend ... if you too desert me I have nobody I can love but Delawarr. If it were not for his sake, Harrow would be a desert.[13]
>
> (Friday, 2 November 1804)

Later he told the whole story of his love for the young chorister at Cambridge, John Edleston, to his new friend and confidante, Eliza Pigot, without the slightest embarrassment. Ian Gilmour points out that when Byron fell in love with Edleston at Cambridge:

> In always stressing that this love was 'pure' he was evidently contrasting it with other loves or relationships. He never claimed that his relationships at Harrow were 'pure'. Secondly, early in 1807, he wrote a short autobiographical poem, 'Damaetas' (whose suppressed title was 'My Character'), which began, 'In law an infant and in years a boy / In mind a slave to every vicious joy.' ... The transition from Byron's heterosexual though unconsummated passion, to a series of homosexual ones was not unusual. Many adolescent boys, especially if they live in an exclusively male society, go through a homosexual phase which does not preclude being attracted to women ...[14]

This account of the matter is the most persuasive although the poem 'Damaetas' is an example of a tendency in Byron throughout his life to present himself as worse than he was – particularly to the censorious:

> In law an infant, and in years a boy,
> In mind a slave to every vicious joy;
> From every sense of shame and virtue wean'd,
> In lies an adept, in deceit a fiend;
> Vers'd in hypocrisy, while yet a child;
> Fickle as wind, of inclinations wild;
> Woman his dupe, his heedless friend a tool;
> Old in the world, though scarcely broke from school;
> Damætas ran through all the maze of sin,
> And found the goal, when others just begin;
> Ev'n still conflicting passions shake his soul,
> And bid him drain the dregs of Pleasure's bowl;
> But, pall'd with vice, he breaks his former chain,
> And what was once his bliss appears his bane.[15]

This is an early example of Byron's habitual *fanfaron des vices* and at least some items in this list of vice can be seen as a literary exercise since deceit, lies and hypocrisy were absolutely foreign to Byron's nature. His openness, especially about his own misdemeanours, and supposed misdemeanours, was so exaggerated as to be almost in itself a misdemeanour.

At Harrow Byron's interest was in boys younger than himself but there is no evidence of any interest in pre-sexual eight-year-old boys, just as we know of no interest in pre-sexual girls at any time in his life.

Whether Byron considered, at this age, unlicensed sexual congress with women a 'vicious joy' is unclear, but years later he teased Thomas Moore by claiming that his book of erotic verse, published anonymously in 1801 under the title *Poetical Works of the Late Thomas Little*, was responsible for all his sexual peccadilloes:

> I have just been turning over Little, which I knew by heart in 1803, being then in my fifteenth summer. Heigho! I believe all the mischief I have ever done, or sung, has been owing to that confounded book of yours...[16]
>
> (Ravenna, 9 June 1820)

When the first cantos of *Don Juan* were met with an outcry of indecency Byron repeatedly protested, often citing Thomas Little as an example of a really immoral production:

> *Don Juan* will be known by and bye for what it is intended a *satire* on *abuses* of the present *states* of Society – and not an eulogy of vice; – it may be now and then voluptuous – I can't help that – Ariosto is worse – Smollett ... ten times worse – and Fielding no better – No Girl will ever be seduced by reading *Don Juan* – no – no – she will go to Little's poems – and Rousseau's romans – for that – or even to the immaculate De Stael – they will encourage her – and not the Don – who laughs at that – and – and – most other things.[17]
>
> (To John Murray, Genoa 25 October 1822)

Paul Elledge is persuasive in his discussion of the relation of Byron's boyish sexual engagements at Harrow to the episode at Newstead in November 1803 when Byron's tenant, Lord Grey de Ruthyn, is generally believed to have made a sexual overture to the fifteen-year-old boy which Byron rejected, either with disgust, distress or at the least some form of disquiet which caused him to leave Newstead and put an end to his friendship with the older man. Elledge writes:

> Now, amorous experimentation with one's school bedmate or dormitory neighbour is a very different order of engagement from the sort historically assumed to have been proposed by Grey. My hunch, however, is that Byron was less neutrally experimental or playful than sentimentally romantic in his Harrow sexual adventures: his poetry of adolescent boy-love is warm but earnest, guileless, almost painfully sincere, without a trace of the carnal nonchalance often imputed to the later Byron, whose love poetry nevertheless, as long as he composed in the genre, continued to show this tender, sentimental bent.[18]

Jerome Christensen takes a very different view:

> Lord Byron learned his homosexuality from books – old books. One of the most impressionable students of the classics the English public schools have ever formed, Byron invested sexual desire only in Greek boys. For Byron – classical in his tastes, anthropological in his desires – *Greek love* meant love of Greeks.[19]

Others have seen Byron not as bisexual but as exclusively homosexual and have claimed that, in making love to women, he was going against his nature, which caused him to treat them with cruelty. It would be interesting to see evidence of this alleged cruelty to women apart from Lady Byron's allegations and insinuations, which were never tested in court.

I do not believe it possible to make any definitive judgement between Christensen and Gilmour on this question but I do not believe the sweeping judgement that Byron was exclusively homosexual allows for all the known facts. To look simply at this supposition as applied to Byron's life at Harrow it must be borne in mind that he was pouring out poetry, most of it concerned with love. Roughly a quarter of these poems are either addressed to boys or concerned with love or friendship with boys, and some are quite impassioned. But the same is true of some of the poems addressed to girls – particularly the ones concerned with his lost love, Mary Chaworth. Some of the poems addressed to girls may be using girls' names to disguise the fact that those addressed are boys, but many of the poems addressed to named girls we know of at Southwell or Newstead or London display that 'tender, sentimental bent' described by Elledge. If Byron was engaged in homosexual love affairs or experimentation it was certainly not an exclusive interest.

I believe it possible that the family affection he was beginning to feel for his half-sister, Augusta Byron, may have been as important to him (though at this stage less thrillingly exciting) as his love for his Harrow favourites. He longed for a family and his pride of lineage made him particularly intrigued by the meeting with a young woman who was so clearly a Byron, so like him and yet so different in her background and her experience of life which gave her a glamour he delighted in. She was six years older than her brother and the love he felt for her at this time had nothing of *eros* in it but was purely friendship and love of family and, gradually, the hope that through her he might be accepted by the Howards, the Osbornes and other great families.

Much as Byron loved, and was loved by, his mother, the years of putting up with her volatility and the violence of her sudden rages were beginning to alienate him. The poem quoted earlier on his 'Childish Recollections' shows how he felt the lack of a father and of brothers and sisters. Now for the first time he saw his half-sister and began writing to her the affectionate letters which usually begin with 'My Dearest Augusta'. This new sister was tall, elegant, fashionable, though 'shy as an antelope' with strangers, full of fun and ready to love, and be loved by, the young brother she had originally known as 'Baby Byron'. Both were Byrons; both mourned the loss of a father they would never admit to have been a worthless character.

Byron wrote to her on 22 March 1804:

> For the Future I hope you will consider me not only as a *Brother* but as your warmest and most affectionate *Friend*, and if ever Circumstances should require it as your *protector*.[20]
>
> (Burgage Manor)

It seemed unlikely at that time that circumstances would ever warrant Augusta's seeking her brother's protection. She was brought up for the most part in the London house of her grandmother, Lady Holderness, on familiar terms with royalty, and was frequently invited to Castle Howard where she was on the closest terms with the young Howards. Her mother had been Baroness Conyers in her own right and was married to the Marquess of Camarthen by whom she had two sons and a daughter. When she ran away to Paris with John Byron (who thus ensured himself an income of at least four thousand a year) she left her children behind. Their father, now Duke of Leeds, welcomed Augusta into the family after her mother's death and his children were her friends. Those who knew her best loved her dearly and the inference is that she was a charming and lovable young woman. Byron was later to write 'there is not a more angelic being on earth.'[21]

Now he treated her as his confidante and she took to confiding in Mr Hanson whenever she felt her brother needed help or advice or a refuge from his mother's vagaries which, Augusta told the lawyer, would have a damaging effect on any boy's character.

Augusta was already in love with her dashing and handsome cousin, George Leigh, son of John Byron's sister, Frances. The Leighs were firmly opposed to the match since George had joined the army and needed a rich wife to support his extravagant lifestyle. Augusta had a minuscule income left her by her grandmother. In Regency times young women with small incomes had a hard time in the marriage market. Augusta was willing to wait for her George. Byron sympathised with her impatience, as we see in a letter from Southwell:

> My Dear Augusta
> As to your Future prospects, my Dear Girl, *may they be happy*. I am sure *you* deserve Happiness and if *you* do not meet with it I shall have to think it is 'a bad world we live in'.[22]
>
> (26 March 1804)

Byron told her he would be a friend to anyone she loved but he wrote with brotherly advice:

> Can't you drive this Cousin of yours out of your pretty little head? ... or give old L'Harpagon the slip, and take a trip to Scotland?[23]
> (Harrow on the Hill, 25 October 1804)

Byron never showed the slightest trace of envy over the contrast between Augusta's upbringing in the grandest of circles and his own provincial childhood. He had no claim on Augusta's step-family but he was secretly wounded by the lack of interest shown by Lord Carlisle in his new ward. His letters to Augusta show that he could be touchy and distant towards his guardian but it is evident that he longed to meet, and be accepted by, all Augusta's grand relations.

> If you see Lord Sidney Godolphin, I beg you will remember me to him, I fancy he has almost forgot me by now as it is rather more than a year since I had the pleasure of seeing him.[24]
>
> (Burgage Manor, 22 March 1804)

> Be sure to Remember me to my formal Guardy Lord Carlisle, whose magisterial presence I have not been into for some years, nor have I any ambition to attain so great an honour.[25]
>
> (Harrow on the Hill, 25 October 1804)

> You mistake me if you think I dislike Lord Carlisle, I respect him and might like him if I knew him better.[26]
>
> (Harrow on the Hill, 11 November 1804)

Then, after Lord Carlisle had helped to persuade Mrs Byron to allow her son to spend a vacation with the Hansons:

> To Lord Carlisle make my warmest acknowledgements. I feel more gratitude, than my feelings can well express, I am truly obliged to him for his endeavours, and am perfectly satisfied with your explanation of his reserve, though I was hitherto afraid it might proceed from personal dislike.[27]
>
> (Harrow on the Hill, 21 November 1804)

Augusta was trying to reconcile Byron with the guardian she loved and Byron writes in January 1805 of dining with his family:

> I on Saturday, dined with Lord Carlisle, and on further acquaintance I like them all very much ... I think your friend Lady G[ertrude] is a sweet girl... Her Ladyship I always liked, but of the junior part of the family, Frederick is my favourite...[28]
>
> (6 Chancery Lane, 3 January 1805)

These meetings did not develop into the friendly relationship Byron had hoped for when he wrote to Augusta, 2 November 1804

> I should like to know your Lady Gertrude as you and she are so great friends. Adieu, my pretty sister. Write soon...[29]

By 1805 Byron was writing to Augusta:

> My Dearest Augusta…
> I hope, however, to have the pleasure of seeing you on the day appointed, but if you could contrive any way that I may avoid being asked to dinner by Ld. C[arlisle] I would be obliged to you, as I hate strangers.
>
> Adieu, my Beloved Sister.[30]
>
> (Burgage Manor, 23 April 1805)

Once he got into the higher forms at Harrow Byron was taught by Dr Drury who, though not particularly gifted academically, had a predilection for 'illustrating the sentiments of classical authors, especially Greek tragedians, by reference to modern English poets. Furthermore, he encouraged his pupils to write free translations of classical poets into English Verse.'[31] Tyerman concludes that 'Byron's education, relentlessly repetitive and boring as much of it may have been, provided him, not merely with material, but with models of form and expression for his early verse.'[32] Byron was still filled with generous idealism which conflicted with a growing scepticism. The opposition between these aspects of his character illustrates the 'mobility' which he himself recognised as a salient feature in his personality. Both characteristics appear in the poem 'Childish Recollections' which was written in late 1806 and revised later.

> Hours of my youth! when nurtur'd in my breast,
> To Love a stranger, Friendship made me blest, –
> Friendship, the dear peculiar bond of youth,
> When every artless bosom throbs with truth;
> Untaught by worldly wisdom how to feign,
> And check each impulse with prudential rein;
> When, all we feel, our honest souls disclose,
> In love to friends, in open hate to foes;
> No varnish'd tales the lips of youth repeat,
> No dear-bought knowledge purchased by deceit;
> Hypocrisy, the gift of lengthen'd years,
> Matured by age, the garb of Prudence wears:
> When, now the Boy is ripen'd into Man,
> His careful Sire chalks forth some wary plan;
> Instructs his Son from Candour's path to shrink,
> Smoothly to speak, and cautiously to think;
> Still to assent, and never to deny –
> A patron's praise can well reward the lie:
> And who, when Fortune's warning voice is heard,
> Would lose his opening prospects for a word?

Although, against that word, his heart rebel,
And Truth, indignant, all his bosom swell.[33]

In his last years at Harrow Byron covered himself with glory by his skill at declamation, which delighted Dr Drury. But he retained his reputation as an unruly pupil, becoming almost as angry with the headmaster's brother, Mark Drury, as he had earlier been with Henry. The master twitted him on his lack of fortune, which seems a strange thing for a schoolmaster to do and one must suspect that Byron offered him provocation, perhaps in the form of some piece of adolescent pretension. He raged to his mother in a letter: 'If my fortune is narrow, it is my misfortune not my fault.'[34] During the early nineteenth century and the Regency wealth may not have been openly worshipped but those without it were deprived of what was described as 'consequence', and 'consequence' was absolutely necessary for commanding respect. Later, Byron was to write, 'riches are power, and poverty is slavery all over the earth.'[35] On the same subject Sydney Smith remarked, 'It was always considered an impertinence in England if a man of less than two or three thousand a year had any opinion at all on important subjects.'[36]

A letter to Augusta shows Byron's fondness for Dr Drury:

> ...this very morning I had a thundering Jobation from our Good Doctor, which deranged my *nervous system* for a least five minutes. But notwithstanding He and I now and then disagree, yet upon the whole we are very good friends, for there is so much of the Gentleman, so much mildness, and nothing of pedantry in his character, that I cannot help liking him and will remember his instructions with gratitude as long as I live...[37]
>
> (Friday, 2 November 1804)

Byron felt no such admiration for George Butler, the new Headmaster who replaced Dr Drury shortly before Byron was due to leave the school. Byron had narrowly escaped being expelled under Drury. His behaviour to Doctor Butler was outrageous. He made a nuisance of himself partly because he was unhappy at the departure of Dr Drury and partly through a snobbish feeling of superiority, customarily felt by the upper classes of the period towards the schoolmaster or 'usher'. He was reconciled with Butler in February 1808, which demonstrates a forgiving nature in the

Headmaster who was pilloried by Byron in his verses on 'Pomposus'. These were subversive of school discipline though even 'Pomposus' himself must have thought they were quite well-turned:

Portrait of Pomposus

...Just half a Pedagogue, and half a Fop,
Not formed to grace the pulpit, but the Shop;
The *Counter*, not the *Desk*, should be his place,
Who deals out precepts, as if dealing Lace;[38]

Dr Butler invited all the older boys to dinner. Byron rejected the invitation, an unheard of rebuff to a Headmaster. When Butler taxed him with it and asked for an explanation Byron replied that, should Dr Butler ever find himself near Newstead, he would certainly not be invited to dinner there. Byron was therefore unable to accept an invitation from his Headmaster to dinner at Harrow.

Soon after this Byron left the school to go on to the University of Cambridge. There he would continue for some time to present to the world such an apparently vain and unendearing attitude that John Cam Hobhouse (who was to become his lifelong friend) detested him on sight.

Byron was desolated at having to leave Harrow, although he was prone to indulging in self-pity over his loneliness there. A couplet from 'Childish Recollections' foretells a theme which would appear in many of his early poems – the lonely hero shunned by his kind – and this developed further into the Satanic heroes of his Oriental Tales.

A Hermit, midst of crowds, I fain must stray,
Alone, though thousand pilgrims fill the way;[39]

Lying on the Peachey tomb, his favourite spot in the churchyard on the hill, it was possible to feel himself a Hermit, but he was nothing of the kind when bellowing out ribald songs at Mother Barnard's tuck shop with his friends or roistering around London with them after losing the cricket match against Eton.

It is interesting to notice a significant point made by C.J. Tyerman who remarks how odd it was that in a school staffed entirely by clerics there was a total lack of religious instruction. It is possible that this seemed odd to the boys too and may have added to

Byron's growing scepticism about supposedly pious people. By 1807 his experience of life led him to write, 'I abhor Religion, though I reverence and love my God, without the blasphemous notions of Sectaries, or a belief in their absurd and damnable Heresies, mysteries and thirty nine articles.'[40]

4

SOUTHWELL AND CAMBRIDGE

'At fifteen I began to think myself a very fine gentleman.'[1]

When Mrs Byron moved into Burgage Manor she brought with her the family portraits from Newstead Abbey but not her son. He flatly refused to settle into the provincial life of Southwell and after a short time in the Lodge with Owen Mealey as his servant accepted the invitation of Lord Grey de Ruthyn to stay with him at Newstead. This did not last long. He returned home abruptly and refused to discuss his reason for leaving the Abbey with either his mother or Augusta, though he assured them both that he would never again have anything to do with Lord Grey. In view of Byron's subsequent behaviour the generally accepted view is that Lord Grey made a sexual advance which shocked the young Byron.

This led to impassioned arguments with Catherine Byron who had enjoyed her acquaintance with Lord Grey and resented the embarrassment caused by her son's contemptuous attitude to his tenant. Byron's relationship with his mother was further soured by his growing suspicion that she was a little in love with the sophisticated young man who was so much more entertaining than the rest of her circle of acquaintances. However, much as she enjoyed the company of Lord Grey Mrs Byron did not lose her head over him. She hoped he would be a good tenant but was determined to make it impossible for him to be a bad one.

At the age of fifteen Byron was five feet eight and a half inches tall, which was tall for his time, and weighed over fourteen stone. He was very shy and quite capable of climbing out of the window and decamping if strangers came to call. His mother tried hard to introduce him into Southwell society, throwing a party for him and introducing him to the Pigot family who lived on the other side of the Green. Tongue-tied at first, he became enchanted with Elizabeth Pigot when she made a literary joke referring cleverly but kindly to his awkward behaviour. He immediately sought her friendship. She was older than Byron by six years, was engaged to a subaltern who was in India, and had no intention of flirting with Byron. She became a confidante and mentor, encouraging him to sing to her playing, to join in the parties, assemblies and amateur theatricals put on for the entertainment of the young people of Southwell and, when she discovered that he had written several poems, encouraging him to go into print. Byron and John Pigot, her brother, who was a medical student at Edinburgh, became close friends.

Contrary to his expectations Byron enjoyed himself at Southwell, played a great deal of cricket and wrote several poems addressed to various of Southwell's young women in a sentimental strain: 'To Emma', 'To Caroline', 'To a Lady with the poems of Camoens', 'On the Death of a Young Lady', 'To Mary', 'To Lesbia', 'To Marian', 'To a Beautiful Quaker'. But some of the titles show that the young troubadour was not incapable of regarding his own productions with an ironic eye: 'To a Young Lady who Presented to the author a lock of hair braided with his own and appointed a night in December to Meet Him in the Garden'.

John Pigot was to tell Thomas Moore, after Byron's death, 'Few people understood Byron but I knew that he had naturally a kind and feeling heart, and that there was not a single spark of malice in his composition.'[2] It was Byron's lack of conceit and open-hearted friendliness at this time which earned Pigot's praise. Pigot felt great sympathy for the shy younger man. He writes later of a visit with Byron to Harrogate: 'He was naturally shy, *very* shy; which people who did not know him mistook for pride.'[3] Pigot tells how delighted Byron was at seeing a professor from Cambridge on the street. He sent his carriage to bring the professor to the theatre and later to a ball at the Granby.

In October 1805 Byron went up to Trinity College Cambridge and from now on his arguments with his mother became more bitter. He began to call her 'Mrs Byron Furiosa' when talking to the Pigots and related how she once threw the fire irons at him and laid him flat. The Pigots offered him refuge and even, on one occasion, helped him to escape from Southwell without her knowledge.

One can only sympathise with Catherine Byron. Instead of becoming more sensible Byron's behaviour became more adolescent and more rebellious after he left Harrow and he even began to put on airs, in direct contrast to his conduct in the past and, indeed, by and large during the rest of his life. Elizabeth and John Pigot saw nothing of this phase in Byron's development though they remained his confidants. If John Pigot had read some of Byron's letters to his mother at this period the rosy picture he gave to Thomas Moore might have undergone some modification.

On going up to Cambridge Byron was afraid that those used to grander acquaintances and higher incomes would despise him. To stave off any humiliating rebuff he determined to take a high tone even with Hanson and his mother. There was no father to depress his pretensions and give him good advice. He was fond of Hanson but Hanson was not of the *haute monde*. Lord Carlisle was too distant a figure to be of any help. The boy had to learn his lesson from experience. In the meantime his mother bore the brunt of his disdain.

Byron compensated for his feeling of inadequacy and the always visible evidence of deformity in his lameness by spending money with wild extravagance: fitting up his rooms at Trinity College with some splendour, ordering down a dozen each of wine, brandy, port, sherry, claret and madeira and buying a horse called Oateater. He planned to cut a dash in Cambridge with a servant, a horse and a white hat (which latter annoyed Hobhouse more than any other of his affectations).

Catherine Byron was alarmed at her son's extravagance. Hanson had managed to organize a grant of £500 a year (paid quarterly to Mrs Byron) for Byron's education when he went to Harrow. Mrs Byron foolishly turned the whole of this sum over to Byron when he went up to Trinity. He was seventeen and a half and the son of a spendthrift. Catherine applied for a grant of £200 for herself. This was refused and her Civil List pension was reduced to £200. She was hard put to it to exist without some addition to her income, which was composed of this £200 and another sum of £200 of Scottish income, and was obliged to live very frugally. Her son obstinately refused to recognise the sacrifices his mother made for him until after her death when it was too late to show his gratitude. He told Augusta that he had one of the best allowances in Cambridge:

> I need scarcely inform you that I am not in the least obliged to Mrs B. for it, as it comes off my property, and she refused to fit out a single thing for me out of her own pocket, my Furniture is paid for and she has moreover a handsome addition made to her own income which I do not in the least regret, as I would wish her to be happy.[4]
>
> (Trinity College, 6 November 1805)

He wrote to Hanson, 'Study is the last pursuit of the Society; the Master eats, drinks and Sleeps, the Fellows *drink*, *dispute* and *pun*; the employments of the under Graduates you will probably conjecture.'[5] (Trinity College Cambridge, 23 November 1805)

Arguments over money caused a coolness between Byron and Hanson. The lawyer who had been so kind to the boy and whose family had welcomed him into their household, became 'that fool, Hanson, in his vulgar idiom', and 'that chattering puppy, Hanson'.

By the time Byron went to London for the Christmas vacation he was so short of money that he asked Augusta to guarantee a loan for him. This she sensibly refused to do, offering instead, to lend him the money. His sense of honour (somewhat inconsistent at this stage in his life) precluded his accepting money from her and he persuaded his landlady at 16 Piccadilly, Mrs Massingberd and her daughter, to act as security for the loan. From this time on, Byron was in the hands of the moneylenders, Mrs Massingberd acting as go-between. By the time he left Cambridge his debts amounted to £5000. The explanation of this foolishly extravagant behaviour is that, during this time and for many years to come, Byron believed – and was encouraged by Hanson in this belief – that his Rochdale lands (which had been illegally sold by the Wicked Lord) would fetch in the region of £60,000 when a lawsuit conducted under Hanson's guidance came to a successful conclusion. More than once Byron was told that he had won the lawsuit but, shortly before his death, he learned that all hope of retrieving the bulk of the money was at an end.

Byron enjoyed himself in London, taking fencing lessons with Henry Angelo and boxing lessons from Gentleman Jackson, and airily announcing to his mother new plans for going abroad. Mrs Byron began to suspect that her beloved son had got into the hands of moneylenders. Augusta was vexed at seeing her brother at the theatre in London when he should have been pursuing his studies at Cambridge. Byron went back to Cambridge but not before the next term was well underway. He wrote later that he was disgusted by 'the commonplace libertinism of the place' – but still took part in it.

Byron finally returned to Southwell bringing with him a manservant and a coach and horses to the consternation of his mother who was expected to house them. He had sent her from London an insufferably patronising letter:

> I intend remaining in Town a month longer, when perhaps I shall bring my Horses and myself down to your residence in that *execrable* kennel. I hope you have engaged a Man Servant – else it will be impossible for me to visit you since my Servant must attend chiefly to his horses, at the same Time you must cut an Indifferent Figure with only maids, in your habitation.[6]
>
> (To Mrs Catherine Gordon Byron, 16 Piccadilly, 26 February 1806)

In fact he returned to Southwell only briefly and not until the Summer vacation, escaping again to London after a scene with Mrs Byron led to his leaving the house in the middle of the night. In September he returned to Southwell and enjoyed himself by taking part in private theatricals, playing Penruddock in Cumberland's *The Wheel of Fortune* and Tristram Fickle in Allingham's *The Weathercock*. Paul Elledge describes *The Wheel of Fortune* as a 'spineless mawkish affair'; nevertheless, it was 'as well-regarded in its day as "Death of a Salesman" in ours'. Elledge regards Allingham's as a much better play from which Byron 'learned something of satiric representation.' Tristram Fickle 'is a colourfully silly fellow.' He becomes 'by turns an actor, a musician, a philosopher, a soldier, a gardener, a Quaker, and ultimately "a buck".' 'He is convinced that "I possess great powers of oratory"' and 'he has summoned his barber to shave half of his head in imitation of "Demosthenes, the Athenian orator".'[7]

In early 1807 a change occurred in Byron's life which was almost as significant as the taking up of his inheritance in 1799. He embarked on a régime for losing weight and the overweight youth was transformed into a 'regular Apollo'. He wrote to Hanson from Southwell:

> You will be surprised to hear that I am grown *very thin* ... I have lost 18LB in my weight ... by violent exercise and Fasting ... I wear *seven* Waistcoats and a great Coat, run and play at Cricket in this Dress ... use the hot Bath daily, eat only a quarter of a pound of Butcher's meat

in 24 hours, no Suppers or Breakfast ... drink no malt liquor, little wine.[8]

(To John Hanson, Southwell, 2 April 1807)

Byron succeeded in getting his weight down to eleven stone. From now on his beauty became legendary and, as a result, he was pursued, even hunted down, by women for the rest of his life. The more famous he became the more devastating was his effect. Women fell desperately in love with him on gazing at him from the far side of a room. Harriette Wilson, the famous courtesan whose beauty was fading by the time she caught sight of the poet, wrote to inform him that while watching his very beautiful face she had imagined his lips pressed to hers, as wild and eager as his poetry.

Coleridge later went into raptures about Byron's eyes, filled with light, and declared his face among the most beautiful he ever saw.

This beauty, combined with his musical speaking voice, his reputation for wild deeds and mysterious love affairs and for having experienced and suffered more than most of his age, enhanced the fame which changed his life on the publication of *Childe Harold's Pilgrimage*.

Byron always had to fight his tendency to put on weight, and for the most part he was successful. His motives for fasting were not simply an obsession with the desirability of a slender figure. He liked to fast because he believed that heavy meals, especially if they contained meat, increased the passions. He did not want to be a slave of passion. Starving himself and then eating vast meals when his hunger became too much for him, had a deleterious effect on his digestion. He once wrote to Samuel Rogers, who had invited the young poet to dinner, 'Will you allow me to come in *after* dinner tomorrow instead of before – for I have so bedevilled my digestion – that your *light* supper – the other night – half killed me.'[9]

An advantage of his loss of weight was that there was much less for his lame foot to carry about. At Harrow he had to hire a pony to go to the bathing place because it was too far for him to walk on his lame leg. In 1815 he would scramble up a steep hill near the beach at Seaham, racing Annabella Milbanke to the top. He remained deeply sensitive about his lameness and this was the cause of his remarking as a young man that no woman could ever love 'such a thing as I am.' (He proceeded to try to give the lie to this statement by consorting with 'lewd loves' in London when he escaped from Southwell). It was only a few years later that he wrote in his Journal:

> [Four or Five Reasons in Favour of a Change]
> 1st At twenty three the best of life is over and its bitters double. 2ndly I have seen mankind in various Countries and find them equally despicable. If anything the Balance is rather in favour of the Turks, 3dly I am sick at heart...
> 4thly A man who is lame of one leg is in a state of bodily inferiority which increases in years and must render his old age more peevish and intolerable. Besides in another existence I expect to have *two* if not *four* legs by way of compensation.[10]
>
> (Malta, 22 May 1811)

Though Byron often suffered from melancholy he was easily made happy by friendship and love. During his first term at Cambridge he spent much of his time with Edward Noel Long who had been at Harrow and was now at Trinity College with him. They would ride and swim together and Long would play the flute and violoncello for Byron in the evenings.

Byron was dismayed when, in May 1807, Long left Cambridge for the army and wrote to tell him he was going to war:

> I am truly sorry the duties of your profession call you to combat, for what? Can you tell me? The ambition of Despotism or the caprice of men placed by chance in the Situation of Governors, and probably inferior to yourself ... I am no *coward*, nor would I shrink from Danger on a proper occasion, indeed Life has too little valuable for me, to make Death horrible; I am not insensible to Glory, and even hope before I am at *Rest*, to see some service in a military Capacity, yet I cannot conquer my repugnance to a Life absolutely and exclusively devoted to Carnage.[11]
>
> (To Edward Noel Long, Southwell, 11 May 1807)

Byron had moved some way from the child who contemplated the glorious future career of 'Byron's Blacks'. Edward Noel Long's military career lasted no more than eighteen months. He was drowned at sea in early 1809 when the transport ship in which he was travelling went down with all hands. Byron was grief-stricken. He wrote later that at Cambridge Edward Long's friendship and a 'violent, though *pure*, love and passion' ... 'were the then romance of the most romantic period of my life.'[12] The 'pure' passion was for a seventeen-year-old chorister who sang in the chapel at Trinity College. Byron included in 'Fugitive Pieces' (his first privately printed book of verse) a poem, 'The Cornelian', which refers to a cornelian ring which was a present from this young man, John Edleston.

G. Wilson Knight explains the idealism of Byron's youthful male loves, contrasting his physical experience later in Greece with Nicolo Giraud with the idealism of his experience with Edleston:

> To Byron youth ... always remained in his mind the age of unsullied insight and valuation. Though in himself and others the early perfection was destined, in various ways and from various causes, to be desecrated, he throughout remained true to this world of ardent friendship, self-sacrifice, and heroism. It was a world of classic, Greek tone. As good an expression of it as any is Vergil's story of Nisus and Euryalus in the *Aeneid* (IX); a translation of it is among Byron's youthful poems.[13]

Jerome Christensen seems to agree with this interpretation of Byron's attitude to love for young males:

> Among the ancient Greeks, according to Dover, the legitimacy that was conferred on a philanthropic relationship between an *erastes* and his youthful *erimenos* was sharply contrasted with 'gross misbehaviour for monetary payment [which] is the act of a *hubristes* and uneducated man' – a vice aptly described by Byron's phrase – (he had in mind his friend Francis Hodgson's penchant for falling in love with prostitutes) 'romantic attachments for things marketable for a dollar.'[14]

Byron wrote of his love for Edleston after his death:

> Ours too the glance none saw beside;
> The smile none else might understand;
> The whispered thought of hearts allied,
> The pressure of the thrilling hand;
> The kiss so guiltless and refined,
> That Love each warmer wish forbore;
> Those eyes proclaimed so pure a mind,
> Ev'n Passion blushed to plead for more.[15]

Only a hypocrite could have written these lines from the *Thyrza* cycle if the relationship with Edleston was in fact physical.

For many years it has been believed that while Byron was away on his travels with Hobhouse Edleston was accused of indecency in London. The conviction arose from a mistaken reading of an entry in Hobhouse's Journal to the effect that 'The Collection has been accused of indecency.' This refers to his collection of poems. The word 'Collection' was mistakenly read as 'Edleston' at least thirty years ago and Edleston has been supposed to have indulged in behaviour which resulted in a charge of indecency. This has undoubtedly led to a misreading of Byron's relationship with the boy and of his sexual affiliations in general and may have convinced readers of the above stanza that Byron was indeed a hypocrite. This valuable piece of clarification we owe to Phyllis Grosskurth who pointed out the mistake to Paul Elledge by whom her discovery has been verified.[16] Whether or not Jonathan Gross was aware of this mistake in the year 2000 when his book *Byron the Erotic Liberal* appeared, his view of Byron's *eros* seems to chime with that of G. Wilson Knight and that of Jerome Christensen:

> Byron's *eros* has little in common with libertinism. This is an important distinction. Where those driven by *eros* become dissatisfied with themselves and strive for self-improvement, libertines regard each new conquest as proof of their intellectual superiority. Erotic lovers are overwhelmed by passion, which they struggle in vain to control; libertines control others by controlling themselves. Plato explains how *eros* leads the lover from loving beautiful bodies to loving beautiful acts. – The libertine's progress is toward hell and damnation ... Byron conformed to Plato's definition of *eros*, to an erotic ladder rather than a libertine descent.[17]

When Edleston left Cambridge Byron was determined to leave it too. He toyed with the idea of living with his protegé and confided in Elizabeth Pigot:

> ... [I] quit Cambridge forever, with little regret, because our *Set* are *vanished*, and my *musical* protegé ... has left the Choir, and is to be stationed in a mercantile house ... in the Metropolis. You may have heard me observe he is exactly to an hour, 2 years younger than myself, I found him grown considerably; and as you will suppose, very glad to see his former patron. – He is nearly my height, very thin, very fair complexion, dark eyes, and light locks ...[18]
>
> (Cambridge, 30 June 1807)

A few days later he wrote:

> . . . at this moment I write with a *bottle* of *Claret* in my *head* and *tears* in my *eyes*, for I have just parted from 'my *Cornelian*' . . . my mind is a *Chaos* of *hope* and *Sorrow* . . . I certainly *love* him more than any human being . . . In short, we shall put Lady E. Butler, and Miss Ponsonby [the ladies of Llangollen] to the *Blush*, *Pylades* and *Orestes* out of countenance.[19]
>
> (To Elizabeth Pigot, Trinity College, Cambridge, 5 July 1807)

While he was at Southwell Byron almost succeeded in putting most of its female population out of countenance by collecting his early verse into a volume called *Fugitive Pieces* which he took to be printed by John Ridge, at Newark. Elizabeth had persuaded him to take this step but she must have been astonished at the verses 'To Mary' – a much naughtier Mary than Mary Chaworth – and surprised at the other poems on love and sex (an unmentionable subject in front of ladies since the middle of the eighteenth century). The Reverend John J. Becher, who was a friend of the young poet, took him gently to task and they agreed that the volume was 'unfit for the perusal of ladies'. Byron destroyed the whole print-run but the Revd. Mr Becher kept his own copy, presumably in the conviction that it was quite fit for the perusal of parsons. The 'Lines to Mary' present a marked contrast to the idealistic poems addressed to Edleston, describing, as they do, the delights of 'love's ecstatic posture' which would have both shocked and intrigued the elderly gossips of Southwell.

Byron was more distressed than he seemed by this débacle. He gave in to the pressure of public opinion but defied his critics on paper – much as he had defied his nurse at the age of four:

> TO A KNOT OF UNGENEROUS CRITICS
> RAIL on, rail on, ye heartless crew!
> My strains were never meant for you;
> Remorseless Rancour still reveal,
> And damn the verse you cannot feel . . .
> Your efforts on yourselves recoil;
> Then Glory still for me you raise,
> Yours is the Censure, mine the Praise.[20]

Byron produced a second privately printed collection, *Poems on Various Occasions* which he described as 'miraculously chaste'. His friends were kind enough to praise these poems and Byron determined to produce a third volume printed not privately but for the public. He called it *Hours of Idleness*. Byron spent the summer vacation in London and could not resist boasting to Elizabeth Pigot about the mild success of *Hours of Idleness*:

> My dear Elizabeth
> ...My Cousin, Lord Alexander Gordon, ... told me his Mother, her *Grace* of *Gordon*, requested he would introduce my *poetical* Lordship, to her *highness*, as she had bought my volume, admired it extremely, in common with the Rest of the fashionable world, and wished to claim her relationship with the Author ... So much for *Egotism*, my *Laurels* have turned my Brain, but the *cooling acids* of forthcoming criticisms, will probably restore me to Modesty ... Southwell, I agree with your Brother, is a *Damned* place, I have done with it and shall see it no more ... excepting yourself, I esteem no-one ... you were my only *rational* companion, and in plain truth I had more respect for you, than the whole *Bevy*, with whose foibles I *amused* myself ... you gave yourself more trouble with me and my *manuscripts*, than a thousand *dolls* would have done, believe me, I have not forgotten your good nature, ... As for the village '*Lasses*' of *every description*, my *Gratitude* is also unbounded, to be equalled only by my *contempt*, I saw the *designs* of all *parties* while they imagined me *everything they wished*.[21]
>
> (Byron to Elizabeth Bridget Pigot)

Byron is referring in this last sentence chiefly to the family of Julia Leacroft, who tried to force him into a proposal of marriage by accusing him of compromising the 'Lesbia' of one or two of his poems. Byron's reply to the lady's brother was that the only remedy was to decline all further intercourse with 'those whom my acquaintance has unintentionally injured ... however careful I am of your Sister's honour, I am equally tenacious of my own.'[22]

Byron's letter to Elizabeth from London was a farewell. Fond as he was of both the Pigots, they belonged to a narrow world he was leaving forever. London and literary fame were intoxicating for a budding poet but he was contemplating further, far-flung and exotic destinations. First, he must complete the work he had conceived as retaliation for the harsh words directed by the *Edinburgh Review* and the *Satirist* against his first published volume.

Note

1. *Hours of Idleness* has been described in the Dictionary of National Biography as 'probably the worst first book ever written by a considerable

poet' and it was savagely reviewed in the *Edinburgh Review*. Modern criticism takes a different view. Brian Nellist writes: 'the whole volume is a digression around the subject of poetry itself, an *eclogue* of potential Byronic voices, appropriate to a first offering in verse.'[1] Michael G. Cooke found Byron's early lyrics worthy of close scrutiny:

> ...they can be shown to encase in a plain, cryptic exterior finely wrought personal positions on time, memory, nature, will, culture, knowledge, and essential being... Many of Byron's lyrical positions turn out to bear comparison with those of Wordsworth, who it may be recalled, was not unsympathetic to *Hours of Idleness*.
>
> 'On a Distant View of the Village and School of Harrow on the Hill' ... looks forward with Wordsworth – Coleridge rather than back to Gray ... the crucial point, however, is that the eighteen-year-old Byron, with no great finesse or feeling as a poet, correctly and sensitively carries out a romantic exercise, and concocts a Wordsworthian flavour. This gives a peculiar extension to a verdict he later passed on himself: 'My earlier poems are the thoughts of one at least ten years older than the age at which they were written: I don't mean for their solidity, but their Experience.[2]

5

THE NEWLY PUBLISHED POET

'The cry is up, and scribblers are my game;'[1]

When Byron went back to Cambridge in June 1807 he intended to pay his College dues, take his leave of John Edleston and leave Cambridge for good. In the event he decided to return to University in the autumn. He could no longer be regarded as the fop he had seemed on his first appearance at Cambridge since he was now a published poet. Charles Skinner Matthews, a brilliant young intellectual whom he had met briefly at Trinity College, introduced him to John Cam Hobhouse, author of an 'Imitation of Juvenal' and son of Benjamin Hobhouse MP. Their lively conversation, mordant wit, interest in literature and politics and membership of the Whig Club (which they had founded themselves) promised a more stimulating time ahead, and Byron was not disappointed.

He returned to Trinity in the autumn, bringing with him a tame bear to annoy the college authorities who had pronounced that Statutes forbade the keeping of dogs in College by the undergraduates. There was nothing in the Statutes about a tame bear.

His new friends made Byron known to Douglas Kinnaird who would become his banker and to Scrope Berdmore Davies, fellow of King's College, a wit, a gambler and a friend of Beau Brummell. Years later when Davies was forced into exile by his gambling debts Byron wrote to Hobhouse from his own exile in Ravenna:

> So – Scrope is gone – down – *diddled* – as Doug. K. writes it – the said Doug being like the Man who when he lost a friend went to the St James's Coffee House and took a new one – but to you and me – the loss of Scrope is irreparable – we could have better spared not just

> 'a better man' but 'the best of Men.' – Gone to Bruges – where he will get tipsy with Dutch beer and shoot himself the first foggy morning – Brummell – at *Calais* – Scrope at Bruges – Buonaparte at St Helena – you in – your new apartments – and I at Ravenna – only think so many great men! – there has been nothing like it since Themistocles at Magnesia – and Marius at Carthage.[2]
>
> (To Hobhouse, Ravenna, 3 March 1820)

Another new friend at Cambridge was Francis Hodgson, a tutor at King's College who intended to take Holy Orders, was easily shocked by Byron's racy conversation and nursed hopes of converting him to a more conventional attitude towards religion. In spite of continuing wide divergences in their outlook they remained close friends until Byron's death.

This last year at Cambridge was a turning-point in Byron's life. Edleston had gone. Long had gone. His younger friends from Harrow days were separated from him by distance or their own avocations. Now he had found the friends who would love him and be loved by him all his life. After his death Hobhouse claimed that no man ever had such devoted friends as Lord Byron.

In spite of his decision to spend another year at Cambridge he spent the Christmas vacation in London and stayed on there in January 1808, returning to Cambridge only for visits to his new cronies and, in July, to take the degree of MA reluctantly awarded to him by the University in spite of his far too frequent and lengthy absences.

Byron was now on the fringes of the literary world of the reviews and magazines which were setting up at the beginning of the nineteenth century as critics of literature and commentators on politics. This was a battle field on which he would first be an eager participant and later an interested onlooker.

In 1802 Francis Jeffrey, Henry Brougham and Sydney Smith had founded the *Edinburgh Review*. By 1812 it had a circulation of 10,000. This alarmed Sir Walter Scott for, as a Tory, he felt that the Whig partisanship of the *Edinburgh Review*'s political commentaries was unedifying. To combat this horrifying tendency he joined John Murray and William Gifford in founding the rival *Quarterly Review*. Supporters of the *Edinburgh* took just as partisan an attitude to the Tory *Quarterly* as Scott took to the *Edinburgh*; Hazlitt wrote of the *Quarterly* that in it nothing was regarded but the political creed or external circumstances of a writer, whereas the *Edinburgh* adverted to nothing but his literary merits. He claimed that the *Quarterly* presents 'one foul blotch of servility, intolerance, falsehood, spite and ill-manners'.[3]

Feelings ran so high that angry literary men challenged each other and Sydney Smith told Lady Holland in a letter of 1809, 'Wordsworth vows personal vengeance upon Jeffrey for his last critique, and blood will flow.'[4]

Hours of Idleness was reviewed briefly in the *Antiquarian Review and Magazine*, December 1807:

> ...the poems exhibit strong proofs of genius, accompanied by a lively but chastened imagination, a classical taste and a benevolent heart.[5]

From now on Mrs Byron, at home in Southwell and later in Newstead Abbey, collected all the reviews of Byron's works. There is no doubt that the reference here to his 'benevolent heart' must have given her great pleasure. She would have been affronted by the critical review in *The Satirist* in January 1808 and would have shared Byron's fury when *The Monthly Monitor* pronounced his poems no more than 'school exercises' and suggested that if Byron escaped whipping for them the masters at Harrow must have 'an undue respect for Lords' bottoms.'[6]

Byron now showed a new solicitude for his mother, writing from London to the Revd John Becher:

> A most violent attack is preparing for me in the next number of the *Edinburgh Review*... Tell *Mrs Byron* not to be out of humour with them, and to prepare her mind for the greatest hostility on their part, it will do no injury however, and I trust her mind will not be ruffled – They defeat their object by indiscriminate abuse, and they never praise except the partizans of Ld. Holland & Co.[7]
>
> (Dorant's, 26 February 1808)

(This conviction was the ground of Byron's attack on Lord and Lady Holland in his projected satire.)

Later he wrote to Becher:

> ...you have seen the *Edinburgh Review*, of course. I regret that Mrs Byron is so annoyed. For my own part, these 'paper bullets of the brain' have only taught me to stand fire.[8]
>
> (Dorant's, 28 March 1808)

John Cam Hobhouse, now Byron's closest friend, told a different story – of extreme distress. Byron believed Jeffrey was the author of the review and he harboured great resentment against him for many years. The writer was in fact Henry Brougham who mocked the young poet unmercifully as much for his nobility as for any literary shortcomings. The *Eclectic Review* sneered at *Hours of Idleness* on the same grounds: 'The book is a collection of juvenile pieces, some of very moderate merit, of very questionable morality; but the author is a nobleman.'[9] Wordsworth objected to such unfair criticism of a young writer. H. Crabb Robinson related that:

> I was sitting with Charles Lamb, when Wordsworth came in with fume in his countenance and the *Edinburgh Review* in his hand. 'I have no patience with these Reviewers,' he said; 'here is a young man, a lord and a minor, it appears, who publishes a little volume of poetry; and these fellows attack him as if no-one may write poetry unless he lives in a garret. The young man will do something if he goes on.'[10]

The young man was about to do something surprising. He wrote a satire attacking most of the writers of the day. Moore's is the best account of this crucial moment in Byron's life, the publication of his first important work, of which a second edition was to follow fast upon the first:

> It was not long, however, before he was summoned back to town by the success of his Satire, – the quick sale of which already rendered the preparation of a new edition necessary. His zealous agent, Mr Dallas, had taken care to transmit to him, in his retirement, all the favourable opinions of the work he could collect; and it is not unamusing, as showing the sort of steps by which Fame at first mounts, to find the approbation of such authorities as Pratt and the magazine writers put forward among the first rewards and encouragements of a Byron.
>
> You are already (he says) pretty generally known to be the author. So Cawthorne tells me, and a proof occurred to myself at Hatchard's, the Queen's bookseller. On enquiring for the latest Satire, he told me that he had sold a great many, and had none left, and was going to send for more ... I asked who was the author? He said it was believed to be Lord Byron's. Did *he* believe it? Yes, he did. On asking the ground of his belief, he told me that a Lady of distinction had, without hesitation, asked for it as Lord Byron's satire. He likewise informed me that he had enquired of Mr Gifford, who frequents his shop, if it was yours. Mr Gifford denied any knowledge of the author, but spoke very highly of it, and said a copy had been sent to him. Hatchard assured me that all who came to his

> reading-room admired it. Cawthorne tells me it is universally well spoken of, not only among his own customers, but generally at all the booksellers. I heard it highly praised at my own publisher's, where I have lately called several times. At Philip's it was read aloud by Pratt to a circle of literary guests, who were unanimous in their applause: The *Antijacobin*, as well as the *Gentlemen's Magazine*, has already blown the trump of fame for you. We shall see it in the other Reviews next month, and probably in some severely handled, according to the connection of the proprietors and editors with those whom it lashes.[11]

English Bards and Scotch Reviewers was an astonishing achievement for so young an author. Byron is setting himself up, powerfully, though imperfectly, as continuing in the tradition of Pope who was always to be the poet he most admired, perhaps from as early as 1803 when his friend Henry Boldero gave him the complete works of Pope at Harrow.

The theme of the Satire was praise of Pope, Congreve and Otway as a préamble to a series of hearty attacks on some of the leading and some of the minor poets of the day. In *English Bards and Scotch Reviewers* Byron is extremely scathing about some who later became friends. One can only admire the forgiving nature of Walter Scott, Moore and Lord and Lady Holland. Byron accuses Scott of racking his brains for lucre, not fame and condemns the 'prostituted Muse' of this 'hireling bard'. Lord Holland is accused of bribing scribblers by inviting them to the famous banquets at Holland House which makes them his 'hirelings'. As for Lady Holland:

> My lady skims the cream off each critique;
> Breathes o'er the page her purity of soul,
> Reforms each error, and refines the whole.[12]

He accuses Strangford of plagiarism in a brilliant metaphor:

> Think'st thou to gain thy verse a higher place,
> By dressing Camoëns in a suit of lace?[13]

His diatribe against Amos Cottle is that of a formidable 'enfant terrible' in full cry:

> Bœotian COTTLE, rich Bristowa's boast,
> Imports old stories from the Cambrian coast,
> And sends his goods to market – all alive!

Lines forty thousand, Cantos twenty-five!
Fresh fish from Hippocrene! who'll buy? who'll buy?
The precious bargain's cheap – in faith, not I.[14]

Wordsworth,

('Who, both by precept and example, shows
That prose is verse, and verse is merely prose')[15]

was briskly dealt with. It is unlikely that the great poet ever forgave Byron for this, and Brougham (although it was he who had written the cruel review of *Hours of Idleness* in the *Edinburgh Review*) certainly never forgave him for these lines:

Beware lest blundering Brougham destroy the sale,
Turns Beef to Bannocks, Cauliflowers to Kail.[16]

If anyone deserved retaliation it was Brougham and this was no more than a glancing blow, though Byron at this time was unaware that Brougham was author of the review which had distressed him. Brougham, however, waited for the appropriate moment and took a damaging, but secret, revenge.

Some readers who resented the hegemony of the *Edinburgh Review* over English letters may have enjoyed the lines:

For long as Albion's heedless sons submit,
Or Scottish taste decides on English wit.[17]

Many more must have enjoyed the sheer gusto and lèse-majesté of the whole performance. Others may have been mollified by the self-deprecation which was a novel attitude for an audience used to poets who tended to place themselves on a pedestal, above the ordinary run of mankind:

E'en I – least thinking of a thoughtless throng,
Just skilled to know the right and choose the wrong,
Freed at that age when Reason's shield is lost,
To fight my course through Passion's countless host,
Whom every path of Pleasure's flow'ry way
Has lured in turn, and all have led astray –
E'en I must raise my voice, e'en I must feel
Such scenes, such men, destroy the public weal:

Altho' some kind, censorious friend will say,
'What art thou better, meddling fool, than they?'
And every Brother Rake will smile to see
That miracle, a Moralist in me.[18]

In these lines Byron shows that he is well aware that he cannot set himself up as a moralist and perhaps he is conceding that his own earlier efforts at verse are no better than some of those he is criticising.

It was not long before he began to repent of the whole satire and in particular of the lines on Carlisle. In the original version he had some lines in praise of his guardian. After having been snubbed by Carlisle on his first appearance in the House of Lords he was so resentful that he replaced them with some outrageous verse referring to Carlisle's attempts at verse as 'the paralytic puling of Carlisle?'[19] This caused a rift with Augusta.

Moore describes Byron's attitude to the Satire on re-reading it during his stay at the Villa Diodati on the Lake of Geneva in the summer of 1816:

> But, whatever may have been the faults or indiscretions of this Satire, there are few who would now sit in judgment upon it so severely as did the author himself, on reading it over nine years after, when he had quitted England, never to return. The copy which he then perused is now in possession of Mr Murray, and the remarks which he has scribbled over its pages are well worth transcribing. On the first leaf we find –
> 'The binding of this volume is considerably too valuable for it contents.
> 'Nothing but the consideration of its being the property of another prevents me from consigning this miserable record of misplaced anger and indiscriminate acrimony to the flames.

Opposite the passage,

'to be misled
By Jeffrey's heart, or Lamb's Boeotian Head,'

is written, 'This was not just. Neither the heart nor the head of these gentlemen are at all what they are here represented.' Along the whole of the severe verses against Mr Wordsworth he has scrawled 'Unjust,' – and the same verdict is affixed to those against Mr Coleridge. On his unmeasured attack upon Mr Bowles, the comment is, – 'Too savage all this on Bowles;' and down the margin of the page containing the lines 'Health to immortal Jeffrey,' &c. he writes, – 'Too ferocious – this is mere insanity;' – adding, on the verses that follow ('Can none remember that eventful day?' &c.), 'All this is bad, because personal.'

Sometimes, however, he shows a disposition to stand by his original decisions. Thus, on the passage relating to a writer of certain obscure Epics (v. 793), he says, – 'All right;' adding, of the same person, 'I saw some letters of this fellow to an unfortunate poetess, whose productions (which the poor woman by no means thought vainly of) he attacked so roughly and bitterly, that I could hardly regret assailing him; – even were it unjust, which it is not; for, verily, he *is* an ass.' – On the strong lines, too (v. 953), upon Clarke (a writer in a magazine called the Satirist), he remarks, – 'Right enough, – this was well deserved and well laid on.'

To the whole paragraph, beginning 'Illustrious Holland,' are affixed the words 'Bad enough; – and on mistaken grounds besides.' The bitter verses against Lord Carlisle he pronounces 'Wrong also: – the provocation was not sufficient to justify such acerbity;' – and of a subsequent note respecting the same nobleman, he says, 'Much too savage, whatever the foundation may be...'

Opposite the paragraph in praise of Mr Crabbe he has written; 'I consider Crabbe and Coleridge as the first of these times in point of power and genius.' On his own line, in a subsequent paragraph, 'And glory, like the phoenix mid her fires,' he says, comically, 'The devil take that phoenix – how came it there?' and his concluding remark on the whole poem is a follows:

The greater part of this Satire I most sincerely wish had never been written; not only on account of the injustice of much of the critical and some of the personal part of it, but the tone and temper are such as I cannot approve.[20]

Byron was exceedingly rude to Jeffrey in the postcript to the second edition of the satire and he later repented of it when he discovered that the review of *Hours of Idleness* had been written not by Jeffrey but by Brougham. He was delighted when he heard that Jeffrey had compared his *Manfred* to the *Prometheus* of Aeschylus.

Once he became an habitué of Holland House and friend of Walter Scott and Thomas Moore he refused to allow any further editions of *English Bards and Scotch Reviewers* to be published and in 1813 he wrote of his repentance:

To-night I went with young Henry Fox to see 'Nourjahad,' – a drama, which the Morning Post hath laid to my charge, but of which I cannot even guess the author. I wonder what they will next inflict upon me. They cannot well sink below a Melodrama; but that is better than a

> Satire, (at least, a personal one,) with which I stand truly arraigned, and in atonement of which I am resolved to bear silently all criticisms, abuses, and even praises, for bad pantomimes never composed by me, without even a contradictory aspect. I suppose the root of this report is my loan to the manager of my Turkish drawings for his dresses, to which he was more welcome than to my name. I suppose the real author will soon own it, as it has succeeded; if not, Job be my model, and Lethe my beverage![21]
>
> (Journal, 27 November 1813)

A year later Byron gave some good advice to a novice writer, telling him not to be discouraged or enraged by the attacks of the critics. He then went on to ensure that the young man would not be as roughly handled as he himself has been. At this time Byron was twenty six but he writes like a sage, firstly to the writer, John Hamilton Reynolds and then to Francis Hodgson:

> The first thing a young writer must expect, and yet can least of all suffer, is *criticism* – I did not bear it – a few years, and many changes, have since passed over my head, and my reflections on that subject are attended with regret. I find, on dispassionate comparison, my own revenge more than the provocation warranted ... the best reply to all objections is to write better – and if your enemies will not then do you justice, the world will. On the other hand, you should not be discouraged – to be opposed, is not to be vanquished, though a timid mind is apt to mistake every scratch for a mortal wound.[22]
>
> (To John Hamilton Reynolds, 20 February 1816)

> There is a youngster – and a clever one, named Reynolds, who has just published a poem called 'Safie', published by Cawthorne. He is in the most natural and fearful apprehension of the Reviewers – and as you and I both know by experience the effect of such things upon a *young* mind, I wish *you* would take his production into dissection and do it *gently*. *I* cannot, because it is inscribed to me; but I assure you this is not my motive for wishing him to be tenderly entreated, but because I know the misery, at his time of life, of untoward remarks upon first appearance.[23]
>
> (To Francis Hodgson, 28 February 1814)

These letters show that Byron was far from being the cold, selfish, egotistical young man so often portrayed by writers who appear to ignore the bulk of the twelve volumes of letters.

The satire was well received by most critics. Hazlitt's criticism was in general opposed to the tradition of satirical verse from Pope onwards so it was to be expected that he would slate *English Bards and Scotch Reviewers* on literary grounds, as an attempt to continue in this tradition. He is even more scathing on the nobility of the young poet:

> We must say we think little of our author's turn for satire. His *English Bards and Scotch Reviewers* is dogmatical and insolent but without refinement... This is the satire of a lord who is accustomed to have all his whims or dislikes taken for gospel and who cannot be at the pains to do more than signify his contempt and displeasure.[24]

Hazlitt continually refers in his criticism to Byron's being a lord and this clouds his judgement, reducing him to the pettiness we find in Leigh Hunt's references to Byron after he had accepted his hospitality in Italy. Hunt seems to have resented his generosity and Hazlitt his aristocracy. Byron was later well aware of all such nuances in the hatred that was borne him by so many of his compatriots and soon after his exile he began to take it lightly, sending back to England 'A sigh to those who love me / And a smile to those who hate.'[25]

6

RETURN TO NEWSTEAD

Newstead! what saddening change of scene is thine!
Thy yawning arch betokens slow decay;
The last and youngest of a noble line,
Now holds thy mouldering turrets in his sway.[1]

In October 1807 Byron's chief worry was his enormous burden of debt. He asked Hanson to remit his quarterly allowance as soon as possible:

> ...for I am at this moment contemplating with a *woeful* visage, one *solitary Guinea, two bad sixpences* and a *shilling*, being all the *Cash* at present in possession of
>
> Yours very truly
> Byron[2]
> (Dorant's Hotel, 19 October 1807)

On leaving Cambridge his debts amounted to £5,000. By the time he set out on his travels in June 1809 they had increased to over £12,000. He described his way of life in London as 'an abyss of sensuality'.[3] He gambled, and he led the life of a man about Town with Scrope Davies, resorting through Mrs Massingberd to the money-lenders to finance his excesses.

He had written of his London life to Elizabeth Pigot:

> The Intelligence of London cannot be interesting to you who *have rusticated* all your life, the annals of Routs, Riots, Balls and Boxing matches, Dowagers and demireps, Cards and Crim-Con, Parliamentary Discussion, Political details, Masquerades, Mechanics, Argyle Street

> Institution and Aquatic races, Love and Lotteries, Brookes's and Buonaparte, Exhibitions of pictures with Drapery, and *women without*, Statues with more *decent dresses* than their *originals*, Opera-singers and Orators, Wine, Women, Waxworks and Weathercocks, cannot accord with your *insulated* ideas of decorum.[4]
>
> (Gordon's Hotel, 13 July 1807)

Byron naturally made no mention to Elizabeth of the deterioration in his health caused by excessive love-making with his 'blue-eyed Caroline'. This damsel claimed to be pregnant and, from some remark he made to them, Byron's friends were afraid he would feel obliged to marry her, but no more was heard of such a plan although he addressed some tender verses to her:

> But Breeze of night again forbear,
> In softest murmurs only sigh:
> Let not a Zephyr's pinion dare
> To lift those auburn locks on high.[5]

In the summer of 1808 Byron spent some weeks recuperating in Brighton with Hobhouse and Scrope Davies and various visitors including Gentleman Jackson and a Miss Cameron who was dressed in boy's clothes and may have been Byron's 'blue-eyed Caroline'. Nanny Smith later revealed that Byron had once brought a girl to Newstead who was dressed as a boy. These masquerades may have been concerned with disguise for practical purposes, with sexual arousal at the sight of a girl dressed as a boy or simply with the fun of hoodwinking all the onlookers.

In Brighton the three young men lodged on the seafront and would plunge into the sea at all hours of the day or night, visit the new theatre, perhaps attend assemblies at the Ship Hotel and even visit the Pavilion. Byron wrote to Augusta (now married and settled at a country house near Newmarket with her handsome Colonel and a baby girl) that he had seen George Leigh in Brighton. George's regiment, the tenth Hussars, was stationed at Brighton and he was in the service of the Prince Regent.

In September 1808 Lord Grey's lease of Newstead Abbey expired and Byron returned to his ancestral home with old Joe Murray (who had been Byron's pensioner most of the time since they had left Newstead) and William Fletcher, his groom, who was now promoted to valet and was to stay with Byron until his death at Missolonghi.

Byron now began spending lavishly on putting several apartments in order and told his mother, when she remonstrated, that it must be done and that she was to live in the renovated part of the Abbey when he went on his travels. Byron omitted to have the roof repaired so the new decorations were soon ruined by damp and rain. In the meantime he invited his friends to visit him. Hobhouse, Matthews, Scrope Davies, were surprised at being greeted not only by Byron's dogs but by the tame bear which his unfortunate mother was to take care of while he was away. Charles Skinner Matthews describes one such visit:

> Our party consisted of Lord Byron and four others, and was, now and then, increased by the presence of a neighbouring parson ... the order of the day was generally this;- for breakfast we had no set hour ... everything remaining on the table till the whole party had done; though had one wished to breakfast at the early hour of ten one would have been rather lucky to find any of the servants up. Our average hour of rising was one... It was frequently past two before the breakfast party broke up. Then, for the amusements of the morning there was reading, fencing, single-stick, or shuttle-cock in the great room; practising with pistols in the hall; walking – riding – cricket – sailing on the lake, playing with the bear, or teasing the wolf. Between seven and eight we dined [arrayed in the monkish robes and beads supplied by Byron]; and our evening lasted from that time till one, two, or three in the morning. The evening diversions may easily be conceived.[6]

Jonathan Gross comments on the self-conscious play-acting of this performance which included the passing round the table of wine in a goblet formed from a human skull:

> Byron's antics at Newstead Abbey and his references to Laurence Sterne, the Medmenham monks and *Choderlos de Laclos* show him emulating a version of eighteenth century libertinism long after it was unfashionable, even politically dangerous, to do so.[7]

The result was rumours of wickedness which spread round the world once Byron became famous and which helped to build up the false image which has influenced biographers and reviewers, and which Byron's friends would never have recognised. In France it was reported that Byron had murdered one of his mistresses and habitually drank wine out of her skull. When George Ticknor called on him in London in 1815 Byron reported with some amusement that the young American was expecting to meet 'a misanthropical gentleman in wolf-skin breeches'.[8] When Byron arrived in Rome after leaving England in 1816 Lady Lidell caught sight of him at St Peter's and ordered her daughter to avert her eyes for it was dangerous to look at him. Teresa Guiccioli's brother, Pietro Gamba, warned his sister to have nothing to do with this dangerous English lord who had shut up his wife for several years in one of his castles.

Nanny Smith, the housekeeper at Newstead, told Washington Irving after Byron's death that he and his friends had 'played some mad pranks but nothing but what young gentlemen do and no harm done.'[9] She explained that with his lame leg Byron was often unable to keep up with the gentlemen and then the only comfort he had was to be with the ladies a little. It is remarkable how much more censorious many modern biographers have been in comparison with this simple, kind-hearted elderly female servant with all the prejudices of her kind and the strictest notions of what constituted decorous and acceptable behaviour in a nineteenth century household. When old Joe Murray began singing lewd songs in front of the housemaids she would read him a lecture and flounce off to bed in a rage. But she was moved to compassion by the obvious suffering and frustration his deformity caused her young master, and made allowances for his need of comfort.

Although Byron was posturing as an eighteenth century libertine the goings-on described by Nanny Smith and Charles Skinner Matthews appear more reminiscent of typical undergraduate misbehaviour than anything more sinister. Sexual congress with willing housemaids may have been reprehensible but it was not unusual. When the youngest of the housemaids, Lucy, became pregnant Byron provided £100 a year for her, later altered to £50 for her and £50 for the boy. This may be compared with the income of £150 a year on which Mrs Byron and her son had lived in Aberdeen.

Wordsworth came to regard Byron as a moral pariah but the younger man was more honest than Wordsworth in admitting his moral failings and, in taking care of his illegitimate offspring, displayed both moral responsibility and kindness.

The suspicion has been aired that Byron and his Cambridge friends were a coterie of homosexuals and that the diversions of the evenings at Newstead were homo-erotic. This may indeed have been the case but it is most unlikely. Romping with the housemaids was one thing but it is hard to imagine the young men indulging in homosexual practices in Byron's ancestral home (which was inhabited by giggling girls, a young page who was the son of one of Byron's tenants, Fletcher, Joe Murray and Nanny Smith) and inviting the local parson to join them on several occasions.

Modern biographers often assume that Byron went in for every form of sexual excess but to imagine the staid Hobhouse (who was so painfully shy that he was unable to approach women of education and social standing and was obliged to resort to prostitutes) making sexual overtures to Byron, or vice versa, appears somewhat ludicrous. There is no hint of erotic tension in their correspondence over many years. As for Matthews, he appears to have set himself up as their professor in matters to do with Greek love. His letters spur his friends on to ever greater interest in the classic relationship of the older man with the younger boy, but there is no hint of erotic intentions towards his correspondents of his own age.

Jonathan Gross warns, in a different context, against the danger of confusing 'licentious language with licentious deeds'. It is not possible here to rule out licentious deeds of this nature but neither can one pronounce with any degree of certainty that such deeds were done.

Hobhouse sets out the ground of the close and loving friendship which linked Byron, himself, Scrope Davies and Douglas Kinnaird over the years as he deals with Lady Byron's prejudice against her husband's friends:

> Her Ladyship had formed an incorrect judgement not only on his Lordship but on his Lordship's friends, who, from not exactly bearing that cast of character which she might have been accustomed to regard as necessary for the communion of married men, she was induced to look upon as the associates of wickedness rather than as the votaries and encouragers of a steady and honourable attachment to the companion of many years.[10]

Byron started planning his travels in earnest, assuring Hanson that living out of England for a year or two would save him much expense. In the meantime Hanson could sell the Rochdale property to pay off his debts and, in particular, to relieve Scrope Davies who had guaranteed a loan for him and was afraid the creditors might come down on him in Byron's absence. This was an excellent plan but Hanson's failure to dispose of the Rochdale property left Scrope in dismal uncertainty for several years; the fact that Hanson did not write to him for long periods during his travels left Byron fuming with anxiety over the outcome.

The money for expenses abroad had to be raised by loans and proved difficult, especially as it was necessary to raise double the amount required since Hobhouse was on bad terms with his father and the quixotic but heedless young debtor offered to raise the money for him too. At this time Mrs Byron was worrying about Byron's creditors in Nottingham, who would be ruined if he failed to pay his bills. Raising the necessary funds took so long that their departure was put off time and again.

While waiting for a passage Byron was thrown once more into melancholy by a meeting at the Infirmary Ball in Nottingham with Mary and Jack Chaworth-Musters, as they were now known. Byron brought Hobhouse with him to the Ball and arranged for Mrs Byron to meet them there, a rare occasion for his mother to bask in the mild success and new-found beauty of her beloved son. It was the first time Mary saw her formerly fat, school-boy admirer in the persona of a divinely beautiful young poet. As a result Byron and Hobhouse were invited to dinner at Annesley Hall, a distressing experience for both Byron and Mary:

> [I] was determined to be valiant and converse with 'Sang Froid', but instead I forgot my valour and my nonchalance, and never opened my lips even to laugh, Far less to speak, and the Lady was almost as absurd as myself, which made both the object of more observation, than if we had conducted ourselves with easy indifference.[11]
>
> (To Francis Hodgson, Newstead Abbey, Notts, 3 March 1808)

Byron's love for Mary inspired several poems one of which described Byron's trysts with Mary on the hill known as Diadem hill because it was crowned with a diadem of trees. When Byron became famous the poem was read all over Europe. Jack Musters had all the trees cut down. His jealousy may well have originated with the strange behaviour of his wife and her guest when Byron and Hobhouse came to dine.

Soon after this episode Byron was writing, 'My dear Hodgson, Boatswain is dead ... I have lost everybody except Old Murray.'[12] Byron was always besotted by his animals and Boatswain, a huge and amiable Newfoundland, was his particular favourite. He nursed him through the rabies attack which killed him, wiping the slaver from his jaws with his bare hands. Boatswain was buried in a vault near the nave of the ruined Priory Church and Byron decreed that he himself, together with old Joe Murray, would be buried beside him. Old Joe demurred saying he would not mind so long as his Lordship lay there with him, 'But I should not like to lie there alone with the dog.'

Before Byron left England he wanted to see the publication of his satire, now entitled *English Bards and Scotch Reviewers*. He was assisted in this object by Charles Dallas who claimed distant kinship with Byron in 1807, had written some minor novels, and now offered to find him a publisher, fixing on James Cawthorne.

Many who met Byron briefly and were regarded by him with a sceptical eye, made haste to produce accounts of their relationship with him after his death. Dallas was no exception. In his book he relates how he called on Byron one day to find him on the point of setting out for the House of Lords to undergo the ceremony of taking his seat for the first time. Byron was in a state of nervousness and melancholy, the explanation being that when he wrote to tell his guardian that he was planning to take his seat, expecting Carlisle to accompany him to the House and introduce him there, Lord Carlisle wrote a letter explaining what steps he must take and describing the ceremony. All Byron's doubts about Carlisle's coldness towards his ward and the reason for it (strong dislike) arose once again. To Byron this rebuff was tantamount to a blow in the face. As a result he was obliged to set about the irksome business of proving his right of succession to the barony and then to proceed alone in his robes to the House of Lords. Byron welcomed Dallas's offer to accompany him to the House. His seat taken, he was ready to leave England as soon as possible after the publication of his satire.

Byron left England with his affairs in a state of confusion. Hanson begged him to postpone his departure until they could be brought into some sort of order. Now was the time for him to take an interest in his estates. He failed to do so and set off on his travels leaving some large debts for work on the Abbey unsettled and instructing Hanson airily to sell the Rochdale property in order to settle them.

Byron had not been brought up as heir to the estate or taught, as were most heirs, to regard his inheritance as a sacred trust.

More importantly, he was so extravagant as a young man that the sale of Newstead became almost inevitable. Just as the fifth baron relied on the marriage of his son to an heiress to save the day, Byron relied on the sale of Rochdale to make him rich. It never did.

John Murray, Byron's publisher, visited Newstead on 5 October 1814 and wrote a description of what he found:

> Not a tree is left standing ... the hall of entrance has about eighteen large niches, which had been filled with statues, and the side walls covered with family portraits and armour. All these have been mercilessly torn down, as well as the magnificent fireplace, and sold. No sum short of £100,000 would make the place habitable ... the whole place is crumbling into dust ... I am far more surprised that Lord Byron should ever have lived at Newstead, than that he should be inclined to part with it ... I came away with an aching heart.[13]

7

THE PILGRIMAGE

'London and the world is the only place to take the conceit out of a man'[1]

Thomas Moore was convinced that Byron suffered from a deep melancholy at this point in his life and he explains away the evidence of sheer youthful energy and high spirits as isolated incidents which concealed a wounded spirit. G.K. Chesterton took the view that this melancholy was a youthful affectation. Byron took pleasure in dramatic storms and stricken peaks because he was very young and very happy.

Byron planned to take with him on his travels old Joe, William Fletcher and his page, Robert Rushton. Shortly before they left England Byron angrily changed his mind about bringing Robert and Fletcher abroad with him. Fletcher, who was supposed to be looking after the boy in London, had actually introduced him to a prostitute. Byron wrote to Mrs Byron from London:

> I have sent the lad to his father; before this occurrence he was good hearted, honest, and all I could wish him, and would have been so still, but for the machinations of the scoundrel who has not only been guilty of adultery; but of depraving the mind of an innocent stripling ... for his wife's sake he shall have a farm or other provision of some kind, but he quits me... Break this business to his wife, who will probably hear it from the boy's relatives in another manner.[2]
>
> (To Mrs Catherine Gordon Byron, 8 St James's Street, 19 May 1809)

Then Byron, who was incorrigibly soft-hearted, wrote to his mother from Falmouth, the first stop on his journey:

Fletcher begged so hard that I have continued him in my service... Pray tell Mr Rushton his son is well, and *doing* well.'[3]

(To Mrs Catherine Gordon Byron, Falmouth, 22 June 1809)

Many authorities have believed the assertion of Lady Caroline Lamb (at a period when she had told Byron, 'You will see how an Englishwoman can revenge.'[4]) that Byron told her he had corrupted Robert Rushton. If this were so, Byron's letter to his mother on the subject of Fletcher's behaviour must have been sheer hypocrisy. The most sensible account of the matter is given by Ian Gilmour:

> [Byron's] rage at Fletcher having taken his page to a whore has been attributed to his having made Rushton his catamite. Rushton was a good-looking lad, who slept in a bedroom next to his master's; and Byron was fond of him – in a will he made before he went abroad he left Rushton £25 a year for life. According to Lady Byron, Lady Caroline Lamb later alleged that Byron had admitted to her that he had 'corrupted' the boy. And there is a remark by Hobhouse which may be stronger evidence.
>
> Even so, it is on the whole unlikely that Byron ever 'corrupted' Rushton. For him to have done that to the son of a tenant would have been far more dangerous than any of his other homosexual escapades. Tongues would surely have been busy, and he would have faced exile like William Beckford, Lord Leicester and other homosexuals involved in scandal. Indeed both his own and Rushton's lives would have been in danger. While other countries were becoming more liberal over homosexuality, England was becoming more draconian; the number of executions for sodomy was growing...

Gilmour also adds that sending Rushton back to his father as Byron did after the incident with the prostitute 'would have been crazily imprudent had he really corrupted the boy.'[5]

Treating the allegation on the subject of Rushton with some scepticism does not entail a belief that Byron was uninterested in Greek love. Both he and Hobhouse discussed with Matthews their intention of experimenting with this fascinating and, to them, romantic subject when they reached Greece. Those who disagree with this analysis and believe that Byron took Rushton with him as his catamite are faced with the question why he should do so on a journey to Greece with the expectation he and Hobhouse harboured of sexual freedom with Greek boys there. Nor can one easily imagine Byron corrupting the boy with Fletcher in his entourage after the angry remonstrances over the visit to the London prostitute.

From Falmouth Byron wrote a lively description of the town to Francis Hodgson, omitting the *bonne bouche* he saved for Charles Skinner Matthews: 'We are surrounded by Hyacinths and other flowers of the most fragrant nature, and I have some intention of culling a handsome Bouquet to compare with the exotics we expect to meet in Asia.'[6] Hodgson, and even Hobhouse were more inhibited or disapproving on this subject than Matthews, and Byron was always tactful in suiting the tone of his letters to their recipients. With Matthews he employed a code derived from the *Satyricon* of Petronius for the achievement of sexual gratification. But, as Jonathan Gross warns, 'licentious language does not necessarily mean licentious deeds.'[7] It may be that Henry Drury was not the most suitable recipient of the joke about Hobhouse which Byron confided to him in yet another letter from Falmouth – 'Hobhouse further hopes to indemnify himself in Turkey for a life of exemplary chastity at home by letting out his "fair bodye" to the whole Divan.'[8]

On 25 June 1809 Byron and Hobhouse sailed from Falmouth in the Lisbon packet with 'two officers' wives, three children, two waiting maids, ditto subalterns for the troops, three Portuguese esquires, and domestics, in all nineteen souls.'[9]

He wrote to Hodgson from Lisbon:

> I am very happy here, because I loves oranges, and talk bad Latin to the monks, who understand it, as it is like their own, – and I goes into society (with my pocket-pistols), and I swims in the Tagus all across at once, and I rides on an ass or a mule, and swears Portuguese, and have got a diarrhoea and bites from the mosquitoes. But what of that? Comfort must not be expected by folks that go a pleasuring.***
>
> When the Portuguese are pertinacious, I say, 'Carracho!' – the great oath of the grandees, that very well supplies the place of 'Damme,' – and, when dissatisfied with my neighbor, I pronounce him 'Ambra di merdo.' With these two phrases, and a third, 'Avra Bouro,' which signifieth 'Get an ass,' I am universally understood to be a person of degree and a master of languages. How merrily we lives that travellers be! ... To-morrow we start to ride post near 400 miles as far as Gibraltar, where we embark for Melita [Malta?] and Byzantium. A letter to Malta will find me, or to be forwarded, if I am absent ... Hodgson! send me the news, and the deaths and defeats and capital crimes and the

misfortunes of one's friends; and let us hear of literary matters, and the controversies and the criticisms.[10]

(To Frances Hodgson, Lisbon, 16 July 1809)

He wrote a long account of his travels to Mrs Byron from Gibraltar. Now that they were separated he ignored their former differences. His letters to her from Greece are unusually friendly and direct:

I find that reserve is not the characteristic of the Spanish belles, who are in general very handsome, with large black eyes, and very fine forms... Intrigue here is the business of life, when a woman marries she throws off all restraint, but I believe their conduct is chaste enough before. – If you make a proposal which in England would bring a box on the ear from the meekest of virgins, to a Spanish girl, she thanks you for the honour you intend her and replies 'wait till I am married and I shall be too happy...' I am going over to Africa tomorrow, it is only six miles from this Fortress. – My next stage is Cagliari in Sardinia where I shall be presented to his S[ardinian] Majesty. I have a most superb uniform as a court dress, indispensable in travelling...

(To Mrs Catherine Gordon Byron, Gibraltar, 11 August 1809)

15 August
I cannot go to Barbary; the Malta packet sails tomorrow and myself in it... Joe Murray delivers this. I have sent him and the boy back, pray show the lad any kindness as he is my great favourite, I would have taken him on (but you *know boys* are not *safe* amongst the Turks–) say this to his father who may otherwise think he has behaved ill.[11]

(To Mrs Catherine Gordon Byron, 13 August 1809)

In Malta Byron was introduced to a pretty and sophisticated young married woman called Constance Spenser Smith who lived in Vienna and had been through adventures which gave her an intriguing glamour. They fell in love but not deeply enough on Byron's side to cause him to postpone his departure. They planned to meet again the following year and Byron wrote several poems about her during his travels, the last of which spoke of a passion that was waning:

XXX
Sweet Florence! could another ever share
This wayward, loveless heart, it would be thine:[12]

They did meet again when Byron returned briefly to Malta, and he went through the embarrassing business of convincing the lady that the undying love they had sworn two years ago was in reality no more than a fleeting romance. In thus writing of his 'loveless heart' Byron did himself less than justice. 'Wayward' it was, but certainly not 'loveless'. Moore rightly characterised his life as a series of 'the most passionate attachments'[13] and he himself later wrote 'I cannot exist without some object of love.'[14]

CHILDE HAROLD'S PILGRIMAGE

Itinerary of Lord Byron and J.C. Hobhouse
(Originally published in E.H. Coleridge's edition of 1905)

1809	CANTO I
July 2	Sail from Falmouth in Lisbon packet. (Stanza 12)
July 6	Arrive Lisbon. (Stanzas 16, 17)
	Visit Cintra. (Stanzas 18–26)
	Visit Mafra. (Stanza 29)
July 17	Leave Lisbon. (Stanza 28)
	Ride through Portugal and Spain to Seville. (Stanzas 28–42)
	Visit Albuera. (Stanza 43)
July 21	Arrive Seville. (Stanzas 14, 46)
July 25	Leave Seville.
	Ride to Cadiz, across the Sierra Morena. (Stanza 51)
	Cadiz. (Stanzas 65–84)
	CANTO II
Aug. 6	Arrive Gibraltar.
Aug. 16	Sail from Gibraltar in Malta packet. (Stanzas 17–28)
	Malta. (Stanzas 29–35)
Sept. 19	Sail from Malta in brig-of-war *Spider*.
Sept. 23	Between Cephalonia and Zante.
Sept. 26	Anchor off Patras.
Sept. 27	In the channel between Ithaca and the mainland. (Stanzas 39–42)
Sept. 28	Anchor off Prevesa (7 p.m.). (Stanza 14)
Oct. 1	Leave Prevesa, arrive Salakhora (Salagoura).
Oct. 3	Leave Salakhora, arrive Arta.
Oct. 4.	Leave Arta, arrive, han St Demetre (H. Dhimittrios).
Oct. 5	Arrive Janina. (Stanza 47)
Oct. 8	Ride into the country. First day of Ramazan.
Oct. 11	Leave Janina, arrive Zitza ('Lines written during a Thunderstorm'). (Stanzas 48–51)

Oct. 13	Leave Zitza, arrive Mossiani (Móseri).
Oct. 14	Leave Mossiani, arrive Delvinaki (Dhelvinaki). (Stanza 54)
Oct. 15	Leave Delvinaki, arrive Libokhovo.
Oct. 17	Leave Libokhovo, arrive Cesarades (Kestouratαes).
Oct. 18	Leave Cesarades, arrive Ereeneed (Irindi).
Oct. 19	Leave Ereeneed, arrive Tepeleni. (Stanzas 55–61)
Oct. 20	Reception by Ali Pacha. (Stanzas 62–64)
Oct. 23	Leave Tepeleni, arrive Locavo (Lacovon).
Oct. 24	Leave Locavo, arrive Delvinaki.
Oct. 25	Leave Delvinaki, arrive Zitza.
Oct. 26	Leave Zitza, arrive Janina.
Oct. 31	Byron begins the First Canto of *Childe Harold.*
Nov. 3	Leave Janina, arrive han St Demetre.
Nov. 4	Leave han St Demetre, arrive Arta.
Nov. 5	Leave Arta, arrive Salakhora.
Nov. 7	Leave Salakhora, arrive Prevesa.
Nov. 8	Sail from Prevesa, anchor off mainland near Parga. (Stanzas 67, 68)
Nov. 9	Leave Parga, and, returning by land arrive Volondorako (Valanidórakhon). (Stanza 69)
Nov. 10	Leave Volondórako, arrive Castrosikia (Kastrosykia).
Nov. 11	Leave Castrosikia, arrive Prevesa.
Nov. 13	Sail from Prevesa, anchor off Vonitsa.
Nov. 14	Sail from Vonitsa, arrive Lutraki (Loutráki). (Stanzas 70, 72, Song 'Tambourgi, Tambourgi'; Stanza written in passing the Ambracian Gulph.)
Nov. 15	Leave Lutraki, arrive Katúna.
Nov. 16	Leave Katúna, arrive Makalá (? Machalas).
Nov. 18	Leave Makalá, arrive Guriá.
Nov. 19	Leave Guriá, arrive Ætolikon.
Nov. 20	Leave Ætolikon, arrive Mesolonghi.
Nov. 23	Sail from Mesolonghi, arrive Patras.
Dec. 4	Leave Patras, sleep at *Han* on shore.
Dec. 5	Leave *Han*, arrive Vostitsa (Œgion).
Dec. 14	Sail from Vostitsa, arrive Larnáki (? Itea).
Dec. 15	Leave Larnáki (? Itera), arrive Chrysó.
Dec. 16	Visit Delphi, the Pythian Cave, and stream of Castaly. (Canto I. Stanza 1)
Dec. 17	Leave Chrysó, arrive Arakhova (Rhakova).
Dec. 18	Leave Arakhova, arrive Livadia (Livadhia).
Dec. 21	Leave Livadia, arrive Mazee (Mazi).
Dec. 22	Leave Mazee, arrive Thebes.
Dec. 24	Leave Thebes, arrive Skurta.
Dec. 25	Leave Skurta, pass Phyle, arrive Athens. (Stanzas 1–15; stanza 74)
Dec. 30	Byron finishes the First Canto of *Childe Harold.*

1810

Jan. 13	Visit Eleusis.
Jan. 16	Visit Mendeli (Pentelicus). (Stanza 87)
Jan. 18	Walk round the peninsula of Munychia.
Jan. 19	Leave Athens, arrive Vari.
Jan. 20	Leave Vari, arrive Keratéa.
Jan. 23	Visit temple of Athene at Sunium. (Stanza 86)
Jan. 24	Leave Keratéa, arrive plain of Marathon.
Jan. 25	Visit plain of Marathon. (Stanzas 89, 90)
Jan. 26	Leave Marathon, arrive Athens.
Mar. 5	Leave Athens, embark on board the *Pylades.*
Mar. 7	Arrive Smyrna.
Mar. 13	Leave Smyrna, sleep at *Han*, near the river Halesus.
Mar. 14	Leave *Han*, arrive Aiasaluk (near Ephesus).
Mar. 15	Visit site of temple of Artemis at Ephesus.
Mar. 16	Leave Ephesus, return to Smyrna
Mar. 28	Byron finishes the Second Canto of *Childe Harold.*[15]

Byron wrote to Hanson from Prevesa in Albania:

> The Consul has gotten me a house here... The bay where we now lie was the scene of the famous battle of Actium. – I have seen Ithaca and touched in the Morea at Patras, where I found the Greeks polite and hospitable... Remember me to all your family, particularly Mrs Hanson, but do not expect to see me soon, I am now above three thousand miles from Chancery Lane.[16]
>
> (To John Hanson, Prevesa in Albania, 29 September 1809)

Byron wrote also at some length to his mother:

> Prevesa, 12 November 1809
>
> My dear Mother –
> I have now been some time in Turkey; ... When I reached Yanina the capital after a journey of three days over the mountains through a country of the most picturesque beauty I found that Ali Pacha was with his army in Illyricum besieging Ibrahim Pacha in the castle of Berat – He had heard that an Englishman of rank was in his dominions and had left orders in Yanina with the Commandant to provide a house and supply me with every kind of necessary, *gratis* ... though I have been allowed to make presents to the slaves etc.

Byron then travelled over the mountains through Zitza 'a village with a monastery where I slept on my return', reaching Tepelene nine days later where he was introduced to Ali Pacha. He describes the scene on entering Tepaleen (as he calls it):

> The Albanians in their dresses ... (a long *white kilt*, gold worked cloak, crimson velvet gold laced jacket and waistcoat, silver mounted pistols and daggers) ... the Tartars with their high caps, the Turks in their vast pelises and turbans, the soldiers and black slaves with the horses ... two hundred steeds ready caparisoned to move in a moment, couriers entering or passing out with dispatches, the kettle drums beating, boys calling the hour from the minaret of the mosque...
>
> [Ali Pacha] told me to consider him as a father whilst I was in Turkey ... – Indeed he treated me like a child, sending me almonds and sugared sherbet, fruit and sweetmeats 20 times a day ... his manner is very kind and at the same time he possess that dignity which I find universal among the Turks. He has the appearance of anything but his true character, for he is a remorseless tyrant, guilty of the most horrible cruelties, very brave and so good a general that they call him the Mahometan Buonaparte...
>
> Two days ago I was nearly lost in a Turkish ship ... – Fletcher yelled after his wife, the Greeks called on all the Saints, the Mussulmen on Alla, the Captain burst into tears and ran below deck telling us to call on God, the sails were split, the mainyard shivered, the wind blowing fresh, the night setting in ... I did what I could to console Fletcher but finding him incorrigible wrapped myself up in my Albanian capote (an immense cloak) and lay down on deck to await the worst ... – Luckily the wind abated...
>
> Fletcher's next epistle will be full of marvels, we were one night lost for nine hours in the mountains in a *thunder* storm.[17]
>
> (To Mrs Catherine Gordon Byron, Prevesa, 12 November 1809)

In Athens the young men took lodgings in the house of Theodora Macri, widow of the late English Vice Consul. These consisted of a sitting room and two bedrooms opening onto a courtyard where there were five or six lemon trees, from which Hobhouse wrote, '...during our residence in the place, was plucked the fruit that seasoned the pilaf and other national dishes served up at our frugal table.'[18] Their landlady had three pretty daughters and Byron fell in love with the youngest of them, Teresa. On leaving Athens to visit Constantinople Byron wrote to his mother from Smyrna:

> I have traversed the greatest part of Greece besides Epirus and resided ten weeks at Athens, and am now on the Asiatic side on my way to Constantinople ... Greece, particularly in the vicinity of Athens, is

delightful, cloudless skies, and lovely landscapes ... I keep no journal, but my friend Hobhouse scribbles incessantly.[19]

(To Mrs Catherine Gordon Byron, Smyrna, 19 March 1810)

Byron failed to mention that he had almost completed Cantos I and II of *Childe Harold's Pilgrimage*, a poem of a wholly different kind and scale than anything he had yet attempted.

Byron and Hobhouse set off from Smyrna to Constantinople in the naval frigate sent to pick up the retiring Ambassador, Robert Adair. When they anchored off Abydos Byron imitated the feat of Leander in swimming from Sestos to Abydos, lamenting that there was no Hero to greet him as he came up out of the water. He was very proud of this performance, boasting of it in letters to several friends. Now he wrote to Henry Drury describing his adventures:

I have been with Generals and Admirals, Princes and Pachas, Governors and Ungovernables, ... I wish to let you know that I live with a friendly remembrance of you and hope to meet you again ... I see not much difference between us and the Turks, save that we have foreskins and they none, that they have long dresses and we short, and that we talk much and they little. – In England the vices in fashion are whoring and drinking, in Turkey Sodomy and smoking, we prefer a girl and a bottle, they a pipe and pathic... Tell Dr Butler I am now writing with the gold pen he gave me before I left England.[20]

(To Henry Drury, Salsette Frigate, 3 May 1810
in the Dardanelles off Abyssinia)

When they arrived in Constantinople Byron proceeded to make himself unpopular by an ill-mannered insistence on his right to precedence as a man of rank. The two young men were treated with immense courtesy by the departing Ambassador to the Porte, Robert Adair, who invited them regularly to dine and then to join the ceremonial procession which accompanied his leavetaking of the Turkish representative of the absent Grand Vizier. Byron was offended at being required to walk behind the first Secretary, Stratford Canning, and stormed off in a fury. Even so the Ambassador invited him to the ceremonial leavetaking from the Sultan. Byron consulted the powers-that-be on protocol and, finding that an English peer was not in these circumstances entitled to precedence, accepted the invitation with an apology for his former discourtesy. It was a discreditable episode which can have done his reputation no good in the English community of the city. When Byron felt at a disadvantage he tended, at this age, to become haughty and belligerent. He refers later to the fact that travel in the world takes 'the conceit out of a man'.[21]

In July 1810 he had received news which depressed him deeply. He heard that Augusta was annoyed at his attack on Lord Carlisle in *English Bards and Scotch Reviewers*. He wrote, 'Had I been aware that she would have laid it to heart, I would have cast my pen and poem both into the flames... But the mischief is done, Lord forgive me! this it is to have tender hearted she-relations.'[22] (To Edward Ellice, Constantinople, 4 July 1810)

He also learned that Hanson had been unable to pay off his creditors and that the Nottingham upholsterer who had refurbished Byron's apartments at Newstead had presented his bill for £1,600 and was threatening an execution. On 30 July he wrote to Mrs Byron from Patras, 'I suppose some arrangement has been made with regard to Wymondham [his Norfolk property] and Rochdale.'[23]

He wrote to Hobhouse:

> [I have had] two billets from Hanson, he wants me to sell Newstead, but I wont. ... My affairs are greatly embarrassed ... Tell Davies, in a very few months I shall be at home to relieve him from his responsibility which he would never have incurred so long, had I been aware 'of the law's delay.'[24]
>
> (To Hobhouse, Athens, 26 November 1810)

Byron had written to Hodgson from the Salsette frigate:

> I hope you will find me an altered personage, I do not mean in body, but in manner, for I begin to find out that nothing but virtue will do in this damned world. I am tolerably sick of vice which I have tried in its agreeable varieties, and mean on my return to cut all my dissolute acquaintance, leave off wine and 'carnal company', and betake myself to politics and Decorum. – I am very serious and cynical, and a good deal disposed to moralize, but fortunately for you the coming homily is cut off by default of pen, and defection of paper.[25]
>
> (To Francis Hodgson, Salsette Frigate, in the Dardanelles off Abydos, 5 May 1810)

This frame of mind is reflected in Canto I of *Childe Harold* where he echoes Shakespeare's 'expense of spirit in a waste of shame' theme:

XXXV

The paltry prize is hardly worth the cost:
  Youth wasted – Minds degraded – Honour lost –
These are thy fruits, successful Passion! these![26]

He looks back to Mary Chaworth:

V

For he through Sin's long labyrinth had run,
Nor made atonement when he did amiss,
Had sighed to many though he loved but one,
And that loved one, alas! could ne'er be his.
Ah, happy she! to 'scape from him whose kiss
Had been pollution unto aught so chaste;[27]

When Byron learned later that Mary had left Jack Musters (who had always been an inveterate womaniser both before and during the marriage) he may have concluded that his own kiss was no more polluted than that of the man she married and to whom she had borne five children.

Byron and Hobhouse left Constantinople with Robert Adair and his suite on the Salsette Frigate. At Zea Hobhouse parted from Byron and went on to England while Byron headed back to Athens. Byron had told Hobhouse not to worry about the sum (in excess of £800) which he was owed for the expenses of the journey, but Hobhouse, more sensible about money matters than his friend, decided that he could not allow the debt to increase any further. When he reached home his father refused to settle his debts unless he would agree to join the Militia. When Byron received the letter with this news he tried hard to dissuade Hobhouse, as a few years ago he had tried to dissuade Long from joining the military:

> You talk of the Militia, – Santissimi Coglioni! the Militia at five and twenty, Boys over your head, and brutes under you, Mess, Country quarters, Courts martial, and quelling of Riots. – If you will be mad or martial ('tis the same thing) go to Portugal again and I'll go with you.[28]
>
> (To John Cam Hobhouse, Volage Frigate, at sea, 19 June 1811)

Having said farewell to Hobhouse Byron returned to Athens. He had fallen in love with the city during his earlier stay there with Hobhouse and had written a famous poem to the youngest daughter of Mrs Macri:

I

Maid of Athens, ere we part,
Give, oh, give me back my heart![29]

On his return Byron would have been happy to resume his love affair with Teresa Macri but Mrs Macri was greedy and wanted to sell her daughter to him. Uneasy and embarrassed, he moved into the Capuchin monastery near the Acropolis which combined a school for the children of foreigners, or Franks, with an inn for Frankish travellers.

Byron made some excursions from Athens during this time, joining Lord Sligo with his vast train of servants and horses in a journey into the Morea and then visiting Veli Pasha at Tripolitzia. He was embarrassed by the young man's sexual overtures but accepted from him the gift of 'a very pretty horse'. Veli Pasha might have saved himself the cost of the horse. He was not a charming Greek youth and there was no lack of beautiful and willing boys in Athens. Byron had been accompanied on an earlier trip by a handsome boy called Eustathius Gregorious who joined him again, much to the scorn of Fletcher who laughed at the boy's holding up a parasol to protect himself from the sun while on horseback. Eustathius was demanding and capricious and, after a parting which entailed much kissing and embracing, he was sent home.

Byron spent several happy weeks in Athens foregathering with the distinguished, intellectual, or simply agreeable Franks of all nationalities who were wintering there. He told his mother:

> Here I see and have conversed with French, Italians, Germans, Danes, Greeks, Turks, Americans etc. etc., etc., and without losing sight of my own, I can judge of the countries and manners of others – Where I see the superiority of England (which by the bye we are a good deal mistaken about in many things) I am pleased and where I find her inferior I am at least enlightened.[30]

On his way back one day from swimming Byron was involved in a bizarre incident which he used later as the basis for his Oriental Tale, *The Giaour*, and which was also the ground for what Byron referred to as 'Old Goethe's husband-killing story'.[31] Goethe believed that Byron had killed the husband of a woman with whom he became involved in Greece or Turkey. This conviction does not seem to have altered the reverence in which he held the younger man: 'When you have an opportunity to give news of yourself to that remarkable man tell him also about me and mine and the exhaustible reverence, admiration and love which we feel for him.'[32] Byron and his party came upon a group of men near the banks of the Bosphorus. A Turkish girl had been sewn up in a sack and they were about to throw her into the river. The incident is mysterious. Byron rescued the girl. He is thought to have had some connection with her plight. No evidence of this has been forthcoming and it is unlikely that we will ever learn more about the incident. Lord Sligo gave an account of it, claiming that Byron forced the men to release the girl by producing a pistol which persuaded them to resort to higher authority for arbitration.

The plan of reformation Byron had described to Francis Hodgson was put on hold once he got to Athens where he disported himself with both Greek and Turkish women as well as romping with the six boys at the Capuchin monastery. He would take his favourite, Nicolo Giraud aged fifteen, to swim with him and Nicolo became his amico and swore undying love. Byron decided to pay for his education and in fact dropped him off at Malta for this purpose on his way home. This is the period during which he went in for Greek love with Greek boys. These boys were sexually experienced but full of fun and mischief. Such practices were regarded as no great aberration in Greece so they were free from guilt and anxiety. They were romantic experiences in a romantic landscape bathed in sunshine, its beaches washed by the blue Mediterranean waters. Byron told Hobhouse to inform the Citoyen (Matthews) '...that I have obtained above two hundred pl & opt Cs and am almost tired of them, for the history of these he must wait for my return', and later, in a letter: 'Mention to M[atthews] that I have found so many of his antiques on this classical soil, that I am tired of pl & opt Cs, the last thing I could be tired of, I wish I could find some of Socrates's Hemlock, but Lusieri tells me it don't poison people nowadays.'[33] The expression pl & opt Cs is the code Byron used for buggery. It derives from Petronius: *coitum plenum et optabilem.*

Byron's boast about his sexual prowess may be accurate but he had time for other diversions:

> Since your departure from the Cyclades, I have been principally in Attica... Here be many English, and there have been more, with all of

whom I have been and *am* on dining terms, and we have had balls and a variety of fooleries with the females of Athens.[34]

(To John Cam Hobhouse, Capuchin Convent, Athens, 10 January 1811)

In March he wrote to Hobhouse:

My fantastical adventures I reserve for you and Matthews and a bottle of Champagne, I parted as I lived friends with all the English and French in Attica and we had balls, dinners, and amours without number.[35]

(To John Cam Hobhouse, Athens, 18 May 1811)

During his travels Byron had misgivings about Hanson's management of his affairs, but for much of the time of his absence from England he was unaware that Rochdale had not been sold. Throughout his time in Albania and in Greece Byron constantly wrote asking Hanson for news of his financial affairs and Hanson constantly failed to reply. A letter from Byron to Hanson from Prevesa, shows that he was unaware then that his optimistic plans for dealing with his debts had come to nothing:

Now for my affairs, – I have received not a single letter since I left England, – my copyholds I presume are sold, and my debts in some train, what surplus may be of Rochdale, I should wish to convert into annuities for my own life on good security, and tolerable interest, or good mortgages, if nothing remains, sorry as I should be and much as I should regret it Newstead must go for the sake of justice to all parties.[36]

(Prevesa, 12 November 1809)

In May 1810 he had still received no news from Hanson and writes from Constantinople:

...if Mrs Byron requires any supply, pray let her have it at my expence, and at all events whatever becomes of me, do not allow her to suffer any unpleasant privation. – I believe I mentioned in my last that I had visited the plains of Troy, and swam from Sestos to Abydos in the Dardanelles ... I came up in an English Frigate, but we were detained in the Hellespont ten days for a wind. Here I am at last, ... I am anxiously expecting intelligence from your quarter, I suppose you are now at Rochdale.[37]

(Constantinople, 23 May 1810)

Byron was reluctant to be too business-like with Hanson and wrote with kind messages for his family:

> Commend me to your family, I perceive Hargreaves is your partner, he always promised to turn out well and Charles I am sure is a very fine fellow. – As for the others I can't pretend to prophesy. I present my respects to all the ladies, and I suppose I may *kiss* Harriet as you or Mrs Hanson will be my proxy, provided she is not grown too tall for such a token of remembrance. – I must not forget Mrs Hanson who has often been a mother to me as you have always been a friend.[38]
>
> (To John Hanson, Athens, 11 November 1810)

Because he was so eager to communicate with people of every class and nation he happened to meet Byron was studying modern Greek and reported that he could gabble Levant Italian, was tolerably fluent in Lingua Franca, middling at Romaic (modern Greek) and could command several Ottoman oaths. Fletcher was less adaptable. Byron gave his mother an amusing account of his principal servant's shortcomings as a traveller:

> Besides the perpetual lamentations after beef and beer, the stupid bigotted contempt for everything foreign, and insurmountable incapacity of acquiring even a few words of any language, rendered him like all other English servants, an incumbrance. – I do assure you the plague of speaking for him, the comforts he required (more than myself by far) the pilaws he could not eat, the wines which he could not drink, the beds where he could not sleep, and the long list of calamities such as stumbling horses, want of tea!!! etc., which assailed him.[39]
>
> (To Catherine Gordon Byron, Athens, 14 January 1811)

Byron sent Fletcher home with papers for Hanson and, characteristically, felt rather lonely without either friend or servant from home to keep him company. His Albanian servants had become attached to him and wept at his decision to return home.

Reluctantly Byron tore himself away from his beloved Greece. On his voyage home he wrote to Hanson when off the Bay of Biscay assuring him that, worried as he was over the plight of his creditors, he would join the Army rather than sell Newstead Abbey:

> In the mean time I am compelled to draw on you for 20 or 30 pounds to enable me to proceed from the Port to London and pay the customs house duties. – There is a Bill of Miller's in Albemarle's which also

must be paid immediately, on my arrival; I do not mean to reproach you, but I certainly thought there were funds to answer so small a draft when I left London, however it has remained in his hands *dishonoured* more than two years, – However when I consider the sums I owe you professionally, I have nothing further to observe, I have made up my mind to bear the ills of Poverty, Two years travel has tolerably seasoned me to privations. – I have one question which must be resolved, is Rochdale mine, or not? Can I not sell it? and why, if it will bring a sum to clear my debts is it not sold![40]

(To John Hanson, Volage Frigate, 4 July 1811, Bay of Biscay)

He was obliged to write again on 31 July from Reddish's Hotel, London:

Dear Sir, – I have called on you with Mr Miller's bill and I do again (as I repeatedly have done) beg you to enable me to settle it, I have used him so ill (God knows unintentionally) pray let him have the whole and speedily, and do not involve me in fresh disgrace in this instance.[41]

(To John Hanson, 31 July 1811)

Byron had written to his mother to announce his return to England:

I have just been two years ... absent from England, and I return to it with ... indifference, but within that apathy I certainly do not comprise yourself, as I will prove by every means in my power. – You will be good enough to get my apartments ready at Newstead ... for a long time I have been restricted to an entire vegetable diet neither fish nor flesh coming within my regimen, so I expect a powerful stock of potatoes, greens, and biscuit, I drink no wine ... I have brought you a shawl and a quantity of Ottar of Roses.[42]

(To Mrs Catherine Gordon Byron, Volage Frigate, at sea, 25 June 1811)

Byron assured his mother that Newstead was her home and she was to regard him simply as a visitor.

Before he could settle his affairs in London Byron was summoned to Newstead Abbey with the news that his mother had fallen ill. Borrowing from Hanson he hastened up to Nottingham but by the time he arrived there she was dead. He was too late to give her the shawl and the attar of roses and to prove his regard for her as he had promised, by every means in his power. Byron was stunned and devastated by the loss of the mother he had so long taken for granted. One of the reasons he had lingered in London was to set up a libel action against *The Scourge* for scurrilous allegations against her. She was described as passing her days in drunkenness. Byron sprang to her defence: '... with a very large portion of foibles and irritability, she was without a Vice.'[43] He instructed Hanson that this case must go ahead. He would allow no slur on his mother's good name.

Now came the news that Charles Skinner Matthews had drowned in the river at Cambridge. Byron was shocked – '... to him all Men I ever knew were pigmies, he was an Intellectual Giant.'[44] Jonathan Gross points out that a poem appeared in the *Morning Chronicle* in 1811 accusing Byron of having failed to write elegiac verse for Matthews because Matthews was not of his own social class.[45] Yet he spoke openly of his love for Edleston, Delawarr and others, confiding his deepest feelings, pouring out poetry and indulging his compulsion for naming the loved one. After Matthew's death Byron wrote to Scrope Davies: 'To me he was much ... to Hobhouse everything ... I did not love quite so much as I honoured him.'[46] 'Byron surely wrote no elegiac verse for Matthews because he was not in love with him. Had he loved Matthews as he loved Edleston he would have written of his love, just as he composed the *Thyrza* cycle of poems for Edleston who was of considerably lower social standing than Matthews. The poems to the 'Citoyen' could have been disguised in the same way as those addressed to Edleston, with a female pseudonym.

Before long came news that his friend Wingfield had died of a fever in the Peninsula.

He wrote to Scrope Davies:

> My Dearest Davies, – some curse hangs over me and mine. My mother lies a corpse in this house, one of my best friends is drowned in a ditch ... My dear Scrope, if you can spare a moment, do come down to me, I want a friend.[47]

He wrote to John Pigot thanking him for his condolences and hoping to meet him.

Now the death of his mother and no fewer than four young friends led Byron to rewrite Cantos I and II of *Childe Harold* in such a way that the poem was transformed. From being a travelogue with a series of vignettes it became an account of his own development through grief and tribulation – a more philosophic, perhaps a sadder but wiser, work.

Note

1. Looking back on his younger self Byron declared that, at fifteen, he began to think himself a very fine gentleman. In writing later about James Hogg, the Ettrick Shepherd, he praises the salutary effect of travel and the experience of a wider world:

> Hogg is a strange being, but of great, though uncouth powers. I think very highly of him, as a poet; but he and half of these Scotch and Lake troubadours, are spoilt by living in little circles and petty societies. London and the world is the only place to take the conceit out of a man.[1]
>
> (To Thomas Moore, Hastings, 3 August 1814)

8

THE MAIDEN SPEECH

'Twelve Butchers for a Jury and a Jeffries for a Judge.'

The air of Greece, Byron said, had made him a poet. His travels changed him in more ways than this, as Ian Gilmour points out:

> ... he had become genuinely broad and cosmopolitan in his outlook. If his prejudices had ever been narrow, they were so no longer as he was himself, they were fully mature. His weeks in Spain and Portugal and his proximity to the war had strengthened his 'detestation of *licensed Murder*' and what he had seen there and in Greece had intensified his love of Freedom and his hatred of oppression. He had become a philhelline and felt himself 'a citizen of the world.'[1]

His plans on returning home were first to deliver his maiden speech in the House of Lords and second to arrange for the publication of *Hints from Horace* (an imitation of the poet he had hated so at Harrow) which he felt to be the best work he had done during his travels. When he showed it to Dallas he was told this was not likely to please a publisher. He was persuaded to hand over *Childe Harold's Pilgrimage*, in which he had little faith. Dallas was enthusiastic and so was John Murray when it was offered to him.

Soon after his mother's death Augusta sent her brother a letter of condolence which ended the long silence between them. The future prospects of the Leighs were bleak. George had been dismissed by the Prince Regent for having cheated him over the sale of a horse. Discovery of impropriety in the handling of the regimental funds forced him to resign his commission. Augusta, who loved him dearly, petted him, commiserated with him and wrote to Colonel McMahon, the Prince Regent's secretary, in defence of his indefensible behaviour. George was by now an inveterate gambler and continued to spend most of his time at the races, leaving Augusta to deal with their household, their children and his debts. Byron assured her, '... you have a brother in me, and a home here.'[2]

He visited Scrope Davies but learned just before setting out for Cambridge that John Edleston had died while he was in Greece. Cambridge was haunted by memories of the boy and of Charles Skinner Matthews dying horribly, entangled in weeds at the bottom of the Cam. He wrote some elegiac poems for Edleston concealing the fact that their subject was a boy by addressing them 'To Thyrza'. This became for some time an enigma to future readers of the poet though the clues to Edleston's identity are clear enough, particularly in the poem 'Away, away, ye notes of woe!' which was inspired by hearing a familiar song.

He went back to Newstead and invited Francis Hodgson and William Harness to join him there. Both were sober companions who would not prevent him from working. For love he turned to a pretty Welsh housemaid called Susan Vaughan with whom he fell sufficiently in love to suffer great distress when she proved unfaithful: 'I do not blame her,' he wrote, 'but my own vanity in fancying that such a thing as I am could ever be beloved.'[3] He wrote some lachrymose lines about this episode. The year before, he had lamented the marriage of Mary Chaworth with histrionic threats. Byron had the sense not to publish this melodramatic tirade. After his death Francis Hodgson, to whom the poem was addressed, crossed out the most menacing lines and wrote on the manuscript to the effect that poor dear Byron had not meant a word of it. It is hard to reconcile this poem with the virtues, originality and energy of the first two Cantos of *Childe Harold* and there is a great chasm between this outpouring of self-pitying rage and the frame of mind in which he was working on the publication of *Childe Harold* and planning his maiden speech in the House of Lords. John Mortimer gives an explanation of what it was in his character which saved him again and again when he might have succumbed to lethargy and self-pity:

> It's the contradictions in Byron's nature that provide its endless fascination. Surely there was never a more puritanical libertine, a more down-to-

earth romantic, a more conservative libertarian, a more self-deriding exhibitionist, a more disillusioned freedom fighter. And beneath it all, keeping him as sane and balanced in the mosquito swamps of Missolonghi as he was among the fighting women and dogs and monkeys of his Palazzo on the Grand Canal, in aristocratic London ballrooms or at the gaming tables of Piccadilly, was his invulnerable, his superb common sense.[4]

It was this common sense which prompted his maiden speech on the Bill to impose the death penalty on the frame-breakers. During 1811 and 1812 there were widespread Luddite riots in Nottinghamshire. Starving workers took to storming into factories at night to break up the recently invented knitting frames, use of which by harsh and greedy employers was putting them out of work. The government reaction was repression. Nottinghamshire was full of army encampments, militia, and Bow Street Runners. Byron did not approve of the violent action taken by the frame workers but he had seen their suffering and believed they were driven to violence by employers and politicians who were indifferent to their plight.

On 27 February 1812, he delivered his maiden speech in the House of Lords, attacking the government proposal to bring in the death penalty for breaking stocking frames. Two days before his appearance before the House Byron wrote to Lord Holland to explain his views on the subject:

For my own part, I consider the manufacturers as a much injured body of men sacrificed to ye views of certain individuals who have enriched themselves by those practices which have deprived the frame workers of employment. – For instance; – by the adoption of a certain kind of frame 1 man performs the work of 7 – 6 are thus thrown out of business. – But it is to be observed that ye. work thus done is far inferior in quality, hardly marketable at home, & hurried over with a view to exportation. – Surely, my Lord, however we may rejoice in any improvement in ye. arts which may be beneficial to mankind; we must not allow mankind to be sacrificed to improvements in Mechanism. The maintenance & well doing of ye. industrious poor is an object of greater consequence to ye. community than ye. enrichment of a few monopolists by any improvement in ye. implements of trade, which deprives ye. workman of his bread, & renders ye. labourer 'unworthy of his hire'. – My own motive for opposing ye. bill is founded on it's palpable injustice, & it's certain inefficacy. – I have seen the state of these miserable men, & it is a disgrace to a civilised country. – Their excesses may be condemned, but cannot be the subject of wonder. – The effect of ye. present bill would be to drive them into actual rebellion.[5]

(To Lord Holland, 8 St James's Street, 25 February 1812)

Having consulted Lord Holland in this letter, Byron went rather further than Lord Holland would have done, declaring in his speech that:

> . . . the framers of such a Bill must be content to inherit the honours of that Athenian lawgiver whose edicts were said to be written not in ink but in blood . . . suppose one of these men . . . dragged into court, to be tried for this new offence, by this new law; still, there are two things wanting to convict and condemn him; and these are, in my opinion, – twelve Butchers for a Jury, and a Jeffries for a Judge![6]

'The poetry of this young aristocrat,' wrote John Mortimer, 'was always at the service of the common people.'[7] His attitude to the common people was made clear in the course of the speech and so was his strong objection to the contemptuous attitude of some of the ruling classes towards 'the mob':

> You call these men a mob . . . Are we aware of our obligations to a *Mob*? – It is the Mob that labour in your fields and serve in your houses, that man your navy, and recruit your army, – that have enabled you to defy all the world, and can also defy you, when Neglect and Calamity have driven them to despair.[8]

The Tories (who were in government) were infuriated by these Radical sentiments uttered by a novice peer with a beautiful voice in a theatrical manner. The Whigs were delighted with him, though Lord Holland was not enchanted with either the speech or the manner in which it was delivered. All the same, he soon called on the young man (an unprecedented honour for a twenty-four-year-old novice peer) and Lady Holland reported how much Lord Holland was growing to like Lord Byron in all his dealings with him. Byron wrote of his experience in Parliament:

> The Impression of Parliament upon me – was that its members are not formidable as *Speakers* – but very much so as an *audience* – because in so numerous a body there may be little Eloquence (after all there were but *two* thorough Orators in all Antiquity – and I suspect still *fewer* in modern times) but must be a leaven of thought and good sense

sufficient to make them *know* what is right – though they can't express it nobly.[9]

(*Detached Thoughts*, 1821)

and of his own feeling during his performance:

> Whatever diffidence or nervousness I felt – (and I felt both in a great degree) arose from the number than the quality of the assemblage, and I thought rather of the *public without* than the persons within – knowing (as all know) that Cicero himself – and probably the Messiah could never have altered the vote of a single Lord of the Bed Chamber or Bishop.[10]
>
> (*Detached Thoughts*, 1821)

Byron was congratulated by many of the Whigs and was invited to sit on a committee for working on amendments to the Bill – a waste of time as the House of Commons threw out all the amendments.

On 2 March 1812 the following poem appeared anonymously in the *Morning Chronicle*. (To publish openly would have jeopardised Byron's political career and the poem did not appear over his name until 1880.)

AN ODE TO THE FRAMERS OF THE FRAME BILL

1.

Oh well done Lord E———n! and better Lord R———r!
Britannia must prosper with councils like yours;
Hawkesbury, Harrowby, help you to guide her,
Whose remedy only must *kill* ere it cures:
Those villains; the Weavers, are all grown refractory,
Asking some succour for Charity's sake –
So hang them in clusters round each Manufactory,
That will at once put an end to *mistake*.

2.

The rascals, perhaps, may betake them to robbing,
The dogs to be sure have got nothing to eat –
So if we can hang them for breaking a bobbin,
'T will save all the Government's money and meat:
Men are more easily made than machinery –
Stockings fetch better prices than lives –
Gibbets on Sherwood will heighten the scenery,
Shewing how Commerce, how Liberty thrives!

3.
Justice is now in pursuit of the wretches,
   Grenadiers, Volunteers, Bow-street Police,
Twenty-two Regiments, a score of Jack Ketches,
   Three of the Quorum and two of the Peace;
Some Lords, to be sure, would have summoned the Judges,
   To take their opinion, but that they ne'er shall,
For LIVERPOOL such a concession begrudges,
   So now they're condemned by *no Judges* at all.

4.
Some folks for certain have thought it was shocking,
   When Famine appeals, and when Poverty groans,
That Life should be valued at less than a stocking,
   And breaking of frames lead to breaking of bones.
If it should prove so, I trust, by this token,
   (And who will refuse to partake in the hope?)
That the frames of the fools may be the first to be *broken*,
   Who, when asked for a *remedy*, sent down a *rope*.[11]

Now Byron was part of the political world in London. He had already been initiated into the literary world by his introduction to John Murray who made him known to William Gifford, his colleague in running the *Quarterly Review*, a man of whom Byron had so high an opinion that he had praised him in *English Bards and Scotch Reviewers*. Hazlitt's view of Gifford was, 'In general his observations are petty, ill-concocted, and discover as little tact as they do a habit of connected reasoning.'[12] Byron's opinion of Gifford was this: 'As Gifford has been ever my "Magnus Apollo", any approbation you mention [from Gifford], would, of course, be more welcome than "all Bokara's vaunted gold, than all the gems of Samarkand".'[13]

Byron was in a better position to judge the abilities of his mentor than Hazlitt. Gifford perceived the strength and originality of Byron's poetry from the beginning and seemed to have no difficulty with the fact that he was a nobleman.

As one of Murray's authors Byron now had the run of the fine front room on the first floor of 50 Albemarle Street where he could consort with some of the most distinguished literary figures of the time such as Walter Scott and look at the latest newspapers and reviews.

In June 1813 he wrote to Murray:

Dear Sir –
I presented a petition to the house yesterday – which gave rise to some debate – and I wish you to favour me for a few minutes with the *Times* and *Herald* to look on their *hostile* report – you will find if you like to look at my *prose* – all my words nearly verbatim in the *Morning Chronicle*.[14]

(To John Murray, 2 June 1813)

Englishmen (and not only the aristocrats and the intelligentsia) were already fixated on their daily newspapers. The general availability of political comment dismayed the government, and in order to stop the spread of Radical ideas and Jacobinism they imposed taxes and stamp duties on newspapers. Those who then found the newspapers too dear promptly resorted to the taverns and coffee houses where they could read them for the price of a mug of ale. Workers' Reform Clubs set up newsrooms where papers were available free. When Byron was in London there were more than ten daily newspapers in the capital, including the *Times*, the *Courier*, the *Sun*, the *Oracle*, the *Morning Post*, the *Morning Herald* and the *Morning Chronicle*. The Government paid subsidies to some of the papers in which it was, accordingly, fulsomely praised. In others it was as enthusiastically blackguarded. Byron must have missed the English papers when he was in Switzerland and Italy.

Samuel Rogers and Thomas Moore were among those who frequented 50 Albemarle Street. Byron had already dined with them at Rogers's house. Moore had taken offence at some mocking lines in *English Bards and Scotch Reviewers* about his abortive duel with Jeffrey of the *Edinburgh Review*, and had sent Byron a challenge before he left England which Francis Hodgson, guessing its purpose, had managed to suppress. On Byron's return Moore wrote again in a more conciliatory tone. Byron replied. Honour on both sides was satisfied and both were invited to dine with Rogers and his friends. Byron was delighted to meet Samuel Rogers whose 'Pleasures of Memory' he admired. Thomas Campbell (another of the writers Byron had praised in his satire) was also present. Hazlitt wrote of the three poets that Campbell '... may be said to hold a place between Lord Byron and Mr Rogers. Mr Rogers as a writer is too effeminate. Lord Byron is too extravagant. Mr Campbell is neither.'[15]

Byron offered both these poets his admiration and homage. With

Moore, who was nearer his own age (Rogers was 49) there was a different level of understanding and liking. They became intimate almost on the spot, laughing together, teasing each other, confiding, grumbling, arguing. This was a friendship that would last without any diminution until death. It was not surprising that Moore and Hobhouse resented each other. Byron loved Hobhouse perhaps more than his new friend but he had more fun with Thomas Moore. Looking back some years later in Italy he wrote:

> In general I do not draw well with Literary men – not that I dislike them but I never know what to say to them after I have praised their last publication. – There are several exceptions to be sure – but they have either been men of the world – such as Scott – & Moore, etc., or visionaries out of it – such as Shelley ... I do not remember a man amongst them – whom I ever wished to see twice.[16]
>
> (*Detached Thoughts*, 1820)

He was enthusiastic about some of the famous men he met at this time:

> Curran! – Curran's the Man who struck me most – such Imagination! – ... I did not see a great deal of Curran – only in 1813 – but I met him at home (for he used to call on me) and in society – at Macintosh's – Holland House etc. etc. etc. And he was wonderful even to me – who had seen many remarkable men of the time.[17]
>
> (*Detached Thoughts*, 1821)

Byron's second speech in the House of Lords was in favour of Catholic Emancipation. On one of his visits to London from Southwell he had listened to the debates in Parliament on this subject in order to inform himself on the wrongs of the Catholics. He later gave to funds for the Irish peasantry and wrote 'The Irish Avator' criticising the Irish in Dublin for the welcome they gave to their 'oppressor', George IV, when he visited Ireland in 1822. He mocks the King in this poem and praises Curran, Sheridan and Grattan:

10

Ever glorious Grattan! the blest of the good!
So simple in heart, so sublime in the rest!
With all which Demosthenes wanted endued,
And his rival, or victor, in all he possess'd.[18]

The speech on Catholic Emancipation was calculated to infuriate most of Byron's fellow-peers:

> It might well be said that the Negroes did not desire to be emancipated; but ... you have already delivered them out of bondage ... I pity the Catholic peasantry for not having had the good fortune to be born black. But the Catholics are contented, or at least ought to be, we are told: I shall therefore proceed to touch on a few of those circumstances which so marvellously contribute to their contentment.[19]

He went on to ask:

> Some persons have compared the Catholics to the beggar in *Gil Blas*: who made them beggars? Who are enriched by the spoils of their ancestors?[20]

He then enlarged on the loss to England of the energies and talents of the Irish people:

> Ireland has done much and will do more. At this moment the only triumph obtained through long years of Continental disaster has been achieved by an Irish general: it is true he is not a Catholic: had he been so, we should have been deprived of his exertions.[21]

His description of the union with England, which had made Lord Castlereagh loathed by his countrymen (including friends of Byron like Thomas Moore, and statesmen he admired like Henry Grattan), was devastating:

> If it must be called a Union it is the union of the shark with his prey; the spoiler swallows up his victim and thus they become indivisible. Thus has Great Britain swallowed up the Parliament, the constitution, the independence of Ireland.[22]

He prophesied the Troubles, expatiating on the consequences of not acceding to the claims of the petitioners:

> You know them, you will feel them, and your children's children when you are passed away.[23]

9

CHILDE HAROLD'S PILGRIMAGE

> *'Childe Harold is perhaps the most original work in the English Language'*[1]
>
> *Edinburgh Review*

> *'Humbug like Childe Harold'* (J.G. Lockhart)[2]

When he burst upon the London scene in March 1812 with an electrifying maiden speech in the House of Lords and two Cantos of a poem which was to make him famous overnight little was known of the young Lord Byron except for *English Bards and Scotch Reviewers*. The satire ends with a challenge to the entire literary establishment and those who had read this challenge must have been astonished at the temerity of the young author who had put a new publication before them without even the protection of anonymity:

> Who conquers me shall find a stubborn foe.
> The time hath been, when no harsh sound would fall
> From lips that now may seem imbued with gall;
> Nor fools nor follies tempt me to despise
> The meanest thing that crawled beneath my eyes:
> But now, so callous grown, so changed since youth,
> I've learned to think, and sternly speak the truth;
> Learned to deride the critic's stern decree,
> And break him on the wheel he meant for me;
> To spurn the rod a scribbler bids me kiss,
> Nor care if courts and crowds applaud or hiss:[3]

In the event the success of the two Cantos was such that the young poet was burdened with great fame at the age of twenty-four. The Cantos have been criticised as affected in style and insincere in content. Byron was himself open to criticism on the first count and assured his publisher, John Murray, '... if there are any alterations in the structure of the versification you would wish to be made, I will tag rhymes, & turn Stanzas, as much as you please,'[4] – but he flatly refused to alter anything in order to conciliate the pious or reactionary among John Murray's customers.

This was bold in a young writer who was already nervous about the reception the poem might expect from those who had been satirised in *English Bards and Scotch Reviewers*:

> 'You must be aware,' he had written to Charles Dallas, 'that my plaguy Satire will bring the North and South Grubstreets down on the "Pilgrimage", but nevertheless if Murray makes a point of it, & you coincide with him, I will do it daringly, so let it be entitled by "the *Author of* E[ngli]sh *Bards* & S[*cot*]ch *R*[*eviewer*]*s*" ... I much wish to avoid identifying Childe Harold's character with mine, & that in sooth is my second objection to my name on the T[itle] Page ... After all I fear Murray will be in a Scrape with the Orthodox, but I cannot help it, though I wish him well through it.'[5]
>
> (To Robert Charles Dallas, Newstead Abbey, 21 August 1811)

Accordingly, when Murray asked for the changes to conciliate his customers Byron replied:

> With regard to the political and metaphysical parts, I am afraid I can alter nothing, but I have high authority for my Errors on that point, for even the *Aeneid* was a *political* poem & written for a *political* purpose, and as to my unlucky opinions on Subjects of more importance, I am too sincere in them for recantation ... As for the '*Orthodox*', let us hope they will buy on purpose to abuse, you will forgive the one if they will do the other.[6]
>
> (To John Murray, Newstead Abbey, Notts., 5 September 1811)

Six months before the Cantos appeared he wrote to Dallas, who was handling negotiations with Murray:

> I also feel that I am sincere, and that if I am only to write '*ad capitandum vulgus*,' I might as well edite a magazine at once, or spin canzonettas for Vauxhall ... My work must make its way as well as it can; I know I have every thing against me, angry poets and prejudices; but if the poem is a *poem* it will surmount these obstacles, and if *not*, it deserves its fate.[7]
>
> (To Robert Charles Dallas, Newstead Abbey, 7 September 1811)

Was it a poem? Jeffrey, some years later, referred to the unprecedented effect produced by the Cantos as 'the sudden blazing forth of his genius'. On the whole the reviewers agreed with this verdict and it was enhanced rather than diminished by the succeeding Cantos when they appeared. There were dissentient voices. J.G. Lockhart wrote in 1821 of '... humbug like Childe Harold,' and Hazlitt declared, 'It would be hard to persuade ourselves that the author of *Childe Harold* and *Don Juan* is not a coxcomb, though a provoking and sublime one.'[8]

The reviewers discussed exhaustively the style, the politics, the philosophy and the morals of the author. One reviewer claimed to have found the secret of the power of the verse:

> The principal of *chiaroscuro* will account for much of the strong effect of his pieces. A sombre thought or image is introduced to give high relief to a lovely description: this is often done with too much show of design, – but it is also sometimes done with consummate skill and feeling.[9]
>
> (John Scott, *The London Magazine*, January 1821)

Ever since the day of publication, there has been constant discussion and disagreement about the value and sincerity of the poem. Byron calls on the Greeks to throw off their bondage:

LXXVI

Hereditary Bondsmen! know ye not
Who would be free *themselves* must strike the blow?
By their right arms the conquest must be wrought?
Will Gaul or Muscovite redress ye? No!
True – they may lay your proud despoilers low,
But not for you will Freedom's Altars flame.
Shades of the Helots! triumph o'er your foe!
Greece! change thy lords, thy state is still the same;
Thy glorious day is o'er, but not thine years of shame.[10]

George Finlay, who had many conversations with Byron shortly before his death in Greece, judged that, although he admired military glory in the abstract, he detested the actuality of war. This hatred of war was not something the young man who admired and sought military glory learned as he grew older and wiser. It was there from the start and appears in Canto I of *Childe Harold*, passionate, denunciatory and inconsistent:

XLI

Three hosts combine to offer sacrifice;
Three tongues prefer strange orisons on high;
Three gaudy standards flout the pale blue skies;
The shouts are France, Spain, Albion, Victory!
The Foe, the Victim, and the fond Ally
That fights for all, but ever fights in vain,
Are met – as if at home they could not die –
To feed the crow on Talavera's plain,
And fertilize the field that each pretends to gain.

XLII

There shall they rot – Ambition's honoured fools!
Yes, Honour decks the turf that wraps their clay!
Vain Sophistry! in these behold the tools,
The broken tools, that Tyrants cast away
By myriads, when they dare to pave their way
With human hearts – to what? – a dream alone.[11]

The anti-war stanzas quoted above (Canto II stanzas 41–43) are preceded by a powerful image of war – the bloody Giant which Jerome Christensen describes as 'Lord Byron's chief essay in sublime war reportage ... By focusing the Peninsular War into a single, mythically charged battle scene, the image of the Giant stretches chivalric motifs toward obscene, Goya-esque caricature.'[12]

XXXVIII

Hark! – heard you not those hoofs of dreadful note?
Sounds not the clang of conflict on the heath?
Saw ye not whom the reeking sabre smote;
Nor saved your brethren ere they sank beneath
Tyrants and Tyrants' slaves? – the fires of Death,
The Bale-fires flash on high; – from rock to rock
Each volley tells that thousands cease to breathe;
Death rides upon the sulphury Siroc,
Red Battle stamps his foot, and Nations feel the shock.

XXXIX

Lo! where the Giant on the mountain stands,
His blood-red tresses deepening in the Sun,
With death-shot glowing in his fiery hands,
And eye that scorcheth all it glares upon;
Restless it rolls, now fixed and now anon
Flashing afar, – and at his iron feet

Destruction cowers, to mark what deeds are done;
For on this morn three potent Nations meet,
To shed before his Shrine the blood he deems most sweet.[13]

Byron had something to say about the fate of freedom in Spain, having first dealt sharply with the perpetrators of the Convention of Cintra:

XXV

Convention is the dwarfish demon styled
That foiled the knights in Marialva's dome:
Of brains (if brains they had) he them beguiled,
And turned a nation's shallow joy to gloom.[14]

It was not surprising that Murray wanted to water all this down, particularly the stanzas where Byron claimed that any class but the nobility would have saved Spain:

LXXXV

Adieu, fair Cadiz! yea, a long adieu!
Who may forget how well thy walls have stood?
When all were changing thou alone wert true,
First to be free and last to be subdued:
And if amidst a scene, a shock so rude,
Some native blood was seen thy street to dye,
A Traitor only fell beneath the feud:
Here all were noble, save Nobility;
None hugged a Conqueror's chain, save fallen Chivalry!

LXXXVI

Such be the sons of Spain, and strange her Fate!
They fight for Freedom who were never free,
A Kingless people for a nerveless state;
Her vassals combat when their Chieftains flee,
True to the veriest slaves of Treachery:
Fond of a land which gave them nought but life,
Pride points the path that leads to Liberty;
Back to the struggle, baffled in the strife,
War, war is still the cry, 'War even to the knife!'[15]

He was not alone in his scepticism on the subject of the Spanish nobility. In 1808 Sydney Smith had written to Lady Holland who was visiting Spain:

Why, my dear Lady Holland do you not come home? It is all over, it has been all over this month; except in the Holland family there has not been a man of sense for some weeks who has thought otherwise... If the Spaniards would murder the nobility and clergy there might be some chance. Linendrapers and shoemakers might save Spain, in the hands of Dukes and Bishops it is infallibly gone.[16]

The stanzas castigating Lord Elgin for removing the marbles from the Parthenon must have been deeply embarrassing to Murray. The more closely one reads the Cantos the more must one admire him for having gone ahead with publication:

XV

Cold is the heart, fair Greece! that looks on Thee,
Nor feels as Lovers o'er the dust they loved;
Dull is the eye that will not weep to see
Thy walls defaced, thy mouldering shrines removed
By British hands, which it had best behoved
To guard those relics ne'er to be restored: –
Curst be the hour when from their isle they roved,
And once again thy hapless bosom gored,
And snatched thy shrinking Gods to Northern climes abhorred![17]

In his notes to *Childe Harold* Byron expresses his outrage at the behaviour of Signor Lusieri, the agent of Lord Elgin, in the removal of the marbles:

While he and his patron confine themselves to tasting medals, appreciating cameos, sketching columns and cheapening gems, their little absurdities are as harmless as insect or fox hunting, maiden speechifying, barouche-driving, or any such pastime: but when they carry away three or four shiploads of the most valuable and massy relics that time and barbarism have left to the most injured and celebrated of cities ... I know of no motive which can excuse ... the perpetrators of this dastardly devastation.[18]

Hobhouse believed that transporting the marbles to London would benefit an infinitely greater number of rising architects and sculptors.[19] Byron's reply to this was: 'I oppose and will ever oppose, the robbery of ruins from Athens, to instruct the English in sculpture (who are as capable of sculpture as the Egyptians are of skating).'[20]

It was not as a political poem that *Childe Harold* found its way into the hands of most of the ladies and many of the men in the

Polite World of the Regency. The passages of description were read aloud and passed from hand to hand.

The farewell song to his native land was a favourite:

I

'ADIEU, adieu! my native shore
 Fades o'er the waters blue;
The night-winds sigh, the breakers roar,
 And shrieks the wild sea-mew.
Yon Sun that sets upon the sea
 We follow in his flight;
Farewell awhile to him and thee,
 My native Land – Good Night![21]

So were the evocations of the Grecian landscape:

LXXXV

And yet how lovely in thine age of woe,
 Land of lost Gods and godlike men, art thou!
 Thy vales of evergreen, thy hills of snow,
 Proclaim thee Nature's varied favourite now:
 Thy fanes, thy temples to thy surface bow,
 Commingling slowly with heroic earth,
 Broke by the share of every rustic plough:
 So perish monuments of mortal birth,
So perish all in turn, save well-recorded *Worth*:

LXXXVI

Save where some solitary column mourns
 Above its prostrate brethren of the cave;
 Save where Tritonia's airy shrine adorns
 Colonna's cliff, and gleams along the wave;
 Save o'er some warrior's half-forgotten grave,
 Where the grey stones and unmolested grass
 Ages, but not Oblivion, feebly brave;
 While strangers, only, not regardless pass,
Lingering like me, perchance, to gaze, and sigh 'Alas!'

LXXXVII

Yet are thy skies as blue, thy crags as wild;
 Sweet are thy groves, and verdant are thy fields,
 Thine olive ripe as when Minerva smiled,
 And still his honied wealth Hymettus yields;
 There the blithe Bee his fragrant fortress builds,

The free-born wanderer of thy mountain-air;
Apollo still thy long, long summer gilds,
Still in his beam Mendeli's marbles glare:
Art, Glory, Freedom fail, but Nature still is fair.[22]

The following description is placed near the monastery at Zitza where Byron and Hobhouse spent the night on their way back from the journey to meet Ali Pasha:

LI

Dusky and huge, enlarging on the sight,
Nature's volcanic Amphitheatre,
Chimaera's Alps extend from left to right:
Beneath, a living valley seems to stir;
Flocks play, trees wave, streams flow, the mountain-fir
Nodding above...[23]

Many in safe and civilised Britain were fascinated at the wild scenes the young nobleman had experienced in the land of 'The wild Albanian kirtled to his knee':

XLII

Morn dawns; and with it stern Albania's hills,
Dark Suli's rocks, and Pindus' inland peak,
Robed half in mist, bedew'd with snowy rills,
Arrayed in many a dun and purple streak,
Arise; and, as the clouds among them break,
Disclose the dwelling of the mountaineer:
Here roams the wolf – the eagle whets his beak –
Birds – beasts of prey – and wilder men appear,
And gathering storms around convulse the closing year.[24]

The descriptions of old battles and acts of heroism in 'the bright clime of battle and of song,' were also full of glamour and fierce action and ended in a nostalgic backward look:

LXXXIX

As on the morn to distant Glory dear,
When Marathon became a magic word;
Which uttered, to the hearer's eye appear
The camp, the host, the fight, the Conqueror's career,

XC

The flying Mede, his shaftless broken bow –
The fiery Greek, his red pursuing spear;
Mountains above – Earth's, Ocean's plain below –
Death in the front, Destruction in the rear!
Such was the scene – what now remaineth here?
What sacred Trophy marks the hallowed ground,
Recording Freedom's smile and Asia's tear?
The rifled urn, the violated mound,
The dust thy courser's hoof, rude stranger! spurns around.[25]

In Cantos I and II of *Childe Harold* the young poet had taken a familiar mode and transformed it. The energy and blazing sincerity of his musings were something new in this sort of topographical poetry. So was the imposition on the poem of the strange and original persona of the poet. It is not surprising that it became a *succès fou.* A letter from a Cambridge professor tends to show that Byron's contemporary readers were intensely moved by the passionate grief he expressed in these verses.

Edward Daniel Clarke, a Professor of Mineralogy at Cambridge with whom Byron had compared notes on their travels in Greece, wrote to him on the publication of the Cantos to tell him that he had asked a friend, 'Surely Lord Byron at this time of life, cannot have experienced such keen anguish as these exquisite allusions to what older men *may* have felt, seem to denote.' This was his answer: 'I fear he has – he could not else have written such a poem.'

Professor Clark goes on, '. . . the eighth stanza [of the second Canto], "Yet if as holiest men," etc., has never been surpassed.'[26]

VII

Well didst thou speak, Athena's wisest son!
'All that we know is, nothing can be known.'
Why should we shrink from what we cannot shun?
Each has its pang, but feeble sufferers groan
With brain-born dreams of Evil all their own.
Pursue what Chance or Fate proclaimeth best;
Peace waits us on the shores of Acheron:
There no forced banquet claims the sated guest,
But Silence spreads the couch of ever welcome Rest.

VIII

Yet if, as holiest men have deemed, there be
A land of Souls beyond that sable shore,
To shame the Doctrine of the Sadducee
And Sophists, madly vain of dubious lore;
How sweet it were in concert to adore
With those who made our mortal labours light!
To hear each voice we feared to hear no more!
Behold each mighty shade revealed to sight,
The Bactrian, Samian sage, and all who taught the Right.

IX

There, Thou! – whose Love and Life together fled,
Have left me here to love and live in vain –
Twined with my heart, and can I deem thee dead,
When busy Memory flashes on my brain?
Well – I will dream that we may meet again,
And woo the vision to my vacant breast:
If aught of young Remembrance then remain,
Be as it may Futurity's behest,
For me 'twere bliss enough to know thy spirit blest![27]

Notes

1. M.K. Joseph writes of *Childe Harold*:

> One of the themes of the poem – the central theme as it finally discloses itself – is the traditional one of lament for lost empire and for the decay of love, and of the triumph of time over human mortality, redeemed only by that quasi-immortality which the human spirit achieves when it 'bodies forth' the forms of art and literature. The scenes of *Childe Harold* are used, in various ways, as developing points for this theme. And, in case we think of this as a method more associated with a certain kind of Augustan didactic poem, it is worth recalling that it is also the essential method of poems like 'The Wild Swans of Coole' or the *Four Quartets*.[1]

As we have seen, Michael G. Cooke discovered a Wordsworthian tinge in Byron's poetry as early as *Hours of Idleness* and the following stanza from Canto II seems as Wordsworthian as anything Byron ever wrote:

XXV

To sit on rocks – to muse o'er flood and fell –
To slowly trace the forest's shady scene,
Where things that own not Man's dominion dwell,
And mortal foot hath ne'er or rarely been;

To climb the trackless mountain all unseen,
With the wild flock that never needs a fold;
Alone o'er steeps and foaming falls to lean;
This is not Solitude – 'tis but to hold
Converse with Nature's charms, and view her stores unrolled.[2]

Byron might have been proud of the comparison since he admitted Wordsworth's power 'to do about any thing'. When he met Wordsworth in 1812 he felt for him nothing but reverence: 'I still think his capacity warrants all you say of *it* only – but that his performances since *Lyrical Ballads* – are miserably inadequate to the ability which lurks within him.'[3]

In later years Byron mocked Wordsworth without mercy. Having welcomed the French Revolution with 'Bliss was it in that dawn to be alive!', Wordsworth had, in Byron's view, become a 'lost leader' who approved the suspension of habeas corpus and behaved like a reactionary. Wordsworth returned Byron's distaste with interest: 'Let me only say one word upon Lord Byron. The man is insane; and will probably end his career in a madhouse.'[4]

In the poem 'Churchill's Grave', commemorating a visit on the eve of his exile from England to the churchyard at Dover where the neglected eighteenth century satirist was buried, Byron paid Wordsworth the (somewhat dubious) compliment of an imitation of his poetry in both style and content, including both its felicities and its failings.

In England Byron's poetry has, over the years, been underrated in comparison with that of Wordsworth but Philip Shaw holds that modern critics tend, on the whole, to prefer 'the unerring honesty of Byron to the uncertain equipoise of Wordsworth'.[5] Jerome McGann repudiates the opinion of Ernest J. Lovell Jr. that Byron's poetry is crippled by its inability to offer us 'a consistent attitude towards life', as Wordsworth's does. McGann believes that 'Byron, like his beloved Montaigne, deliberately sought to avoid the kind of ethical consistency that Wordsworth sought. In the end his poetry embraces alienation, scepticism, constant change, as it were by necessity.'[6]

2. Byron felt so strongly about Lord Elgin's removal of the marbles from Athens that in March 1811, when he was living at the Capuchin convent in Athens, he began to write *The Curse of Minerva*, a tirade against Elgin, in the course of which he dubs the Scotland he had loved so well 'a land of meanness, sophistry and mist.'

The Curse of Minerva is a graceless piece berating Elgin for his 'plunder', likening him to Alaric the Goth and, shockingly, wishing a curse upon his seed so that all his sons might be 'as senseless as their sire'. Should one of them prove otherwise, 'Believe him bastard of a brighter race.'

Since no more than eight copies of this production were printed by Murray for private circulation during Byron's lifetime one can hope that he repented this vitriolic attack. There are occasions when fierce resentment results in the display by Byron of deplorable and sometimes cruel antagonism. In this case he was unfair to Elgin who paid for his 'plunder' and was ruined by it. Evidently John Galt remonstrated with Byron for his treatment of Elgin. Byron replied: 'If you will prove to me that Ld. E[lgin]'s "*is* the error of a liberal mind" the "Muse' shall forthwith eat her own words although they choak her – and me into the bargain.'[7] He did suppress *The Curse of Minerva* on meeting Edward Everett, a friend of Elgin's, in June 1815.[8]

10

WHIG LADIES

LVII

. . . he had that kind of fame
which sometimes plays the deuce with Womankind.[1]

The fame of '*Childe Harold*' opened every door to its author and he stepped into the limelight both a literary and a social lion for, whatever his upbringing might have been, he had the entrée to the Polite World bestowed by high lineage. Even so, it was a precarious position. Captain Gronow describes the vogue of the social lion in Regency London:

> [Alvanley said that] Brummell was the only *Dande*lion that flourished year after year in the hotbed of the fashionable world: he had taken root. Lions were generally annual, but Brummell was perennial, and he quoted a letter from Walter Scott [to the Earl of Dalkeith]: 'If you are celebrated for writing verses, or for slicing cucumbers, for being two feet taller, or two feet less, than any other biped . . . your notoriety becomes a talisman, an "open sesame" which gives way to everything, till you are voted a bore, and discarded for a new plaything.'[2]

Byron was probably aware of this from the outset but it did not prevent him from being ravished by the delights of High Society, the charm and courtesy, the dress as exquisite as the manners, the wit and erudition, the political sophistication of both men and women in this milieu.

There is no more entertaining chronicler of the life led by the great ladies of Regency Society than Harriet Cavendish (known to her friends and family as Hary-O) daughter of Georgiana, Duchess of Devonshire and the fifth Duke. Hary-O is lively, witty, well-read and merciless. Born at the very pinnacle of Society she refers constantly to the luxury, elegance and comfort of her surroundings and the brilliance of the intellectual and artistic pursuits in which she revels. She dwells so consistently on her perfect happiness that one senses a faint note of desperation which may derive from the circumstance that her family married her off to Granville Leweson-Gower, later Lord Granville, who had been the lover of her beautiful aunt, Lady Bessborough, for the past seventeen years. Lady Bessborough kept the portrait of her handsome lover in her closet so that she could gaze at 'Those eyes where I have looked my life away.'[3] (Such arrangements were not unusual in Regency and eighteenth century England. Many of the most aristocratic nurseries contained more than one child born to one or other of the parents out of wedlock).

Hary-O wrote praises of her houses and gardens:

> My new room ... is so pretty and comfortable and quiet ... It hangs out in the sun like a great green and gold cage. It is as full of *ormolu* and Sèvres china as if it belonged to Lady Jersey and I see all the dandy men and women redouble their regard for me when they find me in a room with four looking glasses and clocks that sing...[4]
>
> You have no idea how comfortable we are. We read German, write verses, play at chess and hazard and sometimes sing for very joy.[5]

Her flower garden is sweeter and more beautiful than 'anything but some of the descriptions in Ariosto or *The Faerie Queene*'.[6]

> At four o'clock we all meet. Lady Harrowby drives me in a low coach. Granville, when he is here walks with us and Lord Harrowby and Susan ride.[7]

These idyllic transports are punctuated by sharp comments on other people in the *Haute Monde*:

> Princess Esterhazy is coquette, ... ugly and quite foolish, ... sings pretty, odd Tyrolese airs with no voice, ... talks the veriest German nonsense and ... has a lover or two *par ci par là*.[8]
>
> The *Duc de Berri* [one of the emigrés from France] is clever, sings well, but is *difficile à vivre* and tries Lady Stafford by finding fault. Today the eggs at breakfast were abominable – '*Ma foi, Madame, mesdames vos poules ne s'acquittent pas bien.*'[9]

This sort of gossip was amusing and Hary-O and other ladies would throw off a telling comment on a literary figure. Hary-O wrote of Rousseau that he had too much of looking up at the sky, '*larmes* dans les yeux'.[10]

The headquarters of the Whig party was Holland House, Lord Holland's great red-brick Jacobean mansion in Kensington – a short country ride from Mayfair. The Hollands forgave Byron the rude remarks in his satire about Lady Holland's dinners and Lord Holland's hirelings and he became a welcome visitor. 'Dined at Holland House with Whigs and lawyers,'[11] Hary-O once wrote. But at Lady Holland's table you were as likely to find foreign ambassadors, refugee noblemen, Sheridan, Sydney Smith, Lord Grey, the Melbournes and the Bessboroughs. The conversation was lively and everything enjoyable for those guests who did not object to being bullied by Lady Holland. She had been a great beauty in her youth, had divorced her first husband for the young Henry Fox and technically should not have been received in society, but the Hollands were wealthy and powerful enough to escape ostracism. Hary-O described Lady Holland as 'The only undisputed monarchy in Europe, sitting in a corner, throne and footstool, lords and counsellors-in-waiting, countesses and *dames d'honneur*, all *dans les règles*.'[12]

Sydney Smith would tell nervous people setting off for the first time to attend a dinner at Holland House that there was a chemist in Kensington who made up special pills for people who had been frightened by Lady Holland. Lord Holland himself appeared to be in thrall to his strong-minded wife. Hary-O described him one evening at Holland House, '. . . as merry as a grig though begging in vain for just one glass of Johannisberg.'[13] She ordered her guests about unmercifully, directing one to move from a comfortable to a more distant place, forcing Madame Lieven to pick up the reticule she had dropped on the floor. Byron was never among those bullied or frightened by his hostess. Asked after his death whether Lady Byron had ever loved him Lady Holland retorted that she could not have failed to love him as '. . . he was so lovable. I can see him now sitting under that lamp looking so beautiful.'[14]

Another great lady who might have been ostracised by society (not for her transgressions but for being found out in them) was Lady Melbourne. She was saved by her close friendship with the Duchess of Devonshire and other great ladies as well as the admiration and protection of the Prince Regent. She was also an assiduous hostess whose dinners were exquisite and attended by all the *ton.* It was well known that her second son, William Lamb, was fathered by Lord Egremont. (The rule was that the heir must not be born out of wedlock. In this case Peniston Lamb, Lord Melbourne's son, died young and William became the heir, a tremendous *faux pas* on the part of a lady who seldom made a false move.) Another son, George, was fathered by the Prince Regent but Lord Melbourne would be hard put to it to resent his wife's infidelity in this case as it was by these means she had helped him to his title.

Lady Melbourne's charm, tact and discretion were such that she was received everywhere. Byron may have been thinking of her (the object of his heartfelt admiration and affection although she was over sixty and he twenty-four when they met) when he wrote these lines years later in *Don Juan*:

LXVI

A little genial sparkling of hypocrisy
Has saved the fame of thousand splendid sinners,
The loveliest oligarchs of our Gynocracy:
You may see such at all the balls and dinners
Among the proudest of our aristocracy
So gentle, charming, charitable, chaste –
And all by having *tact* as well as taste.[15]

Lady Melbourne spent her life planning for the advancement of her family. Both Lady Holland and her sister-in-law, Judith Milbanke, compared her with Madame de Merteuil in *Les Liaisons Dangereuses*. Others declared that everyone liked her and she could be exceedingly kind. She wrote to Lord Melbourne's agent in the country (at Melbourne Hall) instructing him in modern methods of husbandry (for which she was highly praised by Arthur Young) always signing herself 'Your friend, E.M.' and going to the trouble of sending him down the 'Trafalgar Gazette'. She sent her son Frederick at the Embassy in Germany a recipe for 84 mince pies. Frederick reciprocated with a gift of Russian sables for her to wear going to the Opera in the winter.[16] After her death William Lamb, now Lord Melbourne, pointed to her portrait, indicating what a wonderful woman she was, 'But not chaste, not chaste.'[17] He might have added that she was by no means unique in this respect. Lord

Egremont wrote that 'There was hardly a woman of fashion who did not think it almost a stain on her reputation if she was not known to have cuckolded her husband.'[18] Byron nursed no illusions about these lovely ladies:

> Went to my box at Covent-garden tonight; and my delicacy felt a little shocked ... It was as if the house had been divided between your public and your *understood* courtesans:- but the Intrigeantes much outnumbered the regular mercenaries ... Now, where lay the difference between [Pauline and her Mama] ... and Lady XXX and daughter? except that the two last may enter Carlton and any *other house*, and the two first are limited to the opera and b—— House.[19]
>
> (*Journal*, 17, 18 December 1813)

He was also aware of the effect of his sudden fame on all those who sought novelty and diversion. His fame had an aphrodisiac effect which caused him some embarrassment. He was pursued by Lady Falkland, who was so astonished at his gift of £500 on her husband's sudden death in a duel that she decided he was in love with her.

LVII

– for he had that kind of fame
Which sometimes plays the deuce with Womankind,
A heterogeneous mass of glorious blame,
Half virtues and whole vices being combined;
Faults which attract because they are not tame;
Follies tricked out so brightly that they blind:[20]

Byron became known to society through his verse but because he was a nobleman he belonged in the grandest circles, as others, however brilliant and famous, never could. Those who did not belong, but were admitted for their talent or some quality which made them unique, were sometimes treated with cruelty and disdain. Hary-O wrote of the actress Miss O'Neill:

> We had a visit from Miss O'Neill, who is odious. She snubbed us all, which is not prepossessing, struts about and throws out sentences in a low tragedy tone, looks short, thick and vulgar, and coolly receives any conversation bearing upon her art.[21]

Hazlitt writes (perhaps a little enviously) of Thomas Moore who, though the son of a Dublin grocer, won his way into every grand drawing room in London by his charm, his verse and the sweet voice in which he sang his own songs. Hazlitt seems yet again to be obsessed with differences in social class:

> He [Moore] ought to write with a crystal pen on silver paper ... Mr Moore has a little mistaken the art of poetry for the cosmetic art ... it is not the style of Parnassus...; but it is the style of our English Anacreon and it is (or was) the fashion of the day! ... He has been so long accustomed to the society of Whig Lords, and so enchanted with the smile of beauty and fashion, that he really fancies himself one of the *set* to which he is admitted on sufferance, and tries very unnecessarily to keep others out of it.[22]

Another in high society on sufferance was Henry Brougham. He had lost his seat in Parliament and was contemplating revenge on his friends and colleagues who had not exerted themselves to get him another. Having been great friends with the Hollands he had withdrawn for several years from Holland House and was now allowed back only to find the young poet he had demolished in the *Edinburgh Review* for a complete lack of talent, the centre of attention among his old friends, always surrounded by 'a circle of stargazers'.[23] Although he was accepted everywhere and admired for his extraordinary mind and talents he was aware that he did not belong as Byron belonged, in such circles. Like Thomas Moore – and even Sydney Smith, who was much loved by the Hollands – he had to sing for his supper.

An episode he must have found humiliating is described by Ward, his colleague on the *Edinburgh Review*:

> We Edinburgh gents ought not to meddle with field sports. Brougham tried it a few weeks ago at Lord Robert's. But he set fire to the powder horn and burnt off his own eyelashes. He tried to explain it on philosophical principles but the more he did so the more the Duke of Argyle and Lord Ponsonby, who are no philosophers, laughed.[24]

Hary-O is often disparaging – 'Sally Jersey thinks he [Brougham] is sometimes quite beautiful, but with his hair and eyebrows grown so long he looks to me like nothing so much as an orang outang.'[25] Lord Holland regarded him as a brilliant colleague and a friend but Brougham would have been beside himself with injured pride if he had read the rhyme Lord Holland made about him:

There's a wild man at large doth roam,
A giant wit, they call him Brougham,
And well methinks they may.
He deals whene'er he speaks or acts
With friends and foes and laws and facts
In such a sweeping way.[26]

Even his friends did not quite trust Brougham. He eventually got back into Parliament but it was galling to him that Byron had inherited his seat in the Lords without the slightest exertion and then proceeded to speak there on the sort of liberal questions – the treatment of the frame breakers, Catholic Emancipation and Parliamentary Reform – which Brougham would have liked to be seen championing in the Commons himself.

As time went on Byron became more and more disillusioned with the life that he was leading. Captain Gronow, whose battalion was stationed in Portman Street Barracks in 1814, remarked that 'good society' at this period was 'wonderfully select'.[27] Sir Arthur Quiller Couch saw it from a rather different point of view: 'The Mayfair of the Prince Regent's day – a tawdry society of war-profiteers swollen upon the misery of a bowed and ruined population – a society to my mind even more hateful, because falser, in its smug godliness than in its vices.'[28] This is a description of the sort of hypocrisy at which Byron was to tilt for the rest of his life. He took up the theme of the war-profiteers a few years later in a splendidly fierce tirade in the *Age of Bronze*:

Alas, the country! how shall tongue or pen
Bewail her now *un*country gentlemen?
The last to bid the cry of warfare cease,
The first to make a malady of peace.
For what were all these country patriots born?
To hunt – and vote – and raise the price of corn?
But corn, like every mortal thing, must fall,
Kings – Conquerors – and markets most of all.
And must ye fall with every ear of grain?
Why would you trouble Buonaparte's reign?
He was your great Triptolemus; his vices
Destroyed but realms, and still maintained your prices;
He amplified to every lord's content
The grand agrarian alchymy, high *rent*.
Why did the tyrant stumble on the Tartars,

And lower wheat to such desponding quarters?
Why did you chain him on yon Isle so lone?
The man was worth much more upon his throne.
True, blood and treasure boundlessly were spilt,
But what of that? the Gaul may bear the guilt;
But bread was high, the farmer paid his way,
And acres told upon the appointed day.
But where is now the goodly audit ale?
The purse-proud tenant, never known to fail?
The farm which never yet was left on hand?
The marsh reclaimed to most improving land?
The impatient hope of the expiring lease?
The doubling rental? What an evil's peace!
In vain the prize excites the ploughman's skill,
In vain the Commons pass their patriot bill;
The *Landed Interest* – (you may understand
The phrase much better leaving out the *land*) –
The land self-interest groans from shore to shore,
For fear that plenty should attain the poor.
Up, up again, ye rents, exalt your notes,
Or else the Ministry will lose their votes,
And patriotism, so delicately nice,
Her loaves will lower to the market price;
For ah! 'the loaves and fishes', once so high,
Are gone – their oven closed, their ocean dry,
And nought remains of all the millions spent,
Excepting to grow moderate and content.
They who are not so, *had* their turn – and turn
About still flows from Fortune's equal urn;
Now let their virtue be its own reward,
And share the blessings which themselves prepared.
See these inglorious Cincinnati swarm.
Farmers of war, dictators of the farm;
Their ploughshare was the sword in hireling hands,
Their fields manured by gore of other lands;
Safe in their barns, these Sabine tillers sent
Their brethren out to battle – why? for rent!
Year after year they voted cent. per cent.
Blood, sweat, and tear-wrung millions – why? for rent!
They roared, they dined, they drank, they swore they meant
To die for England – why then live? – for rent!
The peace has made one general malcontent
Of these high-market patriots; war was rent!
Their love of country, millions all mis-spent,
How reconcile? by reconciling rent!

And will they not repay the treasures lent?
No: down with everything, and up with rent!
Their good, ill, health, wealth, joy, or discontent,
Being, end, aim, religion – *rent* – *rent* – *rent!*[29]

Byron already saw through the gracious social façade, writing from Bath, 'Bedfords – Jerseys – Ossulstones – Greys and the like ... the women ... hating each other and talking. Rogers fell to my share – and we abused everybody ... I never saw anything like it but a print from Dante's *Inferno*.'[30]

All the same Byron thoroughly enjoyed the adulation of the women and the company of the men. He liked the dandies, and for a time frequented the gaming tables, becoming a member of Watier's where the play was very high:

> I was very fond of it [gambling] when young – that is to say 'Hazard' for I hate all *Card* Games even Faro – When macco (or whatever they spell it) was introduced I gave up the whole thing – for I loved and missed the *rattle* and *dash* of the box and dice ... I have thrown as many as fourteen mains running – and carried off all the cash upon the table occasionally – but I had no coolness or judgement or calculation ... Upon the whole I left off in time without being much a winner or loser.[31]
>
> (*Detached Thoughts*, 1821–22)

This was as well since Gronow tells of 'Watier's in the days of Brummell and the dandies' when 'Charles Fox, George Selwyn, Lord Carlisle, Fitzpatrick, Horace Walpole, the Duke of Queensbury, and others, lost whole fortunes at faro, macao, and hazard.'[32]

Byron was clearly liked by his male companions and was happy in male company. But surrounded as he was in the ballrooms and drawing rooms by a 'circle of [female] stargazers' it was likely that so beautiful a young man would be pounced upon by one or other of a host of admiring females and borne off as a sacrifice to her vanity.

Lady Caroline Lamb was known in the Polite World as 'Sprite' or 'Ariel' or 'The Fairy Queen'. Her voice was childlike and lisping, and she spoke with the Devonshire House drawl she had acquired from her mother, Lady Bessborough (sister of Georgiana, Duchess of Devonshire), and from the time she spent in the Devonshire House nurseries with her cousins Georgiana (later Lady Carlisle), Hary-O and 'Hart' (Lord Hartington, the heir), who dearly loved his cousin and was grief-stricken when she married William Lamb. Her early letters show that she was a delightful young woman who might well have developed into Byron's 'mutual mind' if she had not lacked a certain balance. Her vanity was inordinate and because she was so funny and charming she was petted into an obsessive need to be the centre of the stage on every occasion. As a young bride she wrote affectionate letters to Lord Hartington, which are evidence of the charm which had enchanted him over the years as they grew up together.

Caroline's letters are delightful. She scolds her cousin, Hartington (later the sixth Duke of Devonshire) light-heartedly, teases him unmercifully, tells him he is provoking and demands that he should write to her without delay. Her letters are full of rhymes, drawings, threats, promises and the occasional 'God bless you!'. Her warm, loving, lively, inconsequential letters to her mother, Lady Bessborough, are very different from the pert, critical and prosy letters of Byron's future bride, Annabella Milbanke, to her mother, Lady Milbanke.

Ominously, however, Lady Bessborough and her mother, Lady Spencer, confided to each other their anxiety about Caroline's ill-health, strange manners and 'sauvagerie' before her marriage, and her headstrong behaviour as a young married woman. Lady Spencer's conclusion was that Caroline would bring great misery upon herself and her family, not from wickedness, but from inordinate vanity.

The marriage with William Lamb was not a brilliant match for Caroline. Until the death of his brother made him heir William would not have dared to offer for her, though he was eventually to become Viscount Melbourne and Queen Victoria's first Prime Minister. However, William was able to calm her down and for some years they were extremely happy together. She bore him a son, Augustus. This boy, her only child, was an epileptic and his development was later found to be retarded.

No husband could have satisfied Caroline's emotional demands and by the time she met Byron they were leading separate lives, he involved with politics and she inventing dramas with the role of heroine reserved for herself. The most uncomfortable of these for her husband was the flirtation she engineered with Sir Godfrey Webster, Lady Holland's son by her first marriage, a man of dubious reputation but handsome appearance. Caroline made sure that she was seen everywhere with Sir Godfrey and seemed to be intimating to society that she was involved in a passionate affair. William remained calm. He was confident that Caro would never run away with Sir Godfrey and patiently waited until, after a few months, she came to her senses.

In March 1812 Caroline read *Childe Harold's Pilgrimage* and told Samuel Rogers she was determined to meet the new poet. David Cecil, in his illuminating account of the background to all these amours and scandals, points out that Caroline was everything Byron least liked in women:

> Stormy, clever and unfashionably thin... But he had not the strength to withstand her; and he never could refuse the chance of a conquest. Moreover, young as he was, and dazzled by the new and glittering world into which his fame had so suddenly flung him, the prospect of an amour with one of its reigning queens flattered him in a way he was unable to resist.[33]

Byron has been portrayed as the heartless seducer of Lady Caroline. This was not the case. M.K. Joseph rightly pointed out that 'One thing is common to the experience of both Don Juan and his creator – that for both of them it is woman who is the predator not the prey.'[34] In Italy, years later, Byron wrote to Richard Hoppner, 'I should like to know *who* has been carried off – except poor dear *me* – I have been more ravished myself than anybody since the Trojan war.'[35]

Early in 1812 Byron wrote lines to Caroline Lamb describing a frame of mind which is either a posture of some sort or which lasted so short a time that they were contradicted within a few months. Byron felt an urgent desire to name the loved one in his amorous verse (indirectly via the cornelian the boy had given him, in the case of Edleston). Yet even at the outset he declares in the poem that he wants to resist her spell. All the same, he tells her that the chain she has cast on him will last forever.

It was a potent spell. Her background was impressive to a young man who had been brought up in far less sophisticated circles than Melbourne House and Devonshire House. At first Byron found her irresistible but as early as April he was telling her, 'I never knew a woman with greater or more pleasing talents, *general* as in a woman they should be, something of everything and too much of nothing, but these are unfortunately coupled with a total want of common conduct.'[36] Here Byron discloses his sense of decorum, which was as strong as his contrary need to publicise his own transgressions.

Byron wrote to Caroline before the end of April offering to leave London:

> M[oore] is in great distress about us, & indeed people talk as if there were no other pair of absurdities in London. – It is hard to bear all this without a cause, but worse to give cause for it. – Our folly has had the effect of a fault. – I conformed & could conform, if you would lend your aid, but I can't bear to see you look unhappy, & am always on the watch to observe if you are trying to make me so. – We must make an effort, this dream this delirium of two months must pass away, we in fact do not know one another, a month's absence would make us rational, you do not think so, I know it, we have both had 1000 previous fancies of the same kind, & shall get the better of this & be as ashamed of it according to the maxim of Rochefoucalt. – But it is better that I should leave town than you, & I will make a tour, or go to Cambridge or Edinburgh. – Now don't abuse me, or think me altered, it is because I am not, cannot alter, that I shall do this, and cease to make fools talk, friends grieve, and the wise, pity. – Ever most affectionately & sincerely yours.[37]

Byron liked the risk-taking that Caro offered, as he later half revelled in and half shuddered at the risk of his affair with his half-sister. But Caroline was incapable of carrying on her affair with Byron with the discretion that would have prevented it from becoming an open scandal and Byron was forced either to run away with her or to end their liaison. His friends became alarmed at the growing scandal caused by the folly of her behaviour. Byron himself was shocked and embarrassed when she invaded his lodgings dressed in page's clothing. When she ran away from Melbourne House it was Byron who searched for her, found her and restored her to her embarrassed family, thus displaying the contradictory elements in his character.

Lady Bessborough and William Lamb succeeded in whisking Caroline off to Ireland. Caroline wrote frenzied letters to Byron boasting of her conquests there. He wrote to Lady Melbourne who had become his adviser and confidante, 'I cannot write, I would not seem jealous, and it would be . . . improper to appear indifferent.'[38] He admitted generously, 'She never did nor can deserve a single reproach which must not fall with double justice and truth upon myself.'[39]

Byron felt that if Caroline ran away from her husband for his sake he was in honour bound to marry her. '[If after all] I must be hers she shall be *mine* as long as it pleases her ... wretched as it would render me, she should never know it.'[40] This is what he *says* and doubtless he *felt* it in the act of writing it. There is no evidence that he was insincere. But whether he felt it in some stronger sense is hard to determine. This ambiguity is what makes the task of the biographer, who is anxious to explain, pin down and fit into some explanation or theory, all the more difficult.

He was relieved to find that Caroline had no firm intention of leaving her husband. He told Lady Melbourne, 'I am much more unwilling to hurt her feelings now than ever. She has a claim on *me* ... for every respect that she may not feel her own degradation.'[41] But he longed to be free of her – 'If I can *honourably* be off?'[42] Lady Melbourne thought he could. Since Caroline's pursuit of him showed no sign of flagging, Byron determined to escape either by going abroad or by getting married. In March 1812 he had noticed among the young women gathered at Melbourne House for lessons in the new art of waltzing, Annabella Milbanke, a demure and modest-looking girl from the north of England who happened to be a niece of Lady Melbourne. He asked her to sound out his chances with Annabella and later told Medwin that 'there was a simplicity, a retired modesty about her which ... formed a happy contrast to the cold artificial formality and studied stiffness, which is called fashion. She interested me exceedingly.'[43]

Annabella rejected him and this rejection coincided with an invitation to Eywood, the country house of Lord and Lady Oxford in Herefordshire. Lady Melbourne had scolded Caroline when she took to foregathering with ladies of somewhat tarnished reputation, among whom was Lady Oxford. Some of Lady Oxford's tribe of beautiful children were said to be the progeny of various fathers other than Lord Oxford and, the Oxford family name being Harley, they were known by society as 'The Harleian Miscellany.' One of Lady Oxford's lovers was the famous Radical, Sir Francis Burdett. Under his influence Lady Oxford had become a Radical herself and it was at the Hampden Club that she first met Byron who respected Sir Francis so highly as a fair and honourable man that he appointed him some years after he had left London, to be arbiter over the division of the Wentworth inheritance on Lady Noel's death.

Lord Oxford was a conniving husband and Lady Oxford a safe refuge from Caroline. For several months Byron spent much of his time at Eywood or at Kinsham Court, a house he took to be near his 'Armida' without causing 'il sposo' to have 'the crotchets'.

When Caroline returned to London she desperately tried to revive Byron's interest in her, following him, demanding locks of his hair, threatening to stab herself, forging his signature in order to make off with his portrait and forcing her way into his apartments in Albany at all hours. Once when she had entered his rooms in his absence she wrote on the fly leaf of one of his books, 'Remember Me'. Underneath this cry of anguish Byron, driven to fury, wrote the lines:

1.

Remember thee! remember thee!
   Till Lethe quench life's burning stream,
Remorse and Shame shall cling to thee,
   And haunt thee like a feverish dream!

2

Remember thee! Ay, doubt it not.
   Thy husband too shall think of thee:
By neither shalt thou be forgot,
   Thou *false* to him, thou *fiend* to me![44]

Byron and Lady Melbourne had become allies and fast friends, and to her he confided the irritation which had culminated in the writing of *Remember Thee!*: 'Good God – am I to be hunted from place to place like a Russian *bear* or *Emperor*?'[45] Byron was genuinely distressed at being 'stalked' by Lady Caroline Lamb and he certainly felt the desperation displayed in the poem but he was doubtless also delighted to be given the impetus to inhabit so dramatic an attitude. One must remember that in all his experiences of love he was always as much poet as lover – not more so but as much.

Byron wrote a poem addressed not to Lady Oxford but to her eleven-year-old daughter, Lady Charlotte Harley, which was published with the seventh edition of *Childe Harold's Pilgrimage*. It is a very innocent affair which can have caused the child's mother no concern, but it was quoted in Benita Eisler's biography as evidence that Byron was caught by Lady Oxford trying to rape her daughter.

Eisler carefully omits the lines which militate against her theory – lines 3, 4, 5, 12 and 13. Lady Oxford was a particularly devoted mother who would have thrown Byron out of the house if this accusation had been true.

FROM TO IANTHE

Ah! may'st thou ever be what now thou art,
Nor unbeseem the promise of thy Spring –
As fair in form, as warm yet pure in heart,
Love's image upon earth without his wing,
And guileless beyond Hope's imagining!
And surely she who now so fondly rears
Thy youth, in thee, thus hourly brightening,
Beholds the Rainbow of her future years,
Before whose heavenly hues all Sorrow disappears.

Young Peri of the West! – 'tis well for me
My years already doubly number thine;
My loveless eye unmoved may gaze on thee,
And safely view thy ripening beauties shine;
Happy, I ne'er shall see them in decline;
Happier, that, while all younger hearts shall bleed,
Mine shall escape the doom thine eyes assign
To those whose admiration shall succeed,
But mixed with pangs to Love's even loveliest hours decreed.

Oh! let that eye, which, wild as the Gazelle's,
Now brightly bold or beautifully shy,
Wins as it wanders, dazzles where it dwells,
Glance o'er this page; nor to my verse deny
That smile –[46]

Byron wrote to Lady Melbourne of his admiration for the little girl whom –

> – I should love forever if she could always be only eleven years old – & whom I shall probably marry when she is old enough & bad enough to be made into a modern wife. – We have had as yet very few fine days & these I have passed on the water & in the woods – scrambling and splashing about with the children – or by myself – I always feel happier here or at Newstead than elsewhere – & all my plagues are at least 150 miles off.[47]
>
> (Byron to Lady Melbourne, 5 April 1813)

In London he could not escape the worst of his plagues and the Caro Lamb affair remained a scandal of epic proportions.

'Manage her!' he protested to Lady Melbourne, '. . . it is impossible – and as to friendship – no – it must be broken off at once, and all I have left is to take some step which will make her hate me.'[48]

The step he took was the cruel letter – a version of which Caroline made public later in her *roman à clef*, *Glenarvon*. The letter concluded: 'Correct your vanity which is ridiculous, exert your absurd caprices upon others; and leave me in peace.'[49]

It is inexcusable and so is the unpleasant trick he played on Caroline with the connivance of Lady Oxford. When she asked for a lock of Byron's hair they sent one of Lady Oxford's, which was the same colour. Thus Byron allowed resentment to blot out his better nature.

There is in existence, though she never knew it, a poem written in October 1812 which shows that after their parting and when he was already in the toils of his Enchantress, Lady Oxford, Byron could still refer in romantic terms to his liaison with Caroline. It was addressed to her sister-in-law, Mrs George Lamb. This young woman was also a 'Caroline' – Caroline St Jules, daughter of the fifth Duke of Devonshire and Lady Elizabeth Foster, who had been brought up with the Cavendish children at Devonshire House. Because both Lamb brothers lived in separate apartments in Melbourne House the two Carolines were known, to avoid confusion, as Caro William and Caro George.

For a moment Byron seems to have forgotten the pain and aggravation and he looks back fondly on the love he had felt for Caro William. Byron loved to hear a woman sing and Caro George's singing moved him to write:

TO THE HONBLE MRS GEORGE LAMB

1.

The sacred song that on mine ear
   Yet vibrates from that voice of thine,
I heard, before, from one so dear –
   'T is strange it still appears divine.

2.

But, oh! so sweet that *look* and *tone*
   To her and thee alike is given;
It seemed as if for me alone
   That *both* had been recalled from Heaven!

3.
And though I never can redeem
The vision they endeared to me;
I scarcely can regret my dream,
When realised again by thee.[50]

This was not published during Byron's lifetime. If Caro William had seen it she might have been comforted to know that Byron clung to so romantic a memory of her via song. On the other hand it might have tempted her to scratch Caro George's eyes out. In any case Byron could not let her see it, knowing that even so romantic and dream-like an expression of nostalgia would only serve to set her off again. Her subsequent behaviour proved that he was right not to publish.

After a period during which Byron sat at the feet of his Armida, listening to music, talking about books, being lectured about 'his senatorial duties', Lord Oxford began to cut up rough and seems to have threatened to throw his wife out of the house. Although she was well over forty and he in his mid twenties Byron immediately offered her a '*carte blanche*' whereupon, to Byron's intense relief, Lord Oxford '...ate up his own words and intentions and now they are to live happy ever after.'[51] Lord Oxford had for some time been contemplating a sea voyage. The love affair ended with great regret on both sides when Lady Oxford went reluctantly abroad with her husband and Byron stayed reluctantly at home.

11

LOVE AND FRIENDSHIP

'By Mahomet! I begin to think I like everybody ... a sort of social gluttony'[1]

After the departure of Lady Oxford, Byron missed the company of his Enchantress but there were plenty of diversions in London to help him forget the months he had passed with her at Eywood 'like the gods in *Lucretius*'.[2] One of the social lions of that summer was Madame de Staël who had left her château at Coppet in Switzerland to enjoy the adulation of those English who, like Byron, admired her latest book, *De l'Allemagne*, which was published by John Murray since Napoleon had had the Paris edition destroyed. She was greatly respected for her courageous opposition to Napoleon's tyranny which had led to her exile from Paris where she had her literary salon and, as the daughter of Necker (late Director General of Finance to Louis XV and XVI) and possessor of a great fortune, she had been a prominent figure.

Byron found her overpowering, '... a very plain woman forcing one to listen and look at her with her pen behind her ear and her mouth full of *ink*.'[3] When they met at Lady Jersey's she congratulated him on the perfect English constitution and listened in amazement to his reply that the English constitution was mired in corruption and that the King and Pitt between them had destroyed the liberties of the English. 'And you count for nothing the liberty to say all that? And in front of the servants too!'[4]

He left her notes unanswered. 'I admire her abilities, but really her society is overwhelming – an avalanche that buries one in glittering nonsense – all snow and sophistry.'[5] Two notes from Madame de Staël to Byron speak for themselves:

Dinez chez moi dimanche avec vos amis – je ne dirai pas vos admirateurs car je n'ai rencontré que cela de touts parts.

A dimanche
De Staël

A few days later she wrote, no doubt in some exasperation:

Je prends le silence pour oui.[6]

Some years later Madame de Staël was to heap coals of fire on his head by treating him with great kindness when he visited her at Coppet, by then an exile himself. He showed his sympathy for her by remarking that though Madame de Staël thought like a man, unfortunately for her, she *felt* like a woman. Her comment a few years later from Switzerland on the 'Farewell Verses' to his wife shows that he had understood her very well – she wrote of these lines that if they had been addressed to her she would have flung herself into Byron's arms: '*Je n'aurais pu m'y tenir un instant!*'[7]

Lady Melbourne, 'the best friend I ever had in my life, and the cleverest of women',[8] remained his confidante and mentor. He found himself obliged to decline her invitations to dinner at Melbourne House: 'I am rather hungry, having lived on tea and bread and butter ever since I left E[ywood] (where I was under the necessity of conforming to a less Eremetical regimen) and should do justice to your viands – Yet I must resist all this.'[9] A few days later he was unable to accept her invitation since 'I have unfortunately dined for the week yesterday.'[10]

Byron has been diagnosed as anorexic and, though such a diagnosis at long distance in time suffers from the disadvantage that the patient is not present for examination, the argument is persuasive. In his diary for 17 November 1813 he wrote:

I wish to God I had not dined now! – It kills me with heaviness, stupor, and horrible dreams; – and yet it was but a pint of bucellas, and fish. Meat I never touch, – nor much vegetable diet. I wish I were in the country, to take exercise, – instead of being obliged to *cool* by abstinence, in lieu of it. I should not so much mind a little accession of flesh – my bones can well bear it. But the worst is, the devil always comes with it, – till I starve him out – and I will not be the slave of *any* appetite ... I wonder how Buonaparte's dinner agrees with him.[11]

(*Journal*, 17 November 1813)

Nothing could have pleased him more than the arrival in London of Augusta Leigh coinciding with the departure of Lady Oxford. He invited her to come with him to a reception given by Lady Davy (wife of Sir Humphrey Davy, the great chemist) where she would see Madame de Staël – 'some people whom you know – and *me* whom you do *not* know – and you can talk to which you please – and I will watch over you as if you were unmarried ... Now do as you like – but if you chuse to array yourself before or after half past ten I will call for you.'[12] (Byron to Augusta Leigh, 27 June 1813)

He asked Lady Melbourne for vouchers so he could take Augusta to a masque at Almack's. Later he told her, 'I should have been glad of your advice how to untie two or three "*Gordian* knots" tied round me – I shall cut them ... though some are closely twisted round my *heart*.' (He is hinting at his having fallen in love with his half-sister.) 'Perhaps I shall not see you again – if not – forgive my follies and like as much of me as you can.'[13] (Byron to Lady Melbourne, 11 August 1813)

Byron found Augusta utterly beguiling because she looked and behaved like a Byron. She was as shy with strangers as he. He was impressed with the background in which she had been brought up and she was proud of her younger brother's fame and genius. For three weeks they were constantly together and on her return home he went down to Six Mile Bottom, near Newmarket, to visit her. He had been trying to arrange to go abroad again and told Lady Melbourne that his sister was planning to go with him. Byron felt completely at ease with Augusta and told his wife later, 'I only want a woman to laugh. I can make Augusta laugh at anything.'[14] He called her 'Gus' and this soon became 'Goose'. George Leigh neglected Augusta and left her to bear all the burdens of their establishment. Byron understood the inconveniences and humiliations of poverty only too well, and could be unfailingly sympathetic, helpful and generous to her. With Augusta and her children at Six Mile Bottom he found he could enjoy the affectionate domestic life his mother had been unable to provide for him. They could laugh uproariously together and comfort each other in their misfortunes.

Byron was now deeply in love with his half-sister. Her greatest charm for him was her love and affection. She made him no scenes, looked after his comfort and welfare, gave him good advice, continued to love and pity him when he did not take it, laughed him out of his moods and melancholy and made allowances for his failings.

Soon after Augusta's arrival in London Caro Lamb's hysterical behaviour caused the scandal which finally ruined her reputation. Byron wrote to Lady Melbourne the day after Lady Heathcote's ball:

> I have heard a strange story of C's scratching herself with glass – and I know not what besides. What I said or did to provoke her – I know not ... She took hold of my hand as I passed and pressed it against some sharp instrument – and said – 'I mean to use this...' had I guessed her to be serious or had I been conscious of offending I should have done everything to pacify or prevent her.[15]

Gossip spread that Caro Lamb had stabbed herself at Lady Heathcote's ball for love of Byron. This incident caused Lady Westmoreland and Lady Ossulstone, who were present, to conclude that Byron must have done something to offend Caroline. They scolded him and gave him 'angry looks' which were repeated by many other of Caroline's train of 'compassionate countesses' when word of the scandal got out. Sydney Smith's comment was 'And then, of course, he is a poet! What a charming thing to be a poet! I preached for many years in London and was rather popular but I never heard of any Lady who did herself the smallest injury on my account.'[16]

Byron was feeling aggrieved. He wrote a few days later to Thomas Moore, 'The Staël last night attacked me most furiously – said that I had "no right to make love – that I had used [Caroline] barbarously – that I had no feeling, and was totally *in*sensible to *la belle passion*, and had been all my life." I am very glad to hear it though I did not know it before.'[17]

He was then extremely irritated by a rumour that the purchaser Hanson had found for Newstead, a Mr Claughton, was a young man who had been over-reached and ruined over the transaction. The true story was that Claughton was a lawyer, forty five years old, who had bought the estate at his own offer price – '...he evaded and at last drove me into Chancery.'[18]

Annabella Milbanke now decided that she had made a mistake in rejecting Byron so decidedly and wrote from Seaham offering him her friendship, stipulating that their correspondence must remain a secret 'except for Mamma and Papa'. Annabella knew that it was unusual for a young unmarried woman to solicit letters from a single man – in this case one who had been the lover of her cousin-by-marriage, Caroline Lamb, and caused thereby a resounding scandal. She tried to reassure Byron by inventing a previous but hopeless attachment. This lie had a second advantage in that it would, she hoped, obviate any suspicion that she was trying to ensnare him. Byron believed in the hopeless love for another man but he was otherwise undeceived. 'Friendship,' Thomas Medwin reported him as saying, 'is a dangerous word for young ladies. It is Love full-fledged and waiting for a fine day to fly.'[19]

Annabella wrote to him regularly and by the following spring was hinting at a visit to Seaham. The formal invitation from Sir Ralph would follow at a time when he felt little inclination to accept it, much to Annabella's disappointment. She was puzzled as to how to admit that the previous attachment was a fiction without coming down off what Lady Melbourne called 'her stilts' and admitting to a lie. Byron was not as deeply concerned with Annabella as she would have liked. He had confessed his love for his half-sister to Lady Melbourne who told him he would ruin Augusta. Augusta too was having second thoughts and when he went down to Newmarket and found her immovable he cut short his visit. After this there was no more talk of going abroad together; Lady Melbourne persuaded Byron to pay a visit to his friend, Wedderburn Webster, who had a pretty young wife. Lady Frances was to be the saving of Byron by allowing herself to be seduced by him. Lady Melbourne can be forgiven much for her amiable character but this seems an unforgivable act of cynicism. However, it is entirely possible that the shrewd and subtle older woman had heard rumours of Lady Frances, or perhaps had drawn inferences from her own experience of the young woman, which caused her to rate the girl fair game. Byron, however, was incapable of carrying on the game without falling in love. 'I cannot exist without some object of love.'[20] This was to become, in at least some sense, one of the 'series of passionate attachments' described by Thomas Moore. But it was to be short-lived. He wrote to Lady Melbourne to keep her *au fait* with his progress.

He was regularly receiving letters from Annabella and had replied to her questions about his attitude to religion.

> I believe doubtless in God – and should be happy to be convinced of much more – [Annabella was clearly longing to be allowed to convince him] – if I do not at present place implicit faith on tradition and revelation of any human creed I hope it is not from a want of reverence for the Creator but the created ... the *moral* of Christianity is perfectly beautiful – and the very sublime of Virtue – yet even there we find some of its finer precepts in earlier axioms of the Greeks. – particularly 'do unto others as you would they should do unto you'. – the forgiveness of injuries – and more which I do not remember – Good Night.[21]
>
> (To Annabella Milbanke, 26 September 1813)

He was puzzled by Annabella's behaviour and confided to Lady Melbourne:

> The epistles of your mathematician ... continue – and the last concludes with a repetition of a desire that none but Papa and Mamma should know it ... but – observe – here is the strictest of St Ursula's 11000 what do you call 'ems? – a wit – a moralist – and religionist – enters into a clandestine correspondence with a personage generally presumed a great Roué – and drags her aged parents into this secret treaty – it is I believe not usual for single ladies to risk such brilliant adventures – but this come of *infallibility* – not that she ever says anything that might not be said by the Town Cryer – still it is imprudent – if I were rascal enough to take an unfair advantage. – Alas! poor human nature![22]
>
> (Byron to Lady Melbourne, 28 September 1813)

He was to find Lady Frances's behaviour even more puzzling. He wrote from Aston Hall to his confidante:

> I am not exactly cut out for the Lady of the mansion – but I think a stray Dandy would have a chance of preferment – she evidently expects to be attacked – and seems prepared for a brilliant defence – my character as a Roué has gone before me – and my careless and quiet behaviour astonished her so much that I believe she began to think herself ugly – or me blind – if not worse.[23]
>
> (Byron to Lady Melbourne, September–1 October 1813)

During a game of billiards Frances asked him '... an odd question – "how a woman who liked a man could inform him of it without *courting* the *hazards*."' He wrote her a note which '... produced an *answer* – a very unequivocal one too – but a little too much about virtue – and indulgence of attachment in some sort of ethereal process in which the soul is principally concerned ... one generally *ends* and *begins* with Platonism – and as my proselyte is only twenty – there is time enough to materialize...'[24]. Byron wrote indignantly of the husband:

> ...if a man is not contented with a pretty woman and not only runs after any little country girl he meets with but absolutely boasts of it – he must not be surprised if others admire that which he knows not how to value.[25]
>
> (Byron to Lady Melbourne, 8 October 1813)

And again:

> She ... managed to give me a note – and to receive another and a ring before [Webster's] very face – and yet she is a thorough devotee – and takes prayers morning and evening – besides being measured for a new bible every quarter.[26]
>
> (Byron to Lady Melbourne, Newstead Abbey, 10 October 1813)

Now Byron produced one of his extraordinary acts of utterly quixotic generosity. To save Webster from having to apply to the usurers he, though already in the hands of the usurers himself, instructed Hanson to advance a loan of £1000 to James Wedderburn Webster Esquire of Aston Hall, York County.

Matters with Lady Frances became more serious. 'You who know me and my weakness so well – will not be surprised when I say that I am totally absorbed in this passion – that I am even ready to take a *flight* if necessary.'[27] (To Lady Melbourne, 13 October 1813)

He was no longer writing to Augusta. Lady Melbourne's plan seemed to be working. Now came the crisis:

> – it came to this – 'I am entirely at your mercy – I own it – I give myself up to you – I am not *cold* – whatever I seem to others – but I know that I cannot bear the reflection hereafter ... I tell you the truth – now act as you will.' Was I wrong? – I spared her ... There was a something so very peculiar in her manner – a kind of mild decision – no scene – not even a struggle – but still I know not what convinced me she was serious – it was not the mere 'No' which one had heard forty times before ... I love her – if I did not and much too – I should have been more *selfish* ... I have offered to go away with her – and her answer whether sincere or not is 'that on *my account* she declines it' ... she is either the most *artful* or *artless* of her age (20) I ever encountered ... She is so thin and pale ... if she were

once my wife ... a warm climate should be the first resort ... for her recovery. – The most perplexing – and yet I can't prevail upon myself to give it up – is the caressing system – in her it appears perfectly childish – and I do think innocent – but it really puzzles all the Scipio about me to confine myself to the laudable portion of these endearments...[28]

(Byron to Lady Melbourne, Newstead Abbey, 17 October 1813)

Later he wrote, 'I do detest everything which is not perfectly mutual ... Perhaps after all – I was her dupe – if so – I am the dupe also of the few good feelings I could ever boast of.'[29] (Byron to Lady Melbourne, 21 October 1813)

He assured Lady Melbourne, '...you really *wrong* me too – if you do not suppose I would sacrifice everything for *Ph* [Frances] – I hate sentiment – and in consequence my epistolary levity makes you believe me as hollow and heartless as my letters are light – Indeed it is not so.'[30] (Byron to Lady Melbourne, Monday – [25 October 1813?])

In 1815 Byron wrote a poem inspired by the scandal arising from the very public love affair Lady Frances was reported to be conducting in Paris with the Duke of Wellington:

1.

WHEN we two parted
   In silence and tears,
Half broken-hearted
   To sever for years,
Pale grew thy cheek and cold,
   Colder thy kiss;
Truly that hour foretold
   Sorrow to this.

2.

The dew of the morning
   Sunk chill on my brow –
It felt like the warning
   Of what I feel now.
Thy vows are all broken,
   And light is thy fame:
I hear thy name spoken,
   And share in its shame.

3.
They name thee before me,
  A knell to mine ear;
A shudder comes o'er me –
  Why wert thou so dear?
They know not I knew thee,
  Who knew thee too well:–
Long, long shall I rue thee,
  Too deeply to tell.

4.
In secret we met –
  In silence I grieve,
That thy heart could forget,
  Thy spirit deceive.
If I should meet thee
  After long years,
How should I greet thee? –
  With silence and tears.[31]

It has been claimed that Byron felt revengeful because Lady Frances had rejected his love. He admitted to Lady Melbourne that he was unhappy at thinking of the 'not'. But Lady Frances did not reject Byron. She admitted that she was ashamed at having confessed to him that she adored him and, having offered herself to him with various face-saving provisos, she, later, thanked him for having 'spared her'.

Thomas Moore met Lady Frances in 1819. His account of the meeting is interesting:

> She was (or fancied herself) very much in love with him [Byron] ... I should pronounce her cold-blooded and vain to an excess – and I believe her great aim is to attract people of celebrity – if so, she must have been gratified – as the first Poet [Byron] and first Captain [Wellington] of the age have been her lovers – the latter liaison was at all events not altogether spiritual – her manner to me very flattering and the eyes played off most skilfully.[32]

Lady Melbourne tried hard to persuade Byron that the young woman she described as 'This poor little ignorant girl', was truthful, and sincerely in love with him. But she could not resist admitting that Lady Frances was sometimes childish and tiresome. One cannot help suspecting that Lady Melbourne is less than sincere in the opinion she gives of the girl she hopes will charm Byron away from Augusta.

Though Byron claimed to have no very high opinion of women he delighted in the company of Lady Melbourne, Augusta, and, at first, until she threw over the traces, that of Caroline Lamb. All were intelligent women though Augusta found it amusing to appear more scatterbrained than she really was. She had what is called 'emotional intelligence' in high degree. He describes his susceptibility to women of all sorts and classes:

> There is something to me very softening in the presence of a woman, – some strange influence, even if one is not in love with them, – which I cannot at all account for, having no very high opinion of the sex. But yet, – I always feel in better humour with myself and everything else, if there is a woman within ken. Even Mrs Mule, my firelighter, – the most ancient and withered of her kind, – and (except to myself) not the best-tempered – always makes me laugh, –[33]
>
> (*Journal*, 27 February 1814)

Moore writes of Byron's kindness to old Mrs Mule:

> This ancient housemaid, of whose gaunt and witch-like appearance it would be impossible to convey any idea but by the pencil, furnished one among the numerous instances of Lord Byron's proneness to attach himself to any thing however homely, that had once enlisted his good nature in its behalf, and become associated with his thoughts. He first found this old woman at his lodgings in Bennet Street, where, for a whole season, she was the perpetual scarecrow of his visitors. When, next year, he took chambers in Albany, one of the greatest advantages which his friends looked to in the change was that they should get rid of this phantom. But no, – there she was again – he had actually brought her with him from Bennet Street. The Following year saw him married and with a regular establishment of servants in Piccadilly; and here, – as Mrs Mule had not made her appearance to any of the visitors, – it was concluded, rashly, that the witch had vanished. One of these friends, however, who had most fondly indulged himself in this persuasion, happening to call one day when all the male part of the establishment were abroad, saw, to his dismay, the door opened by the same gaunt grim personage, improved considerably in point of habiliments since I last saw her, and keeping pace with the increased scale of her master's household, as a new peruke, and other symptoms of promotion testified. When asked how he came to carry this old woman about with him from place to place Lord Byron's only answer was, 'The poor old devil was so kind to me'.[34]

He was equally kind to old Joe Murray:

> Old Murray, the servant he mentions ... as the only faithful follower remaining to him, had long been in the service of the former Lord and was regarded by the young poet with a fondness of affection which it has seldom been the lot of age and dependence to inspire. 'I have more than once,' says a gentleman who was at this time a constant visitor at Newstead, 'seen Lord Byron at the dinner table fill out a tumbler of madeira and hand it over his shoulder to Joe Murray, who stood behind his chair, saying, with a cordiality that brightened his whole countenance, "Here, my old Fellow".'[35]

Byron told Annabella Milbanke that she was wrong to believe in his '*general despondency*'. '[I] may safely appeal to most of my acquaintance (Ly. M. for instance) in proof of my assertion – "Nobody laughs more".'[36] (Byron to Annabella Milbanke, 6 September 1813)

Moore bears witness to the truth of this assertion:

> Among the many gay hours we passed together this spring, I remember particularly the wild flow of his spirits one evening, when we had accompanied Mr Rogers home from some early assembly, and when Lord Byron, who, according to his frequent custom, had not dined for the last two days, found his hunger no longer governable, and called aloud for 'something to eat.' Our repast, – of his own choosing, – was simple bread and cheese; and seldom have I partaken of so joyous a supper. It happened that our host had just received a presentation copy of a volume of poems, written professedly in imitation of the old English writers, and containing, like many of these models, a good deal that was striking and beautiful, mixed up with much that was trifling, fantastic, and absurd. In our mood, at the moment, it was only with these latter qualities that either Lord Byron or I felt disposed to indulge ourselves; and, in turning over the pages, we found, it must be owned, abundant matter for mirth. In vain did Mr Rogers, in justice to the author, endeavour to direct our attention to some of the beauties of the work: – it suited better our purpose (as is too often the case with more deliberate critics) to pounce only on such passages as ministered to the laughing humour that possessed us. In this sort of hunt through the volume, we at length lighted on the discovery that our host, in addition to his sincere approbation of some of its contents, had also the motive of gratitude for standing by its author, as one of the poems was a warm and, I need not add, well-deserved panegyric on himself. We were, however, too far gone in nonsense for even this eulogy, in which we both so heartily agreed, to stop us. The opening line of the poem was,

as well as I can recollect, 'When Rogers o'er this labour bent,' and Lord Byron undertook to read it aloud; – but he found it impossible to get beyond the first two words. Our laughter had now increased to such a pitch that nothing could restrain it. Two or three times he began; but no sooner had the words 'When Rogers' passed his lips, than our fit burst forth afresh, – till even Mr Rogers himself, with all his feeling of our injustice, found it impossible not to join us; and we were, at last, all three, in such a state of inextinguishable laughter, that, had the author himself been of the party, I question much whether he could have resisted the infection.[37]

A day or two after, Lord Byron sent me the following:

ON LORD THURLOW'S POEMS

1

WHEN Thurlow this damned nonsense sent,
(I hope I am not violent)
Nor men nor gods knew what he meant.

2

And since not even our Rogers's praise
To common sense his thoughts could raise –
Why *would* they let him print his lays?

3

* * * * * * * * * * * * * * * * * * *

4

* * * * * * * * * * * * * * * * * * *

5

To me, divine Apollo, grant – O!
Hermilda's first and second canto,
I'm fitting up a new portmanteau;

6

And thus to furnish decent lining,
My own and others' bays I'm twining –
So, gentle Thurlow, throw me thine in.[38]

He could, as we have seen, enjoy himself in male company of all kinds and this persisted throughout his life.

> Tuesday I dined with Ward and met Canning and all the Wits – and yesterday I dined with the Patrons of Pugilism and some of the professors – who amused me about as much.[39]
>
> (To Lady Melbourne, 25 November 1813)

One of his dearest and most amusing friends was Sheridan who, at this time, was growing maudlin through drink, misfortune and lack of funds. Byron admired Sheridan and looked upon his failings with the most complete understanding and fellow-feeling.

> Poor dear Sherry – I shall never forget the day he and Rogers and Moore and I passed together; when *he* talked and *we* listened without one yawn, from six till one in the morning.[40]
>
> (*Journal*, 16 November 1813)

> Poor fellow! he got drunk very thoroughly and very soon. – It occasionally fell to my lot to convey him home – no sinecure – for he was so tipsy that I was obliged to put on his cock'd hat for him – to be sure it tumbled off again and I was not myself so sober as to be able to pick it up again. –[41]
>
> (*Detached Thoughts*, 15 October 1821)

In those days of high play and deep drinking when young bloods would drink 'a couple of bottles at least at dinner' and 'there were four or even five bottle men', it was just as well that Byron, whose careless spendthrift behaviour and confessed plunge into an 'abyss of sensuality' on his earlier visits to London, had burdened him with enormous debts, was able to summon up the strength of will to avoid constant heavy drinking and to give up gambling altogether, thus escaping the slow, sad, deterioration which made Sheridan a subject for pity and disdain among many who had envied him at the peak of his powers.

'The Monody on the Death of Sheridan' spoken at Drury Lane Theatre in September, 1816, includes a passage which describes the envy and denigration which gather about those who win extraordinary fame:

> The secret Enemy whose sleepless eye
> Stands sentinel – accuser – judge – and spy,
> The foe, the fool, the jealous, and the vain,
> The envious who but breathe in other's pain –

Behold the host! delighting to deprave,
Who track the steps of Glory to the grave,
Watch every fault that daring Genius owes,
Half to the ardour which its birth bestows,
Distort the truth, accumulate the lie,
And pile the Pyramid of Calumny![42]

With *Childe Harold's Pilgrimage* Byron too had won extraordinary fame and he too would suffer from the 'secret enemy' who stands 'accuser – judge – and spy'. He became aware of this as early as 1813:

> C[ampbell] last night seemed a little nettled at something or other – I know not what. We were standing in the ante-saloon, when Lord H. brought out of the other room a vessel of some composition similar to that which is used in Catholic churches, and, seeing us, he exclaimed, 'Here is some *incense* for you.' C. answered – 'Carry it to Lord Byron, *he is used to it*...'
>
> Now, this comes of 'bearing no brother near the throne'. I, who have no throne, nor wish to have one *now* – whatever I may have done – am at perfect peace with all the poetical fraternity; or, at least, if I dislike any, it is not *poetically* but *personally*. Surely the field of thought is infinite; – what does it signify who is before or behind in a race where this is no *goal*?[43]

He wrote to Thomas Moore from Venice defending Sheridan's memory:

> As for his creditors, – remember, Sheridan *never had* a shilling, and was thrown, with great powers and passions, into the thick of the world, and placed upon the pinnacle of success, with no other external means to support him in his elevation. Did Fox*** pay his debts? – or did Sheridan take a subscription? Was the Duke of Norfolk's drunkenness more excusable than his? Were his intrigues more notorious than those of all his contemporaries? and is his memory to be blasted, and theirs respected? Don't let yourself be led away by clamour, but compare him with the coalitioner, Fox, and the pensioner, Burke, as a man of principle, and with ten hundred thousand in personal views, and with none in talent, for he beat them all *out* and *out*. Without means, without connexion, without character, (which might be false at first, and make him mad afterwards from desperation) he beat them all, in all he ever attempted. But alas poor human nature! Good night – or rather, morning. It is four, and the dawn gleams over the Grand Canal and unshadows the

Rialto. I must to bed; up all night – but, as George Philpot says, 'It's life, though, damme it's life!'[44]

Byron became more and more disillusioned with both politics and society. He turned down a request to present another Petition to Parliament. 'Had [Lady Oxford] been here she would have *made* me do it. *There* is a woman who, amid all her fascination always urged a man to usefulness or glory.'[45] But he was 'sick of parliamentary mummeries'[46] and persuaded Lord Holland to present the petition. He was longing to go abroad and had toyed with the idea of visiting Holland which was on the brink of Revolution. 'I should like to listen to the shout of a free Dutchman.'[47] Some months later he wrote to Hobhouse with another plan for escaping from England, a letter which shows the warmth of his friendship and, with its expression of a preference for the company of Hobhouse on his travels, must have hurt the feelings of Thomas Moore if he read the letter after Byron's death:

> now I would wish to set apart £3000 – for the tour – do you think *that* would enable me to see all *Italy* in a gentlemanly way? – with *as few* servants & luggage (except my aperients) as we can help. – And will you come with me? – you are the only man with whom I could travel an hour except an 'ιατροζ' – in short you know my dear H – that with all my bad qualities – (and d—-d bad they *are* to be sure) I like you better than any body – and we have travelled together before – and been old friends and all that – and we have a thorough fellow-feeling & contempt for all things of the sublunary sort – and so do let us go & call the 'Pantheon a cockpit' like the learned Smelfungus. – The Cash is the principal point – do you think that will do – viz £3000 clear from embarkation onwards. I have a world of watches and snuffboxes and telescopes – which would do for the Mussulmans if we liked to cross from Otranto & see our friends again. – They are all safe at Hammersleys. – would my *coach* do? – *beds* I have & all canteens &c. from *your* Man of Ludgate Hill – with saddles – pistols – tromboni – & what not. – I shall know tomorrow or next day – whether I can go – or not – and shall be in town next week – where I must see you or hear from you – if we set off – it should be in October and the earlier the better – Now don't engage yourself – but take up your map – and ponder upon this – ever, dear H.[48]
>
> (Byron to Hobhouse, September 1814)

The plan for this journey never came to fruition since, before it could be put into action, Annabella Milbanke decided to regard a tentative letter from Byron about a possible renewal of his courtship as a proposal of marriage. She sent an acceptance by return of post to Albany, with copy to Newstead Abbey to make assurance doubly sure.

She had captured her poet.

12

BYRON, MOORE AND THE ORIENTAL TALES

'Yes, Love indeed is light from heaven;
A spark of that immortal fire
With angels shared, by Alla given,
To lift from earth our low desire.
Devotion wafts the mind above,
But Heaven itself descends in Love;
A feeling from the Godhead caught,
To wean from self each sordid thought;
A ray of Him who formed the whole;
A Glory circling round the soul!'[1]

Annabella Milbanke told her mother that Byron wrote so beautifully of love in *The Giaour* as to almost make her in love. It was published in June 1813 and ran through fourteen editions by 1815. Described as 'A Fragment of a Turkish Tale'[2] it was based on the mysterious incident of the Turkish girl rescued from death beside the Bosphorus when Byron was in Constantinople. This and the later tales were widely thought to be autobiographical and Byron was generally supposed to have experienced wild adventures and to have indulged in exotic crime. He complained about this in his dedication to Thomas Moore of a later tale, *The Corsair*:

> I have no particular desire that any but my acquaintance should think the author better than the beings of his imaginings; but I cannot help a little surprise ... when several (far more deserving I allow) poets ... quite exempted from all participation in the faults of those heroes who nevertheless might be found with little more morality than the *Giaour*.[3]

Byron writes a note on the passage in the poem beginning, 'He who hath bent him o'er the dead', which he must surely have realised would give rise to suspicions that would make his protests to Thomas Moore somewhat otiose:

> I trust that few of my readers have ever had an opportunity of witnessing what is here attempted in description; but those who have will probably retain a painful remembrance of that singular beauty which pervades, with few exceptions, the features of the dead, a few hours, and but a few hours, after 'the spirit is not there.'

So far so good, but it was unnecessary to add:

> It is to be remarked in cases of violent death by gun-shot wounds, the expression is always that of languor whatever the natural energy of the sufferer's character; but in death from a stab the countenance preserves its traits of feeling or ferocity, and the mind its bias to the last.[4]

Byron may have had this interesting information from the Suliote warriors with whom he foregathered round their camp fires in Albania. Here, whether intentionally or not, he gives the impression that he might himself have been involved in sinister goings-on in the East. Jerome Christensen describes the piece as 'a passage of daring necrophilia':[5]

> He who hath bent him o'er the dead,
> Ere the first day of Death is fled,
> The first dark day of Nothingness,
> The last of Danger and Distress,
> (Before Decay's effacing fingers
> Have swept the lines where Beauty lingers,)
> And marked the mild angelic air,
> The rapture of Repose that's there,
> The fixed yet tender traits that streak
> The languor of the placid cheek,
> And – but for that sad shrouded eye,
> That fires not, wins not, weeps not, now,
> And but for that chill, changeless brow,
> Where cold Obstruction's apathy
> Appals the gazing mourner's heart...[6]

There is no doubt that Byron was fascinated by the transition from life to death but there is surely no justification for describing a loving gaze at the features of a dead person 'ere the first day of Death is fled' as necrophilia.

Byron wrote of his own poem: '*The Giaour* is certainly a bad character – but not dangerous – and I think his fate and his feelings will meet with few proselytes.'[7] In discussing the episode beside the Bosphorus which inspired the poem Byron for once abandoned his 'hatred of sentiment' and 'epistolary levity' and wrote '... to describe the *feelings* of *that situation* were impossible – it is *icy* even to recollect them.'[8]

Annabella Milbanke was one among many young women who yearned over *The Giaour*. Lady Frances Webster told Byron that *The Giaour* was printed on her heart. Byron was surprised at continued messages from this quarter – 'If people will stop at the first tense of the verb "aimer" they must not be surprised if one finishes the conjugation with somebody else.'[9]

The *Edinburgh Review* pronounced on *The Giaour*, criticising the guilt and worthlessness of *The Giaour* himself, deploring the gloomy and revolting subject but praising the poetic power of the author.[10] The *British Review* accused Byron of imitating Scott and Crabbe, which annoyed him more than its criticism of the evil protagonist.[11] The review in *The Satirist* pleased Byron. An author assured that a work of his 'abounds with proofs of genius' could afford to overlook some fair though 'vituperative' remarks.[12]

The Giaour was followed by *The Bride of Abydos* which was highly praised but not on the whole considered as fine as *The Giaour*. The painter, Delacroix, was later delighted with it and wrote in his Journal, 'Poetry is always full of riches; always remember certain passages from Byron, they are an unfailing spur to the imagination ... the end of *The Bride of Abydos* and *The Death of Selim*, his body tossed about by the waves and that hand – especially that hand – held up by the waves as they break and spend themselves upon the shore. This is sublime, and it is his alone. I feel these things as they can be rendered in paint.'[13]

Ten thousand copies of the third Oriental Tale, *The Corsair*, were sold on the day of publication but there were those who disapproved strongly of both subject and manner of all the tales. They reminded Hazlitt of 'flowers strewn over the face of death'.[14] The writer in the *Critical Review* describes the author as the 'poet of sentiment and nature' who should '... despise all affected ornament and elaborate artifice of decoration' ... 'Lord Byron sometimes takes more pains to be *pretty* than a great poet ought to take.'[15] The *Edinburgh Review* wrote of *The Corsair* that Byron '...had adorned a merciless corsair on a rock in the Mediterranean with every virtue under heaven except common honesty.'[16] The *British Critic* prophesied that '...even female admirers would tire of their querulous villainy and misanthropic sensibility.'[17]

Byron's literary mentor, Gifford, admired the narrative skill displayed in the Tales and wrote later of *The Siege of Corinth*, 'It is a dreadful picture, Caravaggio out done in his own way...', but he also declared, 'I keep my old opinion of Lord Byron. He may be what he will. Why will he not will to be one of the finest of poets and men. I lament to see a great mind run to seed and waste itself in rank growth.'[18]

Byron wrote to Thomas Moore:

> I have lately begun to think my things have been strangely over-rated; and, at any rate, whether or not, I have done with them for ever, I may say to you, what I would not say to every body, that the last two were written, *The Bride* in four and *The Corsair* in ten days, – which I take to be a most humiliating confession, as it proves my own want of judgement in publishing, and the public's in reading things, which cannot have the stamina for permanent attention.[19]
>
> (To Thomas Moore, 3 March 1814)

Byron was clearly anxious about the worth of the Tales but what he writes here is not his considered opinion and he had by no means done with them forever. *Lara*, *Parisina* and *The Siege of Corinth* were still to come. He was trying to persuade Moore not to give up his own Oriental poems, sending him reference books and assuring him, 'I need not say to you that your fame is dear to me, – I really might say *dearer* than my own.'[20] Denigrating his own work may have played a part in trying to encourage Moore to persevere.

Jeffery Vail explains the pre-eminence of Moore up to this date – exceeded only by the fame of Walter Scott:

> Moore's satires, his political poems, his prose works or the songs that everyone knew and sang, the lyrics ... His influence on his vast readership as well as on the current of Irish nineteenth century nationalism and culture was incalculably great: as Howard Mumford Jones observes, 'Hundreds who turned a deaf ear to Wordsworth, listened, enraptured, to Moore; thousands to whom Shelley was a filthy atheist learned of tyranny and nationalism from the persuasive Irishman.'[21]

When Byron came on the scene Moore was convinced that Scott would be dethroned, and so he was. *Rokeby* (1813) and *The Lord of the Isles* (1815) were considerably less successful than *The Lay of the Last Minstrel*. Scott bore Byron no malice for this change in the fortunes of his poetry and may have concluded that these new poems were inferior to his earlier efforts. He decided to abandon the field and turn to the novels. Moore on the other hand was worried that his own success would pale before that of Byron, though the latter wrote of his admiration for Moore:

> [Moore] has wonderful powers, and much variety; besides he has lived and felt. To write so as to bring home to the heart, the heart must have been tried.[22]

But Moore had no illusions. He knew that in the realms of poetry this young man was Caesar. When *Lalla Rookh* came out some time after Byron had left England it was much admired but, as Moore had feared, it was judged to be an imitation of Byron. On the other hand, *Beppo* was compared with Moore's *Twopenny Post-Bag*.

Harriet Granville's comment on *Lalla Rookh* is probably representative of the general attitude in London to the poetry of Moore and Byron:

> I have been reading, that is, hearing L... R... K, Moore's poem and I think some of it quite beautiful. There is so much *radiance* and tenderness. Lord Byron has so much thought and passion that it makes everything flat in comparison, but it is also a repose to escape from crime and read of birds of paradise and innocent loves.[23]

It may be that Hary-O heard only the two shorter and lighter of the four tales which make up *Lalla Rookh* since Jeffery Vail points out that the longer tales, *The Haunted Veil* and *The Fire-Worshippers*, are more violent than any of Byron's tales. This may explain Byron's protest at being saddled as author with all the crimes of the characters in his own poems:

> I never heard that my friend Moore was set down for a fire-worshipper on account of his Guebre – that Scott was identified with Roderick Dhu or with Balfour of Burleigh, – or that notwithstanding all the Magicians in Thalaba – anybody has ever taken Mr Southey for a Conjuror.[24]

Byron was easily plunged into gloom from time to time during his years in London. His imagination was haunted by the Orient and he found he could escape from reality by losing himself in the composition of dream-like tales set among the exotic scenes he could never forget. The Giaour, Conrad the Corsair, Lara, Alp, were examples of anti-heroes widely but mistakenly believed by many of his readers to be based on the poet himself. Among these sinister inventions the most popular was probably the Corsair:

Sun-burnt his cheek, his forehead high and pale
The sable curls in wild profusion veil;
And oft perforce his rising lip reveals
The haughtier thought it curbs, but scarce conceals.
Though smooth his voice, and calm his general mien,
Still seems there something he would not have seen:
His features' deepening lines and varying hue
At times attracted, yet perplexed the view,
As if within that murkiness of mind
Worked feelings fearful, and yet undefined;
Such might it be – that none could truly tell –
Too close inquiry his stern glance would quell.
There breathe but few whose aspect might defy
The full encounter of his searching eye; . . .
Slight are the outward signs of evil thought,
Within – within – 'twas there the spirit wrought!
Love shows all changes – Hate, Ambition, Guile,
Betray no further than the bitter smile;
The lips least curl, the lightest paleness thrown
Along the governed aspect, speak alone.[25]

Nostalgia for the climate and the beauty of Greece resulted in such lines as the famous opening of the third canto of *The Corsair*, originally composed for the *Curse of Minerva*:

Slow sinks, more lovely ere his race be run,
Along Morea's hills the setting Sun;
Not, as in Northern climes, obscurely bright,
But one unclouded blaze of living light!
O'er the hush'd deep the yellow beam he throws,
Gilds the green wave, that trembles as it glows.
On old Aegina's rock and Idra's isle,

Mrs. Byron's turbulent boy: Byron at the time he left Harrow.
(The National Historical Museum, Athens)

Byron in 1814, engraving by Robert Graves, after oil painting by Thomas Phillips.

Newstead Abbey by R Harraden. (Nottingham City Museums and Galleries: Newstead Abbey)
'Newstead and I stand or fall together. I have fixed my heart on it.' Byron

Wordsworth by Edward Nashe, 1818.
(by permission of the Wordsworth Trust)
'The young man will do something if he goes on.'
Wordsworth on *Hours of Idleness*

Lady Caroline Lamb by Mary Anne Knight.
(Nottingham City Museums and Galleries: Newstead Abbey)
'A month's absence would make us rational.'
Byron

Lady Melbourne by Thomas Lawrence.
(by kind permission of Lord Ralph Kerr, Melbourne Hall, Derbyshire)
'She is the cleverest of women and her heart I know to be of the kindest.' Byron

Charles James Fox. (National Portrait Gallery)
'Sheridan and Fox - these are great names. I may emulate, I can never equal them.' Byron

The Hon Augusta Leigh by Sir George Hayter.
(© Trustees of the British Museum)
'My Sister! my sweet Sister!' Byron

Lady Byron, engraving by R Page, 1816.
'Every lady could manage my Lord except my Lady' William Fletcher

Napoleon after the Battle of Lodi, 1796, by Appiani. (By permission of the Accademia di Belle Arti di Brera, Milan)
'Since he, miscall'd the Morning Star,
Nor man nor fiend hath fall'n so far.'

Holland House. (V & A Images/Victoria and Albert Museum)
'At Holland House I am always convinced that there will be Revolution before breakfast.'
Lady Caroline Lamb

The god of gladness sheds his parting smile;
O'er his own regions lingering, loves to shine,
Though there his altars are no more divine.
Descending fast the mountain shadows kiss
Thy glorious gulf, unconquered Salamis!
Their azure arches through the long expanse
More deeply purpled met, his mellowing glance,
And tenderest tints, along their summits driven,
Mark his gay course, and own the hues of heaven;
Till, darkly shaded from the land and deep,
Behind his Delphian cliff he sinks to sleep.[26]

'I still sigh for the Aegean,'[27] he told E.D. Clarke, but he was not writing for the pleasure of such memories of the 'living light' of a Grecian sunset but, as he wrote of his state of mind when writing *The Bride of Abydos*, 'to distract my dreams from * *'.[28] In the opening lines to *Lara* he is concerned with the reality which was part cause of all this *angst*:

When she is gone, the loved, the lost, the one
Whose smile hath gladdened though perchance undone;
Whose name, too dearly cherished to impart,
Dies on the lip, but trembles in the heart;
Whose sudden mention can almost convulse
And lighten through the ungovernable pulse,
Till the heart leaps so keenly to the word
We fear that throb can hardly beat unheard,
Then sinks at once beneath that sickly chill
That follows when we find her absent still;
When such is gone, too far again to bless,
Oh God, how slowly comes Forgetfulness!
Let none complain how faithless and how brief
The brain's remembrance or the bosom's grief;
Or, ere they thus forbid us to forget,
Let Mercy strip the memory of regret,
Yet – selfish still – we would not be forgot;
What lip dare say, 'My love – remember not'?
Oh, best and dearest, thou whose thrilling name
My heart adores too deeply to proclaim![29]

The 'she' who is lost is Augusta Leigh.

Wilson Knight writes that *Lara* is a study in personal anguish. But the hero is also a political revolutionary. The poor love him.

He refuses religious consolation. It is clear that he resembles the poet in many important ways:

> With more capacity for love than Earth
> Bestows on most of mortal mould and birth.[30]

Jeffery Vail points out that Byron and Moore shared the same audience and often consulted each other about what their readers wanted: 'This sensibility and responsiveness to their readers' desires often led Byron and Moore to produce poems in a similar genre or style within a year or two or even within months of each other's productions.'[31] With less magnanimity and affection on either side the friendship between the two men might have been destroyed by the interest in Orientalism which they shared, the audience for works inspired by which was divided between them, though some other poets – in particular, Southey – had attempted works of the same genre.

On 10 July 1817 Byron sent Moore the following farewell lyric in a letter:

1.

My boat is on the shore,
   And my bark is on the sea;
But, before I go, Tom Moore,
   Here's a double health to thee!

2.

Here's a sigh to those who love me,
   And a smile to those who hate;
And, whatever sky's above me,
   Here's a heart for every fate.

3.

Though the Ocean roar around me,
   Yet it still shall bear me on;
Though a desert should surround me,
   It hath springs which may be won.

4.

Were't the last drop in the well,
   As I gasped upon the brink,
Ere my fainting spirit fell,
   'T is to thee that I would drink.

5.
With that water, as this wine,
The libation I would pour
Should be – peace to thine and mine,
And a health to thee, Tom Moore.[32]

This tribute was set to music by Henry Bishop and became a popular song, often struck up when Moore was present. 'The song fixed the image of Byron and Moore as close comrades even more firmly in the public mind.'[33]

Byron's dedication of *The Corsair* to Moore had also fixed this image and since the 'Lines to a Lady Weeping' were published with *The Corsair* Moore had suffered some of the vituperation earned by Byron for his lèse majesté.

Notes

1. Paul Elledge writes of the *Oriental Tales* in 1968:

> Byron writes, therefore, at least at this stage in his career, for catharsis and escape. To elude the conflicting, tormenting, and to some degree stultifying emotions of his own mind, he projects them into fictional protagonists who continually flutter between worlds of past and present, dreams and reality, states of action and ennui, poles of passion and intellect.'[1] Yet Elledge dismissed *The Giaour* and *The Bride of Abydos* as 'even cruder experiments in the genre than *The Corsair*.'[2]

2. Jerome J. McGann rescues Byron's *Oriental Tales* from critics who condemned them.

> *The Bride of Abydos*, *The Corsair*, *Lara* and *Parisina* all deal with the same general motifs that appear in *The Giaour*. Contrary to popular belief, however, the ideas and problems are by no means trivial. The tales are repetitive to a fault, but not so much in the matter of theme as of versification. Byron is still learning the fundamentals of language. They are all notable achievements, and if *The Corsair* and *Lara* contain the most memorable passages, *Parisina* is probably, on the whole, the best tale. Each centres round an exploration of the nature and consequences of life that is Eros-directed. Each tells a story of frustrated love and the war of repression within a context where time and contingency in general are strongly emphasized.[3]

McGann explains the fragmentary structure of *The Giaour*. It is an oral poem – 'The performance of one of those storytellers in one of those coffee-houses "that abound in the Levant". What Byron intends us to apprehend in the poem is its narrated quality. The bard sings his tale and avails himself of the privilege of all oral poets from Homer to the present: to assume as many roles as he needs to tell his story, and to enter into the psychology of his characters and present his tale from their point of view.'[4]

3. M.K. Joseph writes of the Byronic hero:

> Behind him lie the titanism of Prometheus and of Milton's Satan; Hamlet, the melancholy dandy in the haunted castle; the sentimental heroes of Rousseau's *Nouvelle Héloise* and of Goethe's *Werther*; the hero-villains of *Otranto* and Gothic melodrama and the Radcliffean tale of terror, as modified by the humanitarianism of Holcroft and Godwin.[5]

4. Some modern critics attribute great significance to the *Oriental Tales*, which might possibly have surprised their author. Eric Daffron observes that:

> In these tales, according to some twentieth century critics he [Byron] contributed to the creation of the modern self.[6]

5. Byron's poetry inspired revolutionaries and Philhellenes during his lifetime and throughout the nineteenth century. It still retains its power. Lines from *The Giaour* were spoken at Gdansk and carved on the Three Crosses monument to the workers who died in the shipyard there when the trades union movement, Solidarity, was founded:

> Clime of the unforgotten brave!
> Whose land from plain to mountain-cave
> Was Freedom's home or Glory's grave!
> Shrine of the mighty! can it be,
> That this is all remains of thee?
> Approach, thou craven crouching slave:
>   Say, is not this Thermopylæ?
> These waters blue that round you lave, –
>   Oh servile offspring of the free –
> Pronounce what sea, what shore is this?
> The gulf, the rock of Salamis!
> These scenes, their story not unknown,
> Arise, and make again your own;
> Snatch from the ashes of your Sires
> The embers of their former fires;

And he who in the strife expires
Will add to theirs a name of fear
That Tyranny shall quake to hear,
And leave his sons a hope, a fame
They too will rather die than shame:
For Freedom's battle once begun,
Bequeathed by bleeding Sire to Son,
Though baffled oft, is ever won.[7]

13

SHOCK-TACTICS

> *There are those who think that the great events which marked the close of the last century, [the American War of Independence and the French Revolution] by giving a new 'impulse to men's minds, by habituating them to the daring and the free, and allowing full vent to 'the flash and outbreak of fiery spirits' had led naturally to the production of such a poet as Byron, and that he was, in short, as much the child and representative of the Revolution in poetry as another great man of the age, Napoleon, was in politics.*[1]

Byron was as liberal in his politics as in his poetry. It was Hobhouse who persuaded him to join the Whig Club in Cambridge but Byron was already an admirer of Charles James Fox, the great liberal Whig known as 'the Man for the People'. (He was so beloved that country people following fox hounds call out 'There goes Charlie!' even today when they catch sight of the fox.)

Fox died when Byron was eighteen. On reading a verse in *The Morning Post* maligning Fox Byron composed a poem in his defence and sent it to *The Morning Chronicle* which declined to publish. The piece then appeared in *Hours of Idleness*. Like Fox, Byron was concerned throughout his life not only with the rights of Englishmen but with the Rights of Man. Like Fox, he ruined his career by advocating liberal principles injudiciously. For years after Fox's death Fox dinners were held annually all over England in his honour. Macaulay said that twenty-five years after his death there were people who could not talk about Charles James Fox for a quarter of an hour without weeping. When Byron died in Greece he was mourned all over the world but there were no annual Byron dinners in England. The French Revolution may have given 'a new impulse' to the minds of some, but the Terror alarmed every one else and government reacted in England with panicky measures of repression. During the long years of war the Secretary of State for home affairs, developed a network of secret agents, spies and informers, the purpose of which was to make sure that any Jacobinical activity in Britain which might lead to revolution would immediately be crushed.

The fears of the government were not totally unfounded. In 1817 the leader of the Derbyshire rising shot dead a servant who refused to get up out of his bed and join the rebels, and in 1820 the plotters of the Cato Street Conspiracy planned to take with them into the room where the Cabinet were dining, several knives and bags for cutting off heads and transporting them to where they could be impaled on pikes.

The spectre of the French Revolution and the Terror had by no means been laid and although Major Cartwright told his followers to 'Stand fast by the laws', it was said that it was safer to be a felon than a Radical. William Cobbett, whose *Weekly Political Register* became available to the poor for twopence in 1816 and sold fifty thousand copies in a week, fled for a time to America in 1817 when habeas corpus was suspended. The government's reaction to the events leading up to the Peterloo Massacre in 1819 was to crush all protest by Gag Acts. When Byron in his maiden speech had told their lordships, 'I have been in some of the most oppressed provinces of Turkey; but never under the most despotic of infidel governments did I behold such squalid wretchedness as I have seen since my return, in the very heart of a Christian country...'[2] government was unmoved, convinced that repression was the only answer to unrest and insurgency because government could do nothing to relieve the misery of the poor. So Gag Acts were followed by Corn Laws and more Enclosure Acts which turned independent small-holders eking out a miserable income by grazing their animals on common land and shooting birds and rabbits for the pot, into poverty-stricken labourers dependent on farmers and landowners for work and thus deprived of independence which made them 'saucy'.

It was not surprising that in such an atmosphere Byron became a marked man – though in spite of attacks on him by the Tory Press this may not have become clear to him until he was visited by an emissary of government shortly before he went into exile in 1816. To be a liberal was suspect but to be so famous a liberal was unacceptable. The publication in 1813 of the first of his Oriental Tales, *The Giaour*, added to his fame. It reached a high point when 'the odious book' [*Childe Harold*] '...attained the *summit* of *fame* by giving a name to a *very slow racehorse*.'[3] If Byron had been an obscure personage his defiance of political decorum might have been ignored but by 1814 he was celebrated all over the world:

> As Moore and I were going to dine with Lord Grey in P[ortman] Square – I pulled out a *Java Gazette* (which Murray had sent to me) in which there was a controversy on our respective merits as poets – it was amusing enough that we should be proceeding peaceably to the same table – while they were squabbling about us in the Indian Seas ... But this is fame, I presume![4]
>
> (*Detached Thoughts*, 1821)

Byron's third speech in the House of Lords outraged both the Whigs and the Tories and put an end to the possibility of a career in Parliament, at least for the time being. It was the presentation of a petition by the famous old Radical, Major Cartwright, for Parliamentary Reform. Byron had no very high opinion of Major Cartwright but supported his right to make the petition.

The old campaigner and his adherents had been forcibly prevented by the military from presenting his petition for Parliamentary reform. Byron told their lordships:

> It is in the cause of the Parliament and people that the rights of this venerable freeman have been violated, and it is, in my opinion, the highest mark of respect that could be paid to the House that to your justice, rather than by appeal to any inferior court, he now commits himself... I have this opportunity of publicly stating the obstruction to which the subject is liable, in the prosecution of the most lawful and imperious of his duties, the obtaining by petition reform in Parliament... Your Lordships will, I hope, adopt some measure fully to protect and redress him, and not him alone, but the whole body of the people, insulted and aggrieved in his person, by the interposition of an abused civil and unlawful military force between them and their right of petition to their own representatives.[5]

This was grasping a very toxic nettle indeed. It was not until 1832 that the first Parliamentary Reform Bill was passed. In 1813 the great Whig landowners still controlled most of the rotten boroughs which allowed them to return their own creatures to Parliament. This was a power they would not easily relinquish. They had not yet begun to understand that the development of a new and prosperous middle class was changing politics forever (though not in ways that Byron would necessarily have approved of).

By the 1830s they were ready to make concessions, not because they believed in or welcomed democracy, but in order to protect their own interests and prevent more sweeping reforms which might put an end to their own ascendancy.

If this was the grudging attitude of the Whigs in 1832, how alarming for the Whig party in 1813 must Byron's shock-tactics on Parliamentary Reform have been. The tactical problems within the party were at least as intractable in 1813 as in the 1830s. As a result of almost twenty years of war with France the Whigs were already in turmoil. Fox had believed (and rightly) that Pitt would use the war to justify repression in England which would set back the cause for liberty for years. The Whig party split over Fox's opposition to the war. The Portland Whigs joined Pitt, judging the danger from France should outweigh the Whig concern for protecting the people from the tyranny of the Crown and its ministers. The Foxite Whigs were reduced to a small minority but their principles and their influence were fundamental to the achievements of the party which, led by Grey and Holland, succeeded in bringing about Catholic Emancipation (passed reluctantly by the Tories), the first steps towards Parliamentary Reform and the abolition of slavery in the British Colonies, by the early 1830s. If Byron had lived and returned to England he would have been with them in all these achievements.

But in 1813/14 he was an embarrassment to both parties. He made matters infinitely worse with eight lines of poetry written and published anonymously in 1812 which, when republished in 1814 under the writer's name, caused a furore by insulting the Prince Regent. As a young man George, Prince of Wales, was known as 'Prince Florizel' for his beauty and as the 'First Gentleman of Europe' for his exquisite manners. In the Twelfth Canto of *Don Juan* Byron looked back with regret on the youth whose promise had been unfulfilled:

LXXXIV

There too, he saw (what'er he may be now)
 A Prince, the Prince of Princes at the time,
With fascination in his very bow,
 And full of promise as the spring of prime.
Though Royalty was written on his brow,
 He had *then* the grace, too, rare in every clime,
Of being, without alloy of fop or beau,
A finished Gentleman from top to toe.[6]

Following the tradition of Hanoverian heirs-apparent, the Prince threw in his lot with the Opposition party, the great Whig earls. He declared in 1811 that it was his glory to have bred up his daughter, Princess Charlotte, in the principles of Fox. In the autumn of 1805 Thomas Creevey had written:

> I remember dining with him (the Prince) at George Johnstone's in Brighton – the Duke of Clarence, old Thurlow, Lord and Lady Bessborough and a very large party, of which Suza, the Portuguese Ambassador, was one. After dinner the Prince, addressing himself to Suza, described himself as being the head of the great Whig party in England and then entered at great length upon the merits of Whig principles and the great glory it was to him, the Prince, to be the head of a party who advocated such principles.[7]

The Whig, Creevey, wrote at this auspicious moment: 'God send we have a Regency and then the cards are in our hands.'[8] But when the Prince became Regent he abandoned the Whigs without warning and retained his father's Tory administration. The Whigs were thunder-struck, although the defects in the character of the Prince had been well known – in 1804 Sheridan was already talking of his unsteadiness and by 1811 the Whigs were talking of his folly and villainy. 'The more one sees of the conduct of this most singular man,' wrote Creevey, 'the more one becomes convinced he is doomed, from his personal character alone, to shake his throne.'[9] These remarks were made by Whigs disappointed in their expectation of taking power. They exaggerated the foibles of the Prince Regent. Some authorities have applauded his decision to retain the Tory administration. The Whigs were critical of the government's handling of the Peninsular War and might have brought it to a disastrous conclusion by recalling Wellesley.

Byron had met the Prince Regent and was aware of his charm but this did not prevent him from writing 'Lines to a Lady Weeping'. The 'lady' is Princess Charlotte, who was distressed at what she regarded as her father's apostasy. Many people hoped the Princess would be the saving of the monarchy. George Lamb remarked that he would like to put the Prince Regent in a boat and send him out to sea so that Princess Charlotte could be Queen.

> WEEP, daughter of a royal line,
> A Sire's disgrace, a realm's decay;
> Ah! happy if each tear of thine
> Could wash a Father's fault away!
> Weep – for thy tears are Virtue's tears –
> Auspicious to these suffering Isles;
> And be each drop in future years
> Repaid thee by thy People's smiles![10]

Byron was as unaccountably surprised at the furore caused by these lines as he had been at the predicted reaction of the ladies of Southwell to his lines 'To Mary'. He wrote to Thomas Moore:

> You can have no conception of the uproar the eight lines on the little Royalty's weeping in 1812 (now republished) have occasioned. The Regent who had always thought them *yours*, chose – God knows why – on discovering them to be mine, to be *affected* 'in sorrow rather than in anger.' The *Morning Post*, *Sun*, *Herald*, *Courier*, have all been in hysterics ever since. Murray is in a fright and wanted to shuffle – and the abuse against me in all directions is vehement, unceasing, loud, some of it good and all of it hearty. I feel a little compunction as to the R's regret – would he had been only angry.[11]
>
> (To Thomas Moore, 10 February 1814)

Byron's compunction for the Regent's sorrow over the 'Lines to a Lady Weeping' led him to make amends some years later. When the Prince (now George IV) repealed the forfeiture imposed on the family of Lord Edward Fitzgerald in consequence of his involvement in the Irish rebellion of 1798, Byron sent a sonnet to John Murray in praise of the King's act:

SONNET TO THE PRINCE REGENT

ON THE REPEAL OF LORD EDWARD FITZGERALD'S FORFEITURE

To be the father of the fatherless,
   To stretch the hand from the throne's height, and raise
   His offspring, who aspired in other days
To make thy Sire's sway by a kingdom less, –
This is to be a monarch, and repress
   Envy into unutterable praise.
   Dismiss thy guard, and trust thee to such traits,
For who would lift a hand, except to bless?
   Were it not easy, Sir, and is't not sweet
   To make thyself belovéd? and to be
Omnipotent by Mercy's means? for thus
   Thy Sovereignty would grow but more complete,
A despot thou, and yet thy people free,
   And by the heart – not hand – enslaving us.[12]

In 1814 he was amazed at the effect of the lines which had upset the Prince Regent:

> Did you ever know anything like this? – at a time when peace and war – and Emperors and Napoleons – and the destinies of the things they have made of mankind are trembling in the balance – the Government Gazettes can devote half their attention and columns day after day to *eight lines* written two years ago – and now republished only – (by an individual) and suggest them for consideration of Parliament probably about the same period with the Treaty of Peace – I really begin to think myself a most important personage – what would poor Pope have given to bring this down upon his *Epistle to Augustus*?[13]
>
> (To Lady Melbourne, 11 February 1814)

Byron was distracted from his own difficulties by 'peace and war – and Emperors and Napoleons'. He was distressed by the defeat of Buonaparte by the allies and deeply distressed by the less than heroic role played by the Emperor in his own débacle and by the restoration of the Bourbons which would destroy all the high hopes brought into being by the Revolution.

This distress is made clear by the entries in his *Journal* during this period:

> To-day I have boxed one hour – written an ode to Napoleon Buonaparte – copied it – eaten six biscuits – drunk four bottles of soda water –
>
> (10 April 1813)

I don't know – but I think *I*, even *I* (an insect compared with this creature), have set my life on casts not a millionth part of this man's. But, after all, a crown may be not worth dying for. Yet to outlive *Lodi* for this!!! Oh that Juvenal or Johnson could rise from the dead! 'Expende – quot libras in duce summo invenies?' I knew they were light in the balance of mortality; but I thought their living dust weighed more *carats*. Alas! this imperial diamond hath a flaw in it and is now hardly fit to stick in a glazier's pencil: – the pen of the historian won't rate it worth a ducat.

Psha! 'something too much of this.' But I won't give him up even now; though all his admirers have, 'like the Thanes, fallen from him'.

(14 April 1813)

There is ice at both poles, north and south – all extremes are the same – misery belongs to the highest and the lowest only, – to the emperor and the beggar, when unsixpenced and unthroned. There is, to be sure, a dammed insipid medium – an equinoctial one – no one knows where, except upon maps and measurement.

'And all our *yesterdays* have lighted fools
The way to dusty death,'

I will keep no further journal of that same hesternal torch-light; and, to prevent me from returning, like a dog, to the vomit of memory, I tear out the remaining leaves of this volume, and write, in *Ipecacuanha*, – 'that the Bourbons are restored!!!' – 'Hang up philosophy.' To be sure, I have long despised myself and man, but I never spat in the face of my species before – 'O fool! I shall go mad'.

(19 April 1813)

What strange tidings from the Anakim of anarchy – Buonaparte! Ever since I defended my bust of him at Harrow against the rascally time-servers, when the war broke out in 1803, he has been a 'Héros de Roman' of mine – on the continent; I don't want him here. But I don't like those same flights – leaving of armies, &c. &c. I am sure when I fought for his bust at school, I did not think he would run away from himself. But I should not wonder if he banged them yet. To be beat by men would be something; but by three stupid, legitimate-old-dynasty boobies of regular-bred sovereigns – O-hone-a-rie! – O-hone-a-rie![14]

(17 November 1813)

Byron was not alone in his distress at the idea of the Bourbons once again restored to the throne of France. Charles James Fox had thought that the French and not the English were the proper persons to determine whether the Bourbons ought to reign in France.

From *Ode to Napoleon Buonaparte*, 1814:

I

'Tis done – but yesterday a King!
  And armed with Kings to strive –
And now thou art a nameless thing:
  So abject – yet alive!
Is this the man of thousand thrones,
Who strewed our earth with hostile bones,
  And can he thus survive?
Since he, miscalled the Morning Star,
Nor man nor fiend hath fallen so far.

X

And Earth hath spilt her blood for him,
  Who thus can hoard his own!
And Monarchs bowed the trembling limb,
  And thanked him for a throne!
Fair Freedom! we may hold thee dear,
When thus thy mightiest foes their fear
  In humblest guise have shown.
Oh! ne'er may tyrant leave behind
A brighter name to lure mankind!

XVIII

But thou forsooth must be a King,
  And don the purple vest,
As if that foolish robe could wring
  Remembrance from thy breast.
Where is that faded garment? where
The gewgaws thou wert fond to wear,
  The star, the string, the crest?
Vain froward child of Empire! say,
Are all thy playthings snatch'd away?

XIX

Where may the wearied eye repose
  When gazing on the Great;
Where neither guilty glory glows,
  Nor despicable state?
Yes – one – the first – the last – the best –
The Cincinnatus of the West,
  Whom Envy dared not hate,
Bequeathed the name of Washington,
To make man blush there was but one![15]

The Ode brought Byron an angry letter which he passed on to Thomas Moore.

> I enclose you an epistle received by me this morning from I know not whom, but I think it will amuse you. The writer must be a rare fellow.
> (To Thomas Moore, 13 Piccadilly Terrace, 12 June 1815)

Moore includes the enclosure:

> My Lord,
> I have lately purchased a set of your works and am quite vexed that you have not cancelled the *Ode to Bonaparte*. It was certainly prematurely written without thought or reflection. Providence has now brought him to reign over millions again, while the same Providence now keeps as it were in a garrison another potentate, who, in the language of Burke, he 'hurled from this throne.' See if you cannot make amends for your folly and consider that, in almost every respect, human nature is the same, in every clime and in every period, and don't act the part of a foolish boy. Let not Englishmen talk of the stretch of tyrants, while the torrents of blood shed in the East Indies cry aloud to Heaven for retaliation. Learn, good sir, not to cast the first stone.[16]

In 1815 Byron wrote three poems calculated to outrage every patriot in Britain (as well as government and establishment) entitled 'Napoleon's Farewell', 'From the French', and 'The Star of the Legion of Honour', all of which purported to be translated from the French. Each was published anonymously in *The Examiner* and then openly in *Poems, 1816*. One hinted at a return by Napoleon, one was an address to the exiled Emperor by one of his faithful soldiers, another prophesied further bloodshed. In writing such poems as these, Byron is exploring possibilities. These are all possible postures he is occupying. He is not being totally insincere but neither is he totally sincere. Arthur Symons wrote of him: 'Byron's thought embraced Europe as another man's thought might have embraced the village from which he had sprung.'[17] His attitude toward Europe might be considered more admirable in a poet than Sydney Smith's attitude in a clergyman:

> How can any man stop in the midst of the stupendous joy of getting rid of Buonaparte and prophecy the little piddling evils that will result from restoring the Bourbons? ... Nor am I quite certain that I don't wish Paris burnt and France laid waste by the Cossacks for revenge and for security.[18]

Those who were outraged by Byron's purported translations might have been mollified if they had known that, as pointed out by Elizabeth Longford:

> ... although Wellington called Napoleon 'the grand disturber', yet he felt that, once peace had been made, the Emperor might still be the best available ruler for France provided he behaved as he promised. Most of the Allied Army, however, took the simpler view of Pakenham that the grand disturber must be 'dethroned and Decapitized [*sic*]'.[19]

Robert Southey thought Napoleon 'a mean-spirited villain' and the 'Ode to Napoloen Bonaparte' convinced him that Byron had arrived at the same opinion. Southey was reckoning without Byron's self-confessed 'mobility'. He could move from one opinion to another but without cancelling the first. All possibilities were valid in explicating a complicated world.

Byron had praised the young Napoleon as the 'Morning Star' and at Harrow he had fought to protect his bust of the Emperor from angry school fellows. He was obliged to accept, by the time he wrote the *Ode*, that his hero had become a tyrant. Yet he still hoped for better from the great man. Jonathan Gross points out that 'Byron condemned tyranny in his own lifetime, whether incarnated by Lord Castlereagh, George III or Napoleon Bonaparte.'[20] The succinct description by this writer of 'the principles of Whiggery' is a condensation of the basis of all Byron's political endeavours: 'resistance to royal power on the one hand and to mob rule on the other...'[21] though one should add the proviso that Byron objected to royal power not because it was royal but where it was tyrannical. He eventually came to believe a republic was probably the best form of government. His resistance to mob rule has infuriated many left-wing politicians and he has been so thoroughly misunderstood that Bertrand Russell thought him almost a Fascist, an unfortunate, and probably influential, misreading of the whole tenor of Byron's life and work. Bertrand Russell observed on the subject of Byron's politics:

> He wrote in later life much noble verse in praise of freedom, but it must be understood that the freedom he praised was that of a German prince or a Cherokee chief; not the inferior sort that might conceivably be enjoyed by ordinary mortals.[22]

Byron's concern with freedom for the Greeks had nothing to do with princes or aristocrats. William Parry who was with him during his last days at Missolonghi reports his saying, 'No system of government in any part of Greece can be permanent which does not leave in the hands of the peasantry the chief part of the political power. They are warmly attached to their country and they are the best portion of the people.'[23] We have seen how he praised the common people of Spain above their leaders and rebuked the members of the House of Lords for their contemptuous attitude to 'the mob'. Later in life he changed his mind about a plan for starting a new life in Venezuela, when he discovered that its economy was based on slavery:

> The accounts sent from England in consequence of my enquiries – discouraged me ... there is *no* freedom – even for *Masters* – in the midst of slaves ... I sometimes wish I was the Owner of Africa – to do at once – what Wilberforce will do in time – viz. – sweep Slavery from her deserts – and look upon the first dance of their Freedom...[24]

Byron was in favour of all oppressed peoples struggling for freedom – the Dutch, the Italians, the Greeks, the South Americans. But he was opposed to lawlessness and wrote of the Radical agitators, Hunt and Cobbett:

> I am glad to hear you have nothing to do with those scoundrels – I can understand and enter into the feelings of Mirabeau and Lafayette – but I have no sympathy with Robespierre and Marat ... I do not think the man who would overthrow all laws – should have the benefit of any.[25]

Byron praised Mirabeau and Lafayette not because they were aristocrats but because they were sensible and moderate in contrast to the cruel tyranny of Marat and Robespierre. He would have applauded the verdict on Cobbett and Hunt of E.P. Thompson:

> The national leaders, Cobbett and Wooler with their pens, Hunt with his voice – were adept at pitching their rhetoric just on the right side of treason: but they laid themselves open to the charge ... of encouraging other men to take illegal or treasonable actions from the consequence of which they themselves escaped...[26]

By October 1819 Byron was writing, 'My taste for revolution is abated – revolutions are not to be made with rosewater – on either side harm must be done before good can come.'[27] But in 1822 he told Thomas Moore, 'There's nothing left for Mankind but a Republic – and I think there are hopes of such ... the two Americas (South and North) have it – Spain and Portugal approach it – and all thirst for it – oh! Washington![28]

14

HEBREW MELODIES: BYRON AND SONG

Hark! the note,
The natural music of the mountain reed –
For here the patriarchal days are not
A pastoral fable – pipes in the liberal air,
Mix'd with the sweet bells of the sauntering herd;
My soul would drink those echoes. Oh that I were
The viewless spirit of a lovely sound,
A living voice, a breathing harmony,
A bodiless enjoyment – born and dying
With the blest tone which made me![1]

'Manfred'

Byron loved to listen to women singing and often burst into song himself. When he was staying at Aston his host asked him to refrain from singing in his bedroom as it made his wife, Lady Frances, cry. Graham Pont describes Byron as 'a natural musician, a collector of songs and improviser of "stanzas for music". He was an amateur singer – a classic "bathroom baritone" – who once described Moore's music as his "matins and vespers": "I won't call it singing", he admitted, "for I never attempt that except to myself".'[2] Thomas Moore remembered that he had watched Byron listening to his own *Irish Melodies* with tears in his eyes.

In September 1814 a collaboration initiated by Douglas Kinnaird between Byron and a young Jewish composer called Isaac Nathan was to produce a series of songs set to music by Nathan with the help of a composer and singer called John Braham.

Graham Pont reminds us that *Hebrew Melodies* belong to the era when 'social music-making was still a civilised recreation' and Nathan describes an evening when he was invited to dine with Douglas Kinnaird and his mistress, Maria Keppel: 'When Lord Byron appeared "we talked a little, drank a little, ate a little, sang a little, drank a little more: the beautiful hostess took part in a trio of one of my *Hebrew Melodies* and her Lothario took the bass part".'[3]

The poems were published in April 1815 with a dedication to Princess Charlotte of Wales and 'soon found their way into ladies' albums or commonplace books ... William St Clair has discovered that, although John Murray's edition [which did not include the music] was not one of Byron's best-sellers, the *Hebrew Melodies* were amongst those most commonly copied into private albums. In her commonplace book (Add. 58802) Augusta Leigh copied several including "She Walks in Beauty".'[4]

The songs were sung in public performances as well as in private drawing rooms and Nathan agreed to the suggestion of John Braham that he should be the performer: 'I should be paying a just tribute of respect to the first poet of the age, by having his verses sung by the greatest vocalist of the day.'[5]

Some of the poems were written on subjects suggested by Nathan, others were lyrics by Byron not necessarily on sacred or Hebrew subjects, which were set to music by the composer. It was a true working collaboration. A friendly relationship grew up between composer and poet. Byron invited Nathan to dinner more than once and Nathan was one of the last people to call at Piccadilly Terrace with a farewell gift for Byron before he left for the continent.

One of the songs Byron gave Nathan for *Hebrew Melodies* was a poem he had written earlier in praise of the wife of his cousin, Robert Wilmot, whom he had seen wearing a dark, spangled frock at a party at Lansdowne House. Lady Byron was involved with the production of *Hebrew Melodies* and copied out some of the poems for Nathan. She must have read this poem soon after her marriage. Byron wrote no poems addressed to Annabella until after their parting and both the young bride and her mother were unhappy at his having neglected to do so. One can give Byron no marks whatsoever for tact:

I

SHE walks in Beauty, like the night
  Of cloudless climes and starry skies;
And all that's best of dark and bright
  Meet in her aspect and her eyes:
Thus mellowed to that tender light
  Which Heaven to gaudy day denies.

II

One shade the more, one ray the less,
  Had half impaired the nameless grace
Which waves in every raven tress,
  Or softly lightens o'er her face;
Where thoughts serenely sweet express,
  How pure, how dear their dwelling place.

III

And on that cheek, and o'er that brow,
  So soft, so calm, yet eloquent,
The smiles that win, the tints that glow,
  But tell of days in goodness spent,
A mind at peace with all below,
  A heart whose love is innocent![6]

One of the most famous of Byron's poems appears in *Hebrew Melodies*. It has been so popular ever since that it has become an 'anthology piece'.

THE DESTRUCTION OF SENNACHERIB

I

The Assyrian came down like the wolf on the fold,
And his cohorts were gleaming in purple and gold;
And the sheen of their spears was like stars on the sea,
When the blue wave rolls nightly on deep Galilee.

II

Like the leaves of the forest when Summer is green,
That host with their banners at sunset were seen:
Like the leaves of the forest when Autumn hath blown,
The host on the morrow lay withered and strown.

III

For the Angel of Death spread his wings on the blast,
And breathed in the face of the foe as he passed;
And the eyes of the sleepers waxed deadly and chill,
And their hearts but once heaved, and for ever grew still!

IV

And there lay the steed with his nostril all wide;
But through it there rolled not the breath of his pride;
And the foam of his gasping lay white on the turf,
And cold as the spray of the rock-beating surf.

V

And there lay the rider distorted and pale,
With the dew on his brow, and the rust on his mail:
And the tents were all silent – the banners alone –
The lances unlifted – the trumpet unblown.

VI

And the widows of Ashur are loud in their wail,
And the idols are broke in the temple of Baal;
And the might of the Gentile, unsmote by the sword,
Hath melted like snow in the glance of the Lord![7]

G. Wilson Knight shows how much more 'The Destruction of Sennacherib' is than an 'anthology piece' with a piece of criticism which is valuable in alerting the reader to overtones some might well miss without his enthusiastic guidance:

> We are made aware of imperial and military glory, of its flash and ambition, its pride and fall. The Assyrian host challenges the stars and sea, man as against the cosmos, its co-equal and rival. But it is, nevertheless, of earth; subject like leaves to the rhythm of the seasons, summer and autumn, life and death...
>
> Much of Byron, apart from his humour, is here compacted: his love of the stellar universe, of the sea, of animal vigour; his sense of human endeavour in magnificence and crime; the repudiation of militarism, coupled with the soft feeling in 'dew' and 'brow', the forgiveness (as at *Don Juan*, III, 109, on Nero); his life-long devotion to the Old Testament; and his sense of an overruling – to use his favourite term – 'Deity.'[8]

Nathan was overjoyed at being invited to collaborate with the celebrated young poet, but he was not so overwhelmed that he dared not make suggestions, or even fairly comprehensive criticisms and Byron was always prepared to listen. 'The Harp the Monarch Minstrel Swept' originally ended with the fifth line of the second verse. This made the second verse five lines shorter than the first. Nathan objected to the resulting lack of balance:

I

The Harp the Monarch Minstrel swept,
  The King of men, the loved of Heaven!
Which Music hallowed while she wept
  O'er tones her heart of hearts had given –
Redoubled be her tears, its chords are riven!
It softened men of iron mould,
  It gave them virtues not their own;
No ear so dull, no soul so cold,
  That felt not – fired not to the tone,
Till David's Lyre grew mightier than his Throne!

II

It told the triumphs of our King,
  It wafted glory to our God;
It made our gladdened valleys ring,
  The cedars bow, the mountains nod;
Its sound aspired to Heaven and there abode!

When Nathan asked for a longer second verse Byron protested, 'Why I have sent you to Heaven – it would be difficult to go further.' Nathan relates that 'My attention for a few moments was called away to some other person, and His Lordship whom I had hardly missed, exclaimed – "Here, Nathan, I have brought you down again", and he immediately presented me with the beautiful and sublime lines which conclude the melody':

Since then, though heard on earth no more,
  Devotion and her daughter Love
Still bid the bursting spirit soar
  To sounds that seem as from above,
In dreams that day's broad light cannot remove.[9]

Michael Cooke describes this as 'a near-mystical statement' and adds that 'Even allowing for Byron's usual fluency in composition the prompt and flawless execution of these last five lines of the poem which bring us "down again" from heaven may well betoken the ripeness of the humanistic idea in his mind.'[10]

In allowing his name to be associated with Jewish songs and a Jewish composer Byron showed his lack of prejudice. He would have no truck with anti-semitism. He was extremely kind to Nathan, particularly on an occasion when Douglas Kinnaird (who had initiated the project) offended the musician by hinting that he might cheat Byron over the standard of production of *Hebrew Melodies*. Nathan wrote in praise of Byron's lack of prejudice in matters of race:

> He was entirely free from the prevalent prejudice against that unhappy and oppressed race of men. [the Jews] On this subject he has frequently remarked that he deemed the existence of the Jews as a distinct race of men the wonderful instance of the effects of persecution. Had they been kindly or even honestly dealt with in the early ages of their dispersion they might, in his Lordship's opinion, have amalgamated with society in the same manner as all other sects and parties have done... This liberality of sentiment was not confined to the Jews alone. His Lordship often regretted the truly distressed state of Ireland. Two thirds of that unhappy country, he observed, had laboured for ages to obtain that liberty which was only extended to a third part of its population and he hoped a time would arrive when religious distinctions in political matters would not prove a barrier to preferment in that country, till which period Ireland would never cordially coalesce with Great Britain but continue as it had been the scene of bloodshed, anarchy and confusion.[11]

Jeffery Vail observes that 'By writing songs that purported to express the feelings of the Jews, a people at least as oppressed and defeated as the Irish, Byron was enabled like Moore to indulge his penchants both for melancholy poetry, and for the advocacy of the downtrodden.' He also remarks that the *Hebrew Melodies* were '...a natural result of his admiration for Moore's work.'[12]

G. Wilson Knight writes illuminatingly on Byron's attitude to the Jews:

> In *The Age of Bronze* Byron's attack on international Jewry corresponds to Alcibiades' reference to 'usury that makes the Senate ugly' (III, V, 101). Byron saw banks beginning to rule the world. But his Jewish sympathies were strong. In 1814 he told Isaac Nathan ... that if the occasion presented itself he was prepared to join in action for the liberation of the Holy Lands. The poems themselves [*Hebrew Melodies*],

made for Hebrew tunes, have been welcomed by the chronicler of Zionism, Nahum Sokolov, as authentic Zionist songs: 'There is in his work an intensity of grief and yearning ... a tenderness which makes him comparable only to the sweet Hebrew muse of Jehuda Halevi. Zionist poetry owes more to Byron than to any other Gentile poet.'[13]

15

AUGUSTA

'There is not a more angelic being upon earth'[1]

Augusta Leigh has received cavalier treatment over the years from many writers on Byron but not from her biographers, Peter Gunn and the Bakewells, who know more about her than most. Those who dismiss her as dull and feather-headed might consider whether Byron could have written such poetry as the opening lines to *Lara* for a feather-headed woman. Augusta's character was firm (albeit gentle). She had a lively humour, an all-embracing kindness and a compelling charm. She was both undemanding and unselfish but she had the courage to defend those she loved and to stand up to those who attacked her where she felt strongly that they were unjust. She had religious principles but did not always live up to them. George's neglect and his frequent absences provided the reason for her need of Byron's love and the opportunity for enjoying the company of her lover. In all else she was a loyal and faithful wife.

Michael and Melissa Bakewell have discovered new facts about her upbringing. For seven years from the age of six she was placed by her grandmother, Lady Holdernesse, in the care of the family chaplain. For this purpose the Reverend and Mrs Alderson were given the living at Eckington in Yorkshire – a remote village where Jack Byron would be unlikely to visit his daughter. It was hoped that the elopement of her mother might be forgotten if Augusta was not in London to remind all Lady Holdernesse's friends of the scandal. The Aldersons, it was felt, would instil in the child moral principles to combat any tendency to emulate her mother.

Brought up with the Alderson children she would have a more natural childhood than alone with her grandmother in Holdernesse House. Mrs Alderson was a motherly woman and Augusta became fond of her daughter Mary. The Bakewells point out that Augusta's life at Eckington must have developed her talent for homemaking and 'her readiness to roll up her sleeves and scrub and scour'.[2] It may also explain the shyness remarked on by her step-sister, Mary Osborne, who, with the rest of her step-family, welcomed her affectionately on her return to London.

When the Prince Regent's gift of the rambling, unpretentious house at Six Mile Bottom, near Newmarket, made it possible for Augusta to marry her George 'she seems to have been blissfully content'. ('She married a fool,' was Byron's comment, 'But she *would* have him...'[3]). George was often absent 'with so many demands on him from the Prince, the regiment, the turf and his friends'.[4] Instead of scolding her husband or repining, Augusta dealt sensibly and intelligently with her unenviable situation. 'She consoled herself ... by writing long letters, sketching and reading; she also began to compile a commonplace book.'[5] Though she was far from the opera, the balls, the milliners and all that constituted the social round she was used to in London her half-brother, Francis Osborne, and his family were within visiting distance at Gogmagog, near Cambridge, and her cousins the Duke and Duchess of Rutland were often at Cheveley, near Newmarket, where the Duke had his racing stables.

The Bakewells describe the love and concern shown Augusta by her step-family. The Chichesters invited her to Stratton Street for her first confinement. Lady Carlisle sent frocks for her little girls. The Duchess of Rutland came to make sure she could manage when George was in the Peninsula during the Corunna Campaign. Augusta consulted her family in every dilemma – a Baby George had arrived, the little girls were unwell, George's debts were mounting and there was not always enough money for paying the servants and the household bills – even discussing with Lady Gertrude Sloane Stanley her early plans for going abroad with Byron. When George was away Augusta was without a carriage. Escape abroad with the brother who adored her must have been tempting indeed. The family were deeply relieved when she decided against the scheme.

In face of all her troubles and privations Augusta did not give way to despondency. It was her serenity, commonsense and playfulness that appealed to Byron. 'One of Augusta's unexpected talents' we are told by the Bakewells, 'was her gift for mimicry and Byron delighted in her irreverent and accurate impersonations, egging her on to do his valet, William Fletcher, Lady Melbourne, Madame de Staël, Lord Carlisle, and, best of all, the heavily accented English of her grandmother, Lady Holdernesse.'[6]

In the spring of 1813 Augusta confessed to Byron that financial problems were destroying her peace of mind. He was mortified at being unable to give her immediate help since Claughton, the prospective purchaser of Newstead Abbey, had not yet paid the deposit on the purchase, let alone the full price. Eventually Claughton disgorged £5000 on account which enabled Byron to clear some of George's debts and to lend Hodgson a sum which would enable him to settle with his creditors and enable him to marry. (Byron had earlier travelled overnight to persuade the mother of Hodgson's beloved to allow her daughter to marry the future Provost of Eton, assuring her that he would pay off Hodgson's debts.)

By November Byron and Augusta found their passion for each other's company growing stronger than their doubts. They used crosses in their letters to convey feelings too strong to be expressed in words. Augusta sent him a lock of her hair. Byron was still confiding in Lady Melbourne, whose hope that Frances Webster or even Mary Chaworth-Musters might succeed in detaching him from Augusta must have been fading fast.

Byron's romantic memories of Mary were being replaced by an embarrassing reality. He wrote to Lady Melbourne:

> Now for a confidence – my old love of all loves – Mrs – [Chaworth-Musters] ... has written to me *twice* – no *love* but she wants to see me – and though it will be a melancholy interview I shall go – we have hardly met and never been on any intimate terms since her marriage – *he* has been playing the Devil – with all kinds of *vulgar* mistresses – and behaving ill enough in every respect ... She is *unhappy* – she was a spoilt heiress – but has seen little or nothing of the world – very pretty – and once simple in character and clever – but with no peculiar accomplishments – but endeared to me by a thousand childish and singular recollections.[7]
>
> (Byron to Lady Melbourne, 8 January 1814)

He asks for advice. Should he see her? Then writes again:

I hear ... they are to be reconciled ... I have no feelings beyond esteem ... and she still fewer for me ... – evidently she does not desire *him* to know anything of the matter. – 'Like C[aroline]' no more than I am like *Wm* and as far *her* superior as ... Wm is to me in every good and praiseworthy quality.[8]

(Byron to Lady Melbourne, 10 January 1814)

Mary and her husband were not yet to be reconciled but Byron was obsessed with his present 'love of all loves' and had little to offer his old one though he wrote to her kindly and told Augusta she would see Mary in Nottingham.

In December Augusta came to London again and Byron went back with her to Six Mile Bottom. Lady Frances Shelley and her husband, Sir John, came to call on Augusta and Lady Frances wrote:

He is decidedly handsome and can be agreeable. He seems to be easily put out and at times looks terribly savage. [Byron may have *felt* savage because these unexpected visitors were intruding on his precious time with Augusta]. He was very patient with Mrs Leigh's children, who are not in the least in awe of him. He bore their distracting intrusions into his room [where he was writing *The Corsair*] with imperturbable good humour. Mrs Leigh had evidently great moral influence over her brother, who listens to her occasional admonitions with a sort of playful acquiescence.[9]

Back in London in early January he was busy preparing *The Corsair* for publication, writing to John Murray, 'When published let the *Notes* be at the *end* as in the other tales – I shall send some mottoes from Dante for each Canto – and one for the title page tomorrow.'[10] Soon he was writing to Augusta:

My Dearest Augusta – On Sunday or Monday next with leave of your lord and president – you will be *well* and ready to accompany me to Newstead – which you *should* see and I will endeavour to render as comfortable as I can for both our sakes – as to time of stay there – suit your own convenience I am at your disposal – Claughton is I believe inclined to settle – if so – I shall be able to do something further for *yours* and *you* - which I need not say will give me ye greatest pleasure – More news from Mrs – [Chaworth-Musters] *all friendship* – you shall see her – Excuse haste and evil penmanship.[11]

Ever yours

Byron

(Byron to Augusta Leigh, 12 January 1814)

Later he asked her:

> Can you tell me ... *how much* G[eorge] *owes* – I trust on C[laughto]n's paying the residue – I shall be able to make some arrangement – for *him* – but at all events you and the Children shall be properly taken care of. – what I did for *him* might be seized etc. anything done for yourself would be safer and more advantageous to both.[12]
>
> (Byron to Augusta Leigh, January 1814)

Augusta was relieved to find her brother able and willing to help her. She was in no way rapacious or prompted by self-interest in her relationship with him but she felt that, as a Byron, she was entitled to some sort of provision if her brother could spare it. Later she wrote quite sharply about George Anson Byron's ungracious resentment over Byron's will (which left to Augusta and her seven children moneys which George Anson believed should have been left to him as heir to the barony). It was not generally understood that the bulk of the legacy would become available to Augusta only after the death of Lady Byron, an event not likely to occur before Augusta's own death. Nevertheless, Augusta became the target for much unfounded jealousy and resentment.

As they drove north from London in Byron's coach they found the roads were already deep in snow. Augusta first saw Newstead Abbey in a heavy snowfall looking more beautiful and romantic than ever. Byron was still trying to sell the Abbey to Claughton and had he succeeded in doing so Augusta's financial difficulties would have been at an end. But, far from encouraging her brother to sell, Augusta begged him to keep 'the dear old Abbey'.

Byron wrote to Murray: '... the roads are impassable and return impossible – for ye. present – which I do not regret as I am much at ease and *six* and *twenty* complete this day – a very pretty age if it would always last. – Our coals are excellent – our fireplaces large – my cellar full – and my head empty.'[13] He told Hanson: 'Mrs Leigh is with me and being in ye. family way – renders it doubly necessary to remain till the roads are quite safe ... we desire our best remembrances to all.'[14] Eventually he revealed to Murray, 'Mrs Leigh is with me – *much* pleased with the place – and less so with me for parting with it.'[15] He even dared to tell Lady Melbourne 'Augusta is here – which renders it much more pleasant – as we never yawn or disagree – and laugh much more than is suitable to so solid a mansion – and the family shyness makes us more amusing companions to each other – than we could be to anyone else.'[16]

Neither Byron nor Augusta would ever be as happy again. Byron's remark that 'she did not know her own peril until it was too late'[17] seems the likeliest explanation of the incest if it did occur. That lovemaking occurred is certain but how far it went will never be known. It was, in any case, not the most culpable of misdemeanours. They were half-brother and sister who had never met in childhood. Both were orphaned and both cherished the memory of the father they had shared and lost.

Byron's habit of flaunting his vices laid him open to the worst possible interpretation of his actions and he would later celebrate in verse a theoretically darker side to their relationship, but some of the critics subscribed to theories of his motives which seem the wildest nonsense. Professor Praz remarks on some who even go so far as to claim that Byron's love affair with his half-sister was a plagiarism because Byron committed in reality the crime (of incest) of which René had only conceived the horrible possibility. In a letter to Thomas Moore Byron referred to his love for Augusta not as a 'horrible possibility' or an 'unthinkable crime' but as 'a new scrape',[18] which seems to support the case for a mutual surrender to the delight of the moment rather than the pursuit of shocking crime for its own sake or in order to rival Chateaubriand, author of the immensely popular Romantic novel, *René*, published in 1802.

Byron expressed his feeling of guilt combined with delight in the relationship in a poem which he sent to Thomas Moore. This poem, which was not published until after his death, and several later poems and letters addressed to Augusta after his parting from her, together with the 'Opening lines to *Lara*', are the record of a most passionate and loving relationship. It has been suggested that Byron's sexual orientation was not bisexual (as most authorities believe) but wholly directed towards male love objects, so that he was going against his own nature when he made love to women. To anyone familiar with the poems and letters addressed to Augusta the theory that Byron was entirely homosexual seems mistaken. Even G. Wilson Knight, who finds the homosexual side of Byron's nature the finer, repudiates this view:

> Whatever the strength of Byron's homosexual instincts there is no question but that heterosexual love often burned in his imagination as,

at least for passion as opposed to idealism, the best. Women could attract him fierily. His actual experience with them may never have drawn level with that that he knew ideally with Edleston and physically with Nicolo Giraud; yet again, Mary Chaworth shone from his youth onwards as a star, and his love for Augusta, whatever its exact nature, was probably his most enduring emotion of all.[19]

STANZAS FOR MUSIC

1

I SPEAK not, I trace not, I breathe not thy name,
There is grief in the sound, there is guilt in the fame;
But the tear which now burns on my cheek may impart
The deep thoughts that dwells in that silence of heart.

2

Too brief for our passion, too long for our peace,
Were those hours – can their joy or their bitterness cease?
We repent, we abjure, we will break from our chain, –
We must part, we will fly to – unite it again!

3

Oh! thine be the gladness, and mine be the guilt!
Forgive me, adored one! – forsake, if thou wilt; –
But the heart which I bear shall expire undebased
And *man* shall not break it – whatever *thou* mayst.

4

And stern to the haughty, but humble to thee,
This soul, in its bitterest blackness, shall be;
And our days seem as swift, and our moments more sweet,
With thee by my side, than with worlds at our feet.

5

One sigh of thy sorrow, one look of thy love,
Shall turn me or fix, shall reward or reprove;
And the heartless may wonder at all we resign –
Thy lip shall reply, not to them, but to *mine*.[20]

Once the thaw came they were obliged to end their idyll. They spent a last night together at the Haycock Inn, Wansford, then Augusta went home to Six Mile Bottom and Byron continued on to London.

Bad weather, lack of inclination and a sudden illness suffered by Mary Chaworth-Musters had prevented Byron from meeting her, though Augusta had urged him to go. Mary had been writing to him, obviously unhappy, obviously in need of comfort. Experienced by now in judging the probable effect of his fame on women to whom he was completely unknown he must have suspected that, in spite of her protestations and her indecision over whether to return to her husband or not, a meeting with the famous poet who had once loved her passionately and unavailingly might result in an embarrassing show of feelings he was unable to return. She wrote, in all, as many as fifty letters to him.

Back in London he wrote to Leigh Hunt whom he had visited in Surrey gaol (imprisoned for a libel on the Prince Regent) in April 1813 at the instigation of Thomas Moore:

> My dear Sir, I have been snow-bound and thaw-swamped ... in Newstead Abbey ... and have not been four hours returned to London. Nearly the first use I make of my benumbed fingers is to thank you for yr. very handsome note in the volume you have just put forth [*The Feast of the Poets*] ... you must think me strangely spoiled – or perversely peevish – ever to suspect that any remarks of yours in the spirit of candid criticism could possibly prove unpalatable. – Had they been harsh – instead of being written as they are in the most indelible ink of good sense and friendly admonition ... as I ... know that you are above any personal bias at least against your fellow bards – believe me – they would not have caused a word of remonstrance ... I have always thought the Italians the *only* poetical *moderns*: – our Milton and Spenser and Shakespeare ... are very Tuscan and surely it is far superior to the French School ... I have been regaled at every Inn on the road by lampoons ... in the ministerial gazettes [this was the furore caused by the 'Lines on a Lady Weeping'] ... *The Morning P*[*ost*] has one copy of devices upon my deformity ... another upon my Atheism ... and another very down-rightly says I am the Devil (*boiteux* they might have added) and a rebel and what not.'[21]
>
> (Byron to Leigh Hunt, 9 February 1814)

To Lady Melbourne he wrote, 'Murray took fright and shuffled in my absence but I made him instantly replace the lines as before – it was no time to shrink now.'[22] A few days later he wrote on another subject – again refusing to 'shuffle' or 'shrink'. Having told Lady Melbourne that she was wrong in thinking that Augusta had tried to persuade him to put an end to his visits to Melbourne House, he added, '... you will easily suppose – that – twined as she is round my heart in every possible manner – dearest and deepest in my hope and my memory – still I am not easy.' But he went on: 'I have not lost all self-command. I am here – and here I *will* remain [London] but it cost me some struggles.'[23] (Byron to Lady Melbourne, 21 February 1814)

Annabella had asked his opinion of Lady Melbourne and he had replied, 'I am not ... an impartial judge of Lady M – but she is doubtless in talent a superior – a *supreme* woman – and her heart I know to be of the kindest ... Her defects I never could perceive as her society makes me forget them and everything else for the time – I do love that woman (*filially* or *fraternally*) better than any being on earth.'[24] (Byron to Annabella Milbanke, 12 February 1814)

Annabella cannot have been pleased with this reply.

At the same time Byron was doing his best to recommend Hobhouse to Lady Holland:

> I think I can prophesy that the more you allow my friend Hobhouse to become acquainted with you the more you will like him ... he is sincere active and unalterable in his friendships – God knows – I have but too often tried his patience very severely. – Nothing can give me greater pleasure than your partiality in his favour?[25]
>
> (Byron to Lady Holland, 12 February 1814)

In March he was writing to James Hogg, the Ettrick Shepherd: 'You seem to be a plain-spoken man, Mr Hogg, and I really do not like you the worse for it. I can't write verses and yet you want a bit of my poetry for your book ... you shall have the verses ... Poetry must always exist, like drink, where there is a demand for it ... You love Southey, forsooth – I am sure Southey loves nobody but himself...'[26] (Byron to James Hogg, Albany, 24 March [1814])

Byron was surprised at the virulence of the continuing attacks on him over the 'Lines to a Lady Weeping'. He told Lady Melbourne, 'I have that within me that bounds against opposition'[27] and expressed to Samuel Rogers his angry determination:

> All the sayings and doings in the world shall not make me utter another word of reconciliation to any thing that breathes. I shall bear what I can and what I cannot I shall resist. The worst thing they could do is to exclude me from society. I have never courted it, nor, I may add, in the general sense of the word, enjoyed it – and 'there is a world elsewhere.'[28]
>
> (To Samuel Rogers, 16 February 1814)

He would not make any attempt to suppress the attacks on him, having earlier written to Lady Melbourne, '*Prosecute?* ... Oh No – I am a great friend to liberty of the press – even at the expense of myself – besides – do I not deserve all this? and am I not in reality much worse...[29]

Claughton having now relinquished the deposit on Newstead and given up the purchase, Byron was able to forward to Scrope Davies the final repayment on his loan. At the same time he was sending heartfelt condolences to the Hanson family on the death of the kindly Mrs Hanson. In April he was lamenting the fall of Napoleon and '...the utter wreck of a mind which I thought superior even to fortune.'[30] He adds a comment which has some bearing on his later reaction to the break-up of his own marriage:

> It is said the Empress had refused to follow him [to Elba] – this is not well – men will always fall away from men – but it may generally be observed that no change of fortune – no degradation of rank or even character will detach a woman who has truly loved – unless there has been some provocation or misconduct towards herself on the part of the man.[31]
>
> (To Annabella Milbanke, Albany, 20 April 1814)

George Leigh now went off to Yorkshire and Augusta summoned Byron to her side. He had just moved into his new apartments in Albany but he went to Six Mile Bottom and stayed five days with her. Soon after this Augusta gave birth to another daughter who was christened Elizabeth Medora.

Byron, however, was trying to make up his mind whether to visit the Milbankes at Seaham. In May and June he was writing *Lara*. Then Moore arrived in London and together they enjoyed the excitement and the revelry of the 'Summer of the Sovereigns' when the Czar, the King of Prussia, Metternich, Marshal Blücher and lesser dignitaries from Europe converged on London to celebrate the banishment of Bonaparte to Elba. Byron liked going to the theatre with Moore and was enthusiastic over the acting of Kean.

In May he sent the Leighs another £3000, which Augusta found embarrassing. He wrote to her:

> I did it on your account – and that I would do for anyone in a similar situation – he need not consider himself under the least obligation – ... I must get you out of debt – and in the mean time ... let him think

> well of some plan for regulating his expenditure – I will have no interest – no bond – no repayment – unless his father left him so rich as to make it easy and pleasant to himself – he can then repay it or not as he likes – I am sure I do not care – if any accident happened to George – I am more deeply interested ... I am also unconnected and less incumbered ... and then, consider the children – and my Georgiana in particular.[32]
>
> (To Augusta Leigh, 24 June 1814)

He makes no mention of Elizabeth Medora who was then nearly two months old and it was not until 3 July when he returned to Six Mile Bottom and saw Augusta's baby daughter for the first time. There they discussed arrangements for a three week holiday at Hastings with all the children. Francis Hodgson, who was in Hastings with his bride-to-be, found them a house by the sea to rent and they were joined there by George Anson Byron, heir to the title. In the course of a happy seaside interlude Byron and Augusta came to the conclusion that he must marry. For Augusta this was the only course which would bring 'redemption' for them both. She wanted him to choose a shy young friend of hers, Lady Charlotte Leveson-Gower, who dithered charmingly for a while, then announced that her family had other plans for her.

Augusta and the children accompanied him back to Newstead and it was there that he composed his tentative proposal to Annabella and received her very determined acceptance. Augusta tried to persuade him to travel straight up to Seaham but he was determined to see Hanson first and settle his financial affairs. He did not despair of Claughton's renewing his offer for Newstead the sale of which was necessary to produce the basis for a generous settlement for Annabella and her children. He and Augusta spent their last hours together at Newstead regretting the loss of the 'dear old Abbey' and the imminent parting from each other. They carved their names on an ancient elm in the park. From now on Augusta did everything she could to persuade Byron to throw himself wholeheartedly into preparations for his marriage. She wanted her beloved brother to be happy, and so Annabella must be happy too.

Note

1. It has often been assumed that the child Augusta bore that spring was Byron's daughter. Byron never behaved to Augusta's little girl, Elizabeth Medora, as if he knew himself to be her father. He showed no more interest in her than in the rest of Augusta's children. At the time when she was born he adored Augusta. It is likely that if he had believed the child was his he would have stayed with her for the birth and would have asked for news of the child and taken an interest in her health and her education as he did later with his other daughters. And surely Augusta would have rejoiced with him over the birth of the little girl and later sent him bulletins about her progress.

George Leigh never questioned that the child was his, absolutely discounted the rumours about Augusta and Byron, and made no difficulties about his wife's staying at Piccadilly Terrace to look after Byron when he was ill after Lady Byron had left for Seaham. It is not impossible that he was prepared to barter his wife in return for financial help from Byron but Byron was still in debt and the failure of the sale of Newstead Abbey made the benefits to be obtained from him in the future quite uncertain.

The only evidence that Elizabeth Medora might have been Byron's daughter is the letter from Byron to Lady Melbourne: 'Oh, but it is "worth while" – I can't tell you why – and it is *not* an *Ape* and if it is – that must be my fault – however, I will positively reform'.[1]

This has been read as a reference to the superstition that the child of incest would be a monster. It could also apply to another superstition – that the appearance and character of an unborn child could be influenced by the experiences of the mother during her pregnancy.

Hary-O tells a story (which illustrates how terrified pregnant women of that period were of evil influences on their babies) about Lady Stuart, wife of the British Ambassador in Vienna, running away from an extremely ugly Austrian count for fear her unborn child would resemble him. She sent for a famous Austrian beauty, Marie Branner, and paid to be allowed to gaze at her for an hour to banish the image of Count Trauttsmandorf from her mind.

The Bakewells' comment on the paternity of Elizabeth Medora is practical and to the point:

> The widely held belief that Byron was unquestionably the father of her fourth child is based on the chivalrous assumption that Augusta, out of romantic consideration for Byron, would not have let George make love to her; but this was not the case. Augusta did not, as Annabella later put it, suffer from 'moral idiocy from birth', but took life as it came and was generally inclined to settle for the easy way out. She had slept with both Byron and George. She would, in any case, have regarded it as her conjugal duty not to deny herself to George, and to do so would only have provoked an unnecessary scene.[2]

16

CHILDE HAROLD AND THE PRINCESS OF PARALLELOGRAMS

She is a very superior woman, and very little spoiled, which is strange in an heiress – a girl of twenty – a peeress that is to be, in her own right – an only child and a savante, who has always had her own way. She is a poetess – a mathematician – and yet withal, very kind, and generous, and gentle, with very little pretension.[1]

In most respects Byron held to this opinion of Annabella throughout the marriage. In March 1816 he defended his wife from the criticisms of his friends, writing to Thomas Moore:

> I must set you right in one point, however. The fault was *not* – no, nor even the misfortune – in my 'choice' (unless in *choosing at all*) – for I do not believe – and I must say it, in the very dregs of all this bitter business – that there ever was a better, or even a brighter, a kinder, or a more aimiable and agreeable being than Lady B. I never had, nor can have, any reproach to make her, while with me. Where there is blame, it belongs to myself, and, if I cannot redeem, I must bear it.[2]
>
> (Byron to Thomas Moore, 8 March 1816)

This testimony by Byron must be accepted. Lady Byron bears little guilt for what happened during the marriage. Byron takes full blame for its collapse. This is not to say that he believed her perfect. Before he asked her to marry him the second time he had realised that he was wrong in thinking her unspoiled:

> She seems to have been spoiled – not as children usually are – but systematically Clarissa Harlowed into an awkward kind of correctness.[3]

This was perceptive. Annabella had been treated like a little queen by her elderly and adoring parents. Judith Milbanke encouraged what she described as Annabella's 'very natural manners' and allowed her daughter to criticise the people around her and to write 'characters' of friends in her journal.

Annabella was very fond of her father who could be swayed into giving her her own way by affectionate cajolery. Her mother was naturally dictatorial and Annabella reacted by telling her she was old-fashioned and addressing her disparagingly as 'Old Lady' or even 'Old Woman'.

An upbringing such as that of the orphaned Augusta at Eckington might have dispelled some of Annabella's complacency but the constant praise she received from family, friends and servants at Seaham could only increase it. Before she was despatched to London for her first season on the marriage market, an older cousin wrote of her prospects: 'It is not every day that she is likely to meet with a *Mind* which ought to claim kindred with one so superior as hers.'[4] Later, Lady Milbanke told her daughter: 'Your character is like *Proof-Spirits* – not fit for common use. I could almost wish the tone of it lowered nearer the level of us every-day people.'[5]

It was hardly surprising after years of such adulation that by the end of her fourth season in London Annabella had rejected no fewer than five eligible suitors, including Lord Byron. Her only remaining *prétendant* at that time was Hugh Montgomery, brother of one of her dearest friends, but no very eligible parti compared with 'the first poet of the age'.

If she was in love with Byron at this stage she was not prepared to admit it. Her ambition was to save his soul and she saw herself as his guide and mentor.

This is not reprehensible. She was young and inexperienced and failed to understand what she was taking on in trying to influence so complex a character as Byron. Her tragedy was her inability to admit a weakness in herself or even a mistake. She was capable of changing neither her attitude nor her behaviour.

By now Byron had become aware of her strong belief in her own infallibility and prophesied that this belief '... will, or may, lead her into some egregious blunder.'[6] The 'egregious blunder' of her life was her acceptance of his proposal. It is hard to understand why, with his eyes open, Byron allowed himself his own 'egregious blunder' in offering to marry a girl with whom he had so little in common. He 'could love anything on earth that appeared to wish it'[7] (a quality not shared by his wife-to-be) and he did develop a sort of love for Annabella, but his early encomium on her spoke not of love but of esteem – 'I never saw a woman whom I *esteemed* so much'[8]). In renewing his addresses to her after his rejection he was ignoring what he had earlier seen clearly – that Annabella required 'all the cardinal virtues'[9] (some of which he might claim, but certainly not all). Annabella was more concerned with esteem than with love. If she had remained with Byron this might conceivably have changed. The separation fixed her on a path towards piety and virtue rather than love.

It is surprising that they ever became engaged. Their reluctance to commit themselves is striking. In August 1814 Annabella informed Byron quite firmly that she ought not to choose him as her companion in life. 'Very well,' he replied, 'now we can talk of something else'. By September she was ready to snap up a tentative renewal of his courtship, treating it as a direct offer of marriage.

The Milbankes were pleased because Annabella seemed happy but they were apprehensive, as well they might be. Their daughter's unrealistic attitude to her conquest appears in a letter she wrote in November to her friend and confidante, Lady Gosford:

> After having had nearly 'the world before me where to choose' I have fixed with mature judgement on the person most calculated to support me in the journey to immortality ... for the blessings we have both received ... we will offer our gratitude to Heaven *together*, during as many years as may be spared to us.'[10]

In making this astonishing forecast of Byron's conversion to her own brand of piety Annabella was busy investing him with the qualities she required in a husband instead of examining with a clear regard the real man with whom she proposed to spend her life.

The real man was busy trying to resolve the question of his debts. He was determined to arrange a proper settlement for Annabella and her children but this depended entirely on the sale of Newstead Abbey. Hanson, as usual, was dilatory. But the Milbankes expected Byron's visit and made it known that they had hoped he would arrive before the departure of Lord Wentworth, Annabella's uncle, who had travelled to Seaham on purpose to meet her future husband. Byron knew the Milbankes hoped Lord Wentworth would leave his fortune to Annabella (who would eventually inherit the title) but he had no intention of dashing up to Seaham before he had organised his own affairs. He was finally obliged to set off to visit his bride-to-be. 'It was very foolish dragging me out of town before my lawyer had arrived.'[11]

Seaham was a village on the bleak east coast where the Milbankes led a cosy provincial existence full of private family jokes, teasing each other about food and visits to the lavatory, taking part in local politics, and parading their strict views on piety and religion. It was no very fit milieu for Annabella's wayward genius of a lover. On one of his visits he wrote to Thomas Moore, 'I must go to tea. – damn tea! I wish it was Kinnaird's brandy.'[12] He wrote more ominously to Lady Melbourne:

> Do you know I have great doubts – if this will be a marriage now. – her disposition is the very reverse of *our* imaginings – she is overrun with fine feelings – scruples about herself and *her* disposition (I suppose in fact she means mine) and to crown all is taken ill once every 3 days with I know not what – but the day before and the day after she seems well – looks and eats well & is cheerful & confiding & in short like any other person in good health & spirits. – A few days ago she made one *scene* – not altogether out of C[aroline]'s style – it was too long and too trifling in fact for me to transcribe – but it did me no good – in the article of conversation however she has improved with a vengeance – but I don't much admire these same agitations upon slight occasions. – I don't know – but I think it by no means impossible you will see me in town soon – I can only interpret these things one way – & merely wait to be certain to make my obeisances and 'exit singly.' I hear of nothing but 'feeling' from morning till night – except from Sir Ralph with whom I go on to admiration – Ly. M[ilbanke] too is pretty well – but I am never sure of A[nnabella] – for a moment – the least word – and you know I rattle on through thick & thin (always however avoiding anything I think can offend her favourite notions) if only to prevent me from yawning – the least word – or alteration of tone – has some inference drawn from it – sometimes we are too much alike – & then again too unlike – this comes of *system* – & squaring her notions to the Devil knows what – for my part I have lately had recourse to the eloquence of *action* (which Demosthenes calls the first part of oratory) & find it succeeds very well & makes her very quiet which gives me some hopes of the efficacy of the 'calming process' so renowned in '*our* philosophy.' – In fact and entre nous it is really amusing – she is like a child in that respect – and quite *caressable* into kindness and

good humour – though I don't think her temper *bad* at any time – but very *self*-tormenting – and anxious – and romantic. ———— In short – it is impossible to foresee how this will end *now* – anymore than 2 years ago – if there is a break – it shall be *her* doing not mine.

ever yrs. truly

B

(Byron to Lady Melbourne, 14 November 1814)[13]

The 'calming process' led Annabella to send her lover away, cutting short his visit because she feared his presence in the house before the wedding ceremony might result in some dangerous impropriety. Before being sent away Byron seems to have got on very well with Annabella's parents.

The engaged couple wrote each other affectionate letters: 'My Heart – We are thus far separated – but after all one mile is as bad as a thousand.'[14] (16 November 1814). 'Well but – sweet Heart – do write & love me – and regard me as thine'.[15] (23 November 1814). Annabella was equally loving in her replies.

But Byron felt himself 'Cold and comfortless as Charity', as he called at Six Mile Bottom on his way back to London from Seaham and even contemplated withdrawing from the engagement. For the next few weeks Annabella, terrified that he might abandon her, wrote repentant letters to him begging him to forgive her and assuring him that she would be all he could wish in a bride. Unfortunately for her, all he could wish as his companion in life was Augusta, Annabella's antithesis in almost every respect.

Hobhouse held that part of Byron's fascination could doubtless be ascribed to '... the entire self-abandonment, the incautious, it may be said, the dangerous sincerity of his private conversation.' Lady Blessington wrote of him: 'The more I see of Byron the more I am convinced that all he says and does should be judged more leniently than the sayings and doings of others – as his proceed from the impulse of the moment and never from premeditated malice. He cannot resist expressing whatever comes into his mind.'[16] His friends agreed that he was 'true-spoken' but deplored his complete lack of discretion. Such a man should never have married one of Shakespeare's 'lords and owners of their faces'. It was fortunate for Lady Byron that she possessed a charm which surrounded her for the rest of her life, after the separation, with a circle of admiring 'stewards of her excellence'.

Byron became fond of Annabella and was often playful with

her. They were even reported to be an affectionate couple. But in the end even Hobhouse came to believe that Byron had behaved very badly to his wife.

On reaching London Byron began to hustle Mr Hanson into preparing the marriage settlements. Sir Ralph was in financial difficulties. Byron wrote:

> I know nothing of her fortune, and I am told that her father is ruined, but my own will, when my Rochdale arrangements are closed, be sufficient for us both, my debts are not £25,000 p[oun]ds and the deuce is in it, if with R[ochdale] and the surplus of N[ewstead] [which he still hoped to sell] I could not contrive to be as independent as half the peerage.[17]

Hanson delayed matters so long that Byron was afraid the marriage would fall through. He proposed to settle £60,000 (or £3,500 a year) on Annabella and her children, the sale of Newstead to supply the requisite capital. Hanson thought £2,500 a year would be perfectly adequate but Byron insisted that it must be done generously. Hanson told him he found the Milbankes grasping. When the sale of Newstead fell through once again, Byron offered to release Annabella from the engagement or to postpone the marriage. For Annabella and her parents such a postponement was out of the question and Byron felt obliged to fulfil their expectations. Byron knew that Annabella would eventually inherit her uncle's fortune, in all probability, and he needed to marry a 'Golden Dolly'. In the short run Annabella was no such thing.

When Annabella told him the bells in Durham had rung a peal for their marriage in the belief that it had already taken place, he replied that the bells were in a pestilent hurry. Annabella was distraught, for she saw that her parents were becoming tight-lipped at the bridegroom's delay. The wedding cake went mouldy and a new one had to be baked before Byron and Hobhouse finally arrived at Seaham after a loitering journey taking in Six Mile Bottom and Cambridge – 'Never,' wrote Hobhouse, 'was lover less in haste.'[18] After the marriage ceremony his words were more ominous: 'I felt as if I had buried a friend.'[19]

Byron had wanted to wait two years – during which time he would have considered himself an engaged man. If the Milbankes had agreed to a postponement until both Rochdale and Newstead (or, at least, Newstead) could be sold, the feeling both at Seaham and in the carriage bearing Hobhouse and Byron to the North might have been happier. Travelling to be married in the knowledge that Hanson had completed the marriage settlements and that the sale of Newstead had provided 'a surplus for necessities' Byron might have felt the rejoicing and the pealing of the bells to be appropriate.

17

THE MARRIAGE

'I mean to reform most thoroughly and to become "a good man and true" ... I will endeavour to make your niece happy.'[1]

If one excludes the practical problems which wrecked the Byron marriage one is still left with the incompatibility which would have made its success unlikely even if everything had gone smoothly. Byron was unpleasantly surprised when Annabella informed him in a letter from Seaham that she had engaged a cook for them. Byron had no intention of sitting down to regular meals with his wife and though he enjoyed dining with his friends he did not go in for formal social events at home and did not invite ladies. He had no desire to change his ways in this respect.

Both of them had an abnormal attitude towards food and hers would end after the separation in what sounds very like bulimia. Edith Mayne comments on Annabella's love of certain foods:

> Her letters are pervaded by a theme which so often reappears – even in the after-stages of the Separation-Drama – that it is worth dwelling on for a moment. That theme is mutton-chops. From Wetherby, in this February, she told Sir Ralph that she had dined on 'Fleecy mutton-chops'. Enough, one would think, to make her order anything else when she got to Grantham next day. But no. She ordered mutton-chops, ate 'twice two and frightened the waiters'. And afterwards mutton chops are so often reported on for praise or blame that one cannot but recall Byron's dislike to see a woman eat – and remember too that (as he wrote to Lady Melbourne during his first stay at Seaham as Annabella's betrothed) she 'was never well for two days together'. It does emerge from her letters that she was inclined to be greedy. We read of her

> eating too many peaches (with her own commentary of Beast!) of a goose-pie being clamoured for both by her and 'B' ... All through Annabella's correspondence with her parents, especially after the separation, food plays a large part, with a frequent corollary of 'biliousness' and its various remedies.[2]

To find that she was not to dine regularly with her husband must have been insulting to her pride and produced a feeling of loneliness and rejection. She was used to the pleasant meal times in her parents' house. Nor was she perceptive enough to work out for herself that, having married a genius she ought perhaps to try to adapt herself to his ways and not to repine. It is interesting to learn that Lady Noel was more tolerant than her daughter of Byron's odd behaviour – at Seaham she would always arrange for him to eat alone if he wished.

Again, if Annabella had allowed him the freedom to go to London or to Six Mile Bottom on his own after the honeymoon at Halnaby and then let him consort with his friends quite freely as he had done before the marriage, he would probably have changed his ways and invited her to join him. But this would have required superhuman wisdom and self-sacrifice on the part of the young bride.

He introduced his friends to her and she expected him to meet her own, who were for the most part pious middle-aged ladies. He claimed to have sometimes returned home to find his wife sitting with '...half a dozen Old Blues who thought a man damned if he made a joke.'[3] Annabella had been worried, as a girl, about being in the same room as Lady Holland even though she was determined to reject any introduction. Now she was actually introduced to that lady and expected to be friends with her. She detested Lady Melbourne who was one of Byron's dearest friends.

With goodwill and forbearance they might have dealt successfully with these problems but the financial difficulties in which Byron found himself as a result of marrying before his financial affairs were satisfactorily arranged, proved disastrous.

When Byron and his bride moved into the grand house at 13 Piccadilly Terrace his creditors thought he had married money and descended on him with writs. In April Lord Wentworth died and the creditors assumed that Lady Byron had inherited. Instead, every penny went to Lady Milbanke for her lifetime. The Milbankes (from now on to be known as the Noels) could offer no immediate financial aid as the legacy was tied up and it would be some time before it became available. Sir Ralph did not manage to pay the agreed £6000 advance on the modest dowry agreed by the lawyers until after the terrible year of financial disasters, and the arrival of the bailiffs. Distraught with shame, Byron tried to dispel the feeling of disgrace by drinking heavily and taking laudanum. Perhaps as a result of these excesses he fell ill with some sort of neurological complaint possibly connected with his lameness, the symptoms of which were headaches and bouts of uncontrollable irritation. Augusta remarked how one eye appeared much smaller than the other.

Augusta tried to soothe him and Annabella made little of their financial problems. This was admirable in her, but irritating for Byron who felt the marriage responsible for all his tribulations. He wanted sympathy, not stoicism. All the same, they were reported to be an affectionate couple and some of Byron's friends thought they were too inseparable. This changed when Annabella became pregnant and when Byron took on responsibilities at Drury Lane Theatre. Annabella objected to Byron's interest in the theatre and took to referring to him disparagingly as 'The Manager'. Her objections were proved to have some weight when Byron confessed to her that he had had a brief affair with one of the actresses, for which she forgave him.

The attempt at disposing of Rochdale and Newstead in July 1815 fell through when neither property reached the reserve price. By November a bailiff was sleeping in the house. Byron told Annabella he must break up the establishment and threatened to go abroad alone. Augusta-Ada was born in late December and the Noels offered them refuge at Kirkby Mallory or at Seaham. Byron suggested to Annabella that she should settle on a date for her departure with the child as soon as convenient to her. This was communicated to Annabella in a note and caused angry remonstrance from her. However, Byron believed this difference was resolved and he reported later that he and his wife had lived together on conjugal terms up to the day of her departure. This is borne out by the two playful and loving letters Annabella sent to him, one during the journey and one from Kirkby Mallory. Byron said he would join her there in the near future. Before he could do so a letter arrived from Sir Ralph Noel announcing that his daughter wanted a separation.

These are the bare bones of the story of the marriage. Over the years a superstructure of comment and assertion has been built on this basis, most of which is supported solely by the testimony of Lady Byron and her confidants (of whom there were many). Byron's *Memoirs* were burned in the fireplace at 50 Albemarle Street, unread by most of the perpetrators of this action. Thus Byron's side of the story was not only suppressed but destroyed. Relating the story of the marriage which has been told and re-told over the years is equivalent to accepting the evidence of the injured party in a divorce case without hearing the evidence for the defence, which is unjust.

[Extracts from Harriet Beecher Stowe's *Vindication of Lady Byron*: an account of the marriage conveyed to her by Lady Byron in 1851, will be found in the appendix.]

18

ANNABELLA THROUGH THE LOOKING GLASS

'Augusta … speaks of my conduct as that of an Angel.'[1]

One cannot avoid the impression that throughout the marriage Annabella was a kind of Alice in Wonderland, lost in a world she was unable to understand, and lacking the common sense that enabled Alice to deal with all the anomalies and the wonders she encountered. Annabella completely misunderstood her husband:

> …founding her opinions on sundry playful paradoxes of which a total inapprehension of irony and humour of any kind prevented her from appreciating the true value. It is true that Lord Byron upon discovering that his new companion did not understand him so entirely as his old friends, should have desisted from those extravagances of expression and manner which were set down to the account of a depraved mind rejoicing in the contemplation of every enormity.[2]

Byron's friend, William Harness, explains Byron's moods. Talking of Byron as he behaved in normal circumstances he says, 'He had a childish weakness for dramatic effect and excitement and indulged in fantastic rhapsodies full of tragic extravagance. If paid no attention he soon stopped.'[3] Augusta knew how to handle her brother's wild flights. She simply laughed at them and thus teased him into a better frame of mind. Annabella came to the conclusion that her huband was depraved. It is difficult to imagine how she got through the year of marriage with its loving as well as its difficulties if this is the conviction she was forming while she was with Byron. One can only wonder how she later interpreted his going to Greece.

Hobhouse explained how mistaken she was:

> His friends had long been acquainted with his singular love of the marvellous in morals which Lord Byron evinced in his conversation and his compositions, but which he was so far from carrying into his own conduct that no man was ever more commonplace than himself in an habitual display of kindness, generosity, and all the every-day virtues of civilised life. He had the habit of marking in his books traits of depravity, and poor Lady Byron mistook these marks for notes of admiration ... they came to the conclusion that Lord Byron had not been guilty of any enormity. They added that his offences might be regretted as subversive of matrimonial felicity but would not render him amenable to the laws of any court, whether of justice or equity.[4]

Hanson, as reported by Hobhouse, relates how Annabella came to see him just before leaving London and told him she believed her husband was mad and, to his amazement and horror, even talked of the possibility of having him put under restraint. This was not rational behaviour. Annabella knew that Byron was drinking heavily and taking laudanum to assuage his despair over the arrival of bailiffs in the house. It would surely occur to a common sense onlooker that his alarming moods were caused by alcohol and drugs rather than by insanity. His behaviour must have been distressing for an inexperienced young woman, though she was supported by maids and nurses and serving men, and Augusta brought in George Byron to help keep her brother in order. But there is no evidence of any act of violence against Annabella or anybody else during this whole period, though Annabella told the lawyers she had a strong conviction of danger while she was with Byron. It would be interesting to know how defending counsel would have dealt with this vague conviction.

Annabella drew up a paper of questions for Augusta and George Byron seeking an admission that they believed she would be in danger of her life if left alone with Byron at Piccadilly Terrace, and *had* been in danger from him both before, during and after, the birth of their child. Lady Noel positively stated to her daughter that Augusta and George Byron had testifed that her life was in danger.

If we are to believe Hobhouse's account, Lady Noel was lying. Hobhouse questioned George Byron and Augusta about this accusation against Byron and he gives their account of the matter:

> Mrs Leigh avowed that there was occasionally something in his Lordship's manner, when talking of his embarrassments as a married man, which terrified her, and might terrify Lady Byron. She mentioned particularly one instance when Lord Byron desired his wife to walk out of the room with him when his air and tone were such as to make her glad when she saw them come back again. Captain Byron had a general impression that Lady Byron believed Lord Byron hated her, but neither Captain Byron nor Mrs Leigh was aware of any individual act tending to prove the least violence.[5]

Such behaviour to a pregnant woman is inexcusable but it is of a different order from physical violence. Since the matter was never brought before a court it is impossible to establish the truth of the matter. If Lady Noel was not lying in stating that Captain Byron and Augusta said Annabella was in danger then we must believe that Augusta and George Byron, in answering Hobhouse, lied to protect Byron. This is unlikely. Augusta wanted to help Annabella to prove Byron mad in the hope that her sense of duty would induce her to pity him and forgive him rather than cast him off. So she would not have denied any act of violence she had witnessed. George Byron's sympathies tended towards Lady Byron.

Annabella's maid, Ann Rood, spent a few months at Piccadilly Terrace and was now married to Byron's valet. She returned to Seaham with her mistress and the baby when they left Piccadilly Terrace. Her deposition is recorded in Hobhouse's account of the separation. Hobhouse is firmly in the Byron camp, but his account is extremely fair and includes material which is not to Byron's credit. The new Mrs Fletcher accuses the Noels of dishonesty in building their case against Byron. She describes how Lady Noel said to her, 'You know you told Mrs Clermont that her Ladyship was in danger of her life while she remained in the house with Lord Byron.' Ann Fletcher replied that she had said no such thing but that Mrs Clermont had said it to her. Lady Noel thereupon flew into a rage and kept repeating, 'You know it was so.'[6]

Hobhouse relates how, soon after this, from motives of policy, Lady Noel began to pay great attention to the girl, sending her to the coach station in her own carriage and arranging to provide a dinner for her when she travelled to London.

Lady Byron may have felt that in these circumstances the Clermont testimony was not sufficiently convincing on the danger in which she claimed to stand from Byron. She produced a statement claiming that her maternity nurse used to lock the doors leading to her room at night. 'It was decidedly her opinion that my life was in danger.'[7] Then, possibly aware that the nurse might give a conflicting account, she covered herself by adding, 'On the other hand she would probably say that she has seen Lord Byron appear personally fond of me during the few minutes she has seen us together.'[8] In spite of the lurid tales about Byron's cruelty to her during her confinement Lady Byron had told Lady Melbourne that her confinement had been so comfortable, owing to Augusta's care for her, that she had no desire to leave Piccaddily Terrace.

The testimony alleged to be that of the maternity nurse, Mrs Shackleton, is to be found among the Lovelace Papers, the hoard of documents concerning the marriage and the separation collected by Lady Byron and preserved by her grandson, Lord Lovelace. Among these documents is a paper purporting to be a statement by the nurse, which is neither signed nor witnessed and contains alterations and interpolations in a different hand, none of them to Byron's credit.

The last word on whether Lady Byron thought herself to be in danger of her life rests with Lady Byron herself. When she visited Mr Hanson, shortly before she left Piccadilly Terrace with her child, to tell him she thought Byron was mad, Hanson, as reported by Hobhouse, asked her whether she laboured under any personal fear for herself, to which she instantly replied, 'Oh no! My eye can always put down his.'[9]

Byron answered these allegations very clearly in a letter to Lady Byron of 10 April 1816. To omit Byron's defence while printing Lady Byron's allegations would amount to misrepresentation. The letter helps to explain Byron's anger against 'the genial spy', Mrs Clermont. (He refers to Ann Fletcher as Mrs R.):

> Enclosed is an extract from Rood's deposition or examination – or whatever it is technically to be called: – from this it will appear that Mrs Clermont did misstate to Lady Noel what Mrs R. had said – or rather attributed to Mrs R. words which she did not say – but which Mrs Clermont herself had used – words of doubled falsehood – false as attributed to Mrs R. – false in point of fact whoever asserted them. You – Lady Byron – know – and I know – that you never were in 'peril of your life' from me – that in the extremest withering of mind which distemper of body – distress of circumstances and exasperation of stimulus singly or united struck through me – you never thought so

> – you never were so – no violence was ever even contemplated by me – from the first day of our connection to that of your desertion – towards *you* or anyone near to you – except myself.[10]

There is no doubt that Lady Byron and her supporters were now intent on giving the impression that the separation was caused by great wickedness on the part of Lord Byron. Considering that they were blackening the reputation of Ada's father it seems extraordinary that this seemed to them necessary. Perhaps the answer is simple. Annabella was afraid that Byron would take the child away from her, as the laws of the period might have allowed him to do. Lady Noel went so far as to take precautions against any attempt to kidnap the baby from Kirkby Mallory. Byron never made any attempt to abduct the child but Augusta unwisely told Annabella that he meant to have her in the end (possibly to frighten Annabella into coming back to Byron with the baby). Annabella believed in the threat and conceived it her duty to destroy her husband in order to protect her child. When Augusta told her she was afraid Byron would take his own life she replied she could not help it. She must do her duty. She then told her father, 'I'm told he is threatening his friends with suicide. A *professed* intention of that sort is rather amusing'[11] and, 'My mother says that if he does take laudanum so much the better. It is not fit such men should live.'[12]

The most potent method of blackening Byron's name was the withholding of the reason why Annabella had sought a separation. It was well known, by whatever means, that Dr Lushington had recommended a reconciliation until Lady Byron travelled to London and told him something which caused him to change his mind. Since no one was ever to be allowed to find out what this was, it was widely believed that Byron had committed some enormity so appalling that it could not be mentioned. This naturally caused avid speculation. Even today there is no agreement on what this terrible secret could have been. Jerome Christensen writes, 'What awful secret did Lady Byron tell? Speculation first produced the rumour of a murder; it then hunted out incest; it has since settled comfortably on the suspicion of homosexuality. – None of those explanations, as G. Wilson Knight was the first to show, is satisfactory.'[13]

'[Byron] is more jealous of his character than anyone in the world,' wrote Lady Byron to her mother. 'How far may he therefore be brought to terms?'[14] 'I am sure few have been libelled as I have been,' Byron wrote from Italy years later. 'Time sets things to rights.'[15] Time has never done so. Lady Byron could instantly have set things to rights in March 1816 when she wrote, 'The silence of my friends has been very *dis*advantageous to Lord Byron ... since worse than the true causes are supposed.'[16] But she took no steps to contradict these false suppositions because she was intent on destroying Byron's reputation for her own purposes.

Though the lawyers were silent on the charge of something so horrible that it could not be talked about, the silence of Lady Byron's friends was in fact a myth. She chose confidantes who would join her in covert character assassination – mostly single women who found Byron's behaviour deeply shocking.

A letter containing extravagant charges of brutality against Byron, written by Selina Doyle, a close friend of Annabella's who was staying with the Noels at the time, was read out at a party in London with the consent of Miss Doyle who stipulated only that her name should not be mentioned as its writer.

Some of the damaging charges spread abroad by such methods concerned Annabella's version of the honeymoon journey [see Appendix – Harriet Beecher Stowe] on which Byron's comment, according to Medwin, was: 'If I had made so cavalier, not to say so brutal a speech, I am convinced that Lady Byron would instantly have left the carriage to me and the maid.'[17] Alfred Austin claimed that '...anyone who rejected this statement by Byron and believed one of Lady Byron's contradictory accounts must be constitutionally incapable of weighing evidence or be of the settled opinion that accusation of guilt is equivalent to proof of it.'[18]

The mention of the maid is puzzling. It is virtually incredible that Byron would have behaved as Lady Byron claimed he did, with the maid in the carriage. The butler at Halnaby claimed that Lady Byron was a pitiable sight of unhappiness when she got out of the carriage. The maid, Mrs Minns, testified years later that Lady Byron was buoyant and cheerful as any bride should be.[19] The butler was dependent on the Milbanke family and, as we have seen, Lady Noel was not above bullying the servants in order to get from them the testimony she required. Of the differing versions of these events given by Lady Byron Alfred Austin wrote:

> I should very much have liked to see either Sir Samuel Romilly or Dr Lushington [Annabella's lawyers] who both so readily believed whatever

> it may be that Lady Byron told them, with a witness under cross-examination who had given two such contradictory accounts of the same transaction ... Why, such evidence, if brought against a pick pocket, would ensure his acquittal.[20]

Lady Byron's is the only account we have of the visit to Augusta at Six Mile Bottom on the way back to London after the honeymoon. If we are to believe her, Byron was cruel both to her and to Augusta, flaunted his passion for his half-sister and taunted his wife with his preference for Augusta. If Byron's behaviour was as outrageous as it appears in this account it is quite incomprehensible that his young bride did not immediately return to her parents. (She claims to have already suspected that incest had occurred.) Instead she accompanied Byron to the newly rented house on Piccadilly Terrace and invited Augusta to come and visit them there for several weeks. Yet the melodramatic account given by Annabella of the stay at Six Mile Bottom – with its description of her fear of hearing Byron's 'terrible step' as he left Augusta and came up to her in bed, and her statement that he swore at Fletcher so that she feared for his life, just as the 'testimony' of the maternity nurse claimed that she feared for Lady Byron's life when Byron came to her room – has been accepted by many biographers as if it were statement of fact or sworn testimony proven in court. Few of these writers have mentioned what is pointed out by Malcolm Elwin, that all such accounts of the marriage were written by Lady Byron after the event either with litigation in view, or to justify her own actions. This is not to suggest that Byron's behaviour was acceptable. The correspondence between Augusta and Annabella as well as Augusta's letter to Francis Hodgson immediately after the visit to Six Mile Bottom shows that both women were deeply concerned about Byron's state of mind which was clearly far removed from that of a newly and happily married bridegroom.

Various accusations were made about Byron's wishing his baby dead, trying to disturb the baby's sleep, declaring that in her he had acquired an instrument for torture of Lady Byron. As Hobhouse reports, they are refuted by Mrs Clermont herself who said, soon after Ada's birth, that she never saw a father so proud and so fond of his child as Lord Byron.[21] Annabella echoed this when she suggested that Byron was fonder of the child than she was – even fonder of it than he was of her.[22] Mrs Fletcher, as reported by Hobhouse, claimed to have seen no disagreements between Lord and Lady Byron at Piccadilly Terrace. She would not, however, have seen them together often, or for long periods.[23]

Lady Byron gives various accounts of her reason for leaving Piccadilly Terrace. In one she leaves because Byron turns her out of the house. In another she leaves on the recommendation of the doctors who believe her presence exacerbates Byron's nervous condition. The attempt to give the impression that she was in danger of her life is intended to insinuate a third version – that she fled to her parents from Byron's violence – and this is the version that was generally believed in 1816.

Her belief in her husband's depravity upheld her in the conviction that she was doing right. She was unable to see that her campaign against him was changing her into an obsessive and deluded woman. Byron saw clearly what was happening to his wife – a tragic deterioration. In the poem 'Lines on hearing that Lady Byron was Ill' (written in 1816 in Switzerland and first published in 1831, after his death) Byron gives his changed view of her 'veracity':

> But of thy virtues didst thou make a vice,
>   Trafficking with them in a purpose cold,
>   For present anger, and for future gold –
> And buying other's grief at any price.
> And thus once entered into crooked ways,
> The early truth, which was thy proper praise,
> Did not still walk beside thee – but at times,
> And with a breast unknowing its own crimes,
> Deceit, averments incompatible,
> Equivocations, and the thoughts which dwell
>   In Janus-spirits – the significant eye
> Which learns to lie with silence – the pretext
> Of prudence, with advantages annexed –
> The acquiescence in all things which tend,
> No matter how, to the desired end –
>   All found a place in thy philosophy.
> The means were worthy, and the end is won –
> I would not do by thee as thou hast done![24]

This strikes home dead centre. It describes with devastating accuracy the way Lady Byron had conducted herself during the separation and how she was to conduct herself over the long and lonely years to come. Witness to this is a letter to the editor of the *Pall Mall Gazette* in 1869. The writer, John Robertson, was a friend of Lady Byron who was so shocked by the publication of Mrs Beecher Stowe's revelations that he decided to make public his doubts about Lady Byron's veracity. He revealed that Lady Byron confided details of two separate crimes to six or seven of her friends, three of whom were Americans. One of these crimes had never been mentioned by her before. She told her listeners that these revelations were not to be treated as secrets but to be used to defend her conduct. Mr Robertson told that in 1847:

> ...one of her friends asked me to talk to her of the liability to error of private judgement when deciding questions involving criminal charges, which can only be properly investigated by public tribunals. No one, I told her, has the right to repeat such charges except as decisions of a court of law. [A word to the wise for the modern biographer and reviewer]. Her stories differed, her memoranda were given away right and left. The confidantes who knew her best, her peculiarities, her troubles with her daughter, her eldest grandson, her servants, never would have repeated her stories with pen and types. They thought her mind was touched. Suspicions had become delusions.[25]

Annabella's attitude to her husband had changed completely after she returned home to her parents. In October 1815 she had written to her mother, who had suggested she should come home for her confinement and bring Byron with her:

> He is in great anxiety about me and would have me go by myself which I *will* not. [Byron could not go with her at that time since, the moment he left London, executions in the house which were being held back, would immediately go into effect.] As long as I am with him I am comparatively comfortable.[26]

Later she wrote that although she would be sorry to see Byron's books go she didn't care about it for herself. Then came the playful and loving letters sent during her journey to the north and on her arrival at Seaham.

It is not easy to reconcile her loving behaviour during the marriage with the unfeeling attitude exhibited towards Byron a few months later. On considering the matter carefully, in combination with accounts of her later history, one is led to the conclusion that Byron was being punished. So was Hobhouse. So were other of his friends.

Looking back at her earlier history, her upbringing, the deep conviction of infallibility, one can surmise that anyone who seriously criticised her or seemed to oppose her will, however unconsciously, merited punishment in her eyes. This is later quite clear in the case of her son-in-law and Ada. It started with Ann Fletcher, who was dismissed and then denied a reference because she refused to be suborned by Lady Noel into giving the evidence Annabella needed.

In 1819 Byron wrote to his wife on her behalf:

> Fletcher has complained to me of your declining to give his wife a character – on account of your 'doubts of her veracity' in some circumstances a short time before she left you. – If your doubts allude to her testimony in your case during the then discussions, *you* must or at least ought to be the best judge how far she spoke the truth or not; – I can only say that she never had directly or indirectly, through me or mine – the slightest inducement to the contrary – nor am I indeed perfectly aware of what her Evidence was ... I presume that you will weigh well your justice before you deprive the woman of the means of obtaining her bread – no one can be more fully aware than I am of the utter inefficacy of any words of mine to you on this or on any other subject, – but I have discharged my duty to Truth in stating the above – and now do yours.[27]
>
> (Byron to Lady Byron, Ravenna, 20 July 1819)

Annabella had built up a picture of herself as the martyred wife, her conduct that of an angel – 'It is my happiness to think that in some degree I live for others.'[28] She could not forgive Byron for calling her 'unforgiving' in the *Separation Poems*. Hobhouse showed only too plainly what he thought of Annabella. He dared to write remonstrating with her and advising her to go back to Byron.

At some stage during the marriage, or possibly not until after the separation, her imagination began to lose all touch with reality on the subject of her husband and his friends. She believed that Byron had committed some crime – probably murder – during his travels with Hobhouse. During the separation crisis she wrote that she had been aware for some time that '... under the guise of friendship Hobhouse was endeavouring Byron's ruin.'[29] Hobhouse, Kinnaird and Frances Hodgson became 'the Piccadilly crew of blackguards'.[30]

One must consider the possibility of some degree of personality disorder here, or at least a breakdown in proper perception of reality (which does not necessarily entail the presence of mental illness).

Obsessed with the breakdown of her marriage and a compulsion to absolve herself of all blame and establish the wrongdoing of everyone else, Lady Byron ignored her own statement to the effect that Augusta was not the cause of the separation. By 1818 she was vehement in declaring that Augusta had tried to engineer the separation for love of money and that she had pretended to reject Byron's love-making during the marriage while secretly giving in to him. By then Annabella had convinced herself that 'there was no secret good' even 'at the bottom of his [Byron's] heart'.[31]

All this was motivated by her pressing need to prove to the world that in leaving her husband she had done right, and to prove to herself that she had never departed from her own standard of perfection.

As time went on, she developed a surprising ability to present extremely dubious actions in a favourable light. After Byron's death she was even able to assert that she had been his only true friend.

The brooding vindictiveness Annabella developed over the years may have been in her stars, but Byron bears a heavy responsibility for the ruin of her life. He should never have offered to marry her to save himself and Augusta. Having married her he should have concentrated on trying to make her happy, as he had promised Lady Melbourne he would do – and especially so during her pregnancy. Though there are strong mitigating circumstances to be taken into account there is no doubt that Byron was the guilty, and Annabella the injured, party in the shipwreck of their marriage.

However, there is one extremely significant letter from Augusta to Hodgson, written during Annabella's visit to London, two months after she had left Byron:

> I never can describe Lady Byron's appearance to you but by comparing it to what I should imagine a being of another world. She is positively reduced to a skeleton, pale as *ashes*, a deep hollow tone of voice and a *calm* in her manner quite supernatural. She received *me* kindly, but that really appeared the only SURVIVING feeling – all else was *death-like* calm. I can never forget it, never.[32]

No one ever described Annabella in such terms during the marriage. She appeared well and even happy, with a face 'round and rosy as a pippin'. It was the leaving Byron forever that changed her to 'a being from another world', not whatever happened during the marriage.

19

BYRON FOR HIS OWN DEFENCE

'I have seen the Blackwood: but I still think it a pity to prosecute ... yet am sure few have been so libelled as myself. – Time sets things to rights.'[1]

Byron tried hard to win Annabella back:

> Dearest Bell – No answer from you yet – perhaps it is as well – but do recollect – that all is at stake – the present – the future – & even the colouring of the past: – The whole of my errors – or what harsher name you choose to give them – you know – but I loved you – & will not part from you without your *own* most express & *expressed* refusal to return to or receive me. – Only say the word – that you are still mine in your heart – and 'Kate! – I will buckler thee against a million' –
>
> ever yours dearest most
>
> B
>
> (To Lady Byron, 5 February 1816)[2]

On the 15th he wrote to her what must, since his memoirs were burned immediately after news of his death arrived in London, be regarded as his answer to the accusations about him circulating in London at the time of the separation – at a moment when, as he later wrote to John Murray, 'my health was declining – my fortune embarrassed – and my mind had been shaken by many kinds of disappointment – while I was yet young and might have reformed what might be wrong in my conduct – and retrieved what was perplexing in my affairs.:[3]

> How far your conduct is reconcileable to your duties & affections as a wife and a mother – must be a question for your own reflection – the

> trial has not been very long – a year – I grant you – of distress – distemper – and misfortune – but these fall chiefly on me – & bitter as the recollection is to me of what I have felt – it is much more so to have made you a partaker in my desolation. – On the charges to be preferred against me – I have *twice* been refused any information by your father & his advisers: – it is now a fortnight – which has been passed in suspense – in humiliation – in obloquy – exposed to the most black and blighting calumnies of every kind: – without even the power of contradicting conjecture & vulgar assertion as to the accusations – because I am denied the knowledge of all or any particulars, from the only quarter that can afford them – in the mean time I hope your ears are gratified by the general rumours. – I have invited your return – it has been refused – I have entreated to see you – it is refused – I have requested to know with what I am charged – it is refused – is this mercy – or justice? – We shall see. – And now – Bell – dearest Bell – whatever may be the event of this calamitous difference – whether you are restored to – or torn from me – I can only say in the truth of affliction – & without hope – motive – or end in again saying what I have lately but vainly repeated – that I love you: – bad or good – mad or rational – miserable or content – I love you – & shall do to the dregs of my memory & existence.[4]

Lady Byron was not unmoved by Byron's repeated appeals. Her maid, Ann, who was now married to Byron's Fletcher, wrote to her husband that Lady Byron was 'rolling on the floor in a paroxysm of grief'. All the same, with a tenacity, inflexibility and obstinacy, extraordinary in so young a woman and so new a bride and mother, she stuck to her guns, thereby destroying her own chance of happiness and depriving Byron of his wife, his child, his lands and his country.

On 12 February 1816 Hobhouse talked to George Byron who told him of Byron's neglect and bad behaviour towards his wife. He persuaded his friend to admit to some of the accusations and soon after this Byron prepared a statement:

> Lady Byron may have had cause to complain of my temper. My manner may have been harsh and rude, perhaps occasionally insulting. My pecuniary distresses and my ill state of body, increased by no very infrequent excesses resorted to for the sake of oblivion, may have made me appear half frantic, but my violence was never directed towards my wife. I made no secret of my hating marriage, but was equally explicit in avowing my love for her. If she can prove that each day I said or did something to give her pain, I can prove that not a day passed without my appearing at least to afford her satisfaction. She may have

seen me sullen, silent or morose but she has often been herself surprised sitting on my knee with her arm around my neck. If I was often neglectful I was more often fond. I may have been indiscreet – perhaps too much so. I poured out all my confessions into her ear, told her of all my failings, never committed a fault without making her my confidante. Even those errors which must have been most offensive to herself, whether in word or deed, were communicated with an unreserve which may have been mistaken for insult but which was not meant for such. The allegations at which she hints, my respect for her character and confidence in her veracity, almost make me think must have some foundation and I am therefore inclined at times to believe that at some periods of my married life I might have been deprived of reason for I solemnly protest that I am unconscious of the commission of any enormity which can have prompted Lady Byron to desert me thus suddenly, thus cruelly.[5]

Later Byron changed his mind about his wife's veracity:

> I have been, and am now, utterly ignorant of what description her allegations … are, and am as little aware for what purpose they have been kept back – unless it was to sanction the most infamous calumnies by silence.[6]

Hobhouse writes:

> A horrid story of Lord Byron having asked his wife when in labour whether the child was dead, having become common, his friends put the question to him and his sister. He answered that he was content to rest the whole merits of his case upon Lady Byron's simple assertion in that respect, 'She will not say so,' he frequently repeated, 'though, God knows, poor thing – it seems now she will say anything: but she would not say that.'[7]

Of some of the rumours, Byron wrote to his wife that they '…imply a treatment which I am incapable of inflicting – and you of imputing to me.'[8] He was incapable of conceiving how far Annabella would go in her efforts to blacken his character in the belief that it was her duty to do so for the sake of her child. In these endeavours she was supported by Brougham.

In 1814 Byron had written of the Westminster election: 'Brougham is a candidate. I fear for poor dear Sherry. Both have talents of the highest order, but the youngster has *yet* a character. We shall see, if he lives to Sherry's age, how he will pass over the red hot ploughshares of public life.'[9] (Brougham had defended Leigh Hunt on the question of his criticisms of the practice of flogging in the army. Byron still knew nothing of Brougham's authorship of the review of *Hours of Idleness* in *The Edinburgh Review*.)

In 1817 he wrote from Venice, 'She is surrounded by people who detest me – Brougham the lawyer – who never forgave me for saying Mrs G[eorg]e Lamb was a damned fool (by the way I did not then know he was in love with her) in 1814 – and for a former savage note in my foolish satire;'[10] – and, 'I was not till lately aware of *all the things* B[rougha]m has *said* and *done* ... he shall answer it – not as Lady B[yron]'s advocate – for to all as such she had a right – but for his conduct and assertions ... he has gone out of his character as an advocate – and been guilty of very improper language.'[11] The lawyer eventually became 'that blackguard Brougham.'

Stories were carefully spread about by Annabella's friends and Byron's enemies – among whom were two of Lady Byron's legal advisers, Dr Lushington as well as Brougham, who did not scruple to reveal scandalous details from the case they were preparing – They succeeded in winning over people who had at first taken a more commonsense view of the matter. In March 1816 the Dowager Duchess of Devonshire wrote from Rome:

> We are all astonished at the separation of Lord and Lady Byron. No one knew the cause when my last letters from England were written but everybody seems to pity her. So do I but I think that if I had married a profligate man knowing him to be so and I had a child and I was not ill treated by him I would not part from him.[12]

Soon after this she heard some of the rumours from London and changed her mind: '...he must be a Caligula. Caro [Mrs George Lamb, who was romantically attached to Henry Brougham] will have told you some of the stories. It is too shocking and her life seems to have been in danger whilst with him from his cruelty.'[13]

Byron himself wrote of the 'black and blighting calumnies' circulating in early 1816: 'My name has been as completely blasted as if it were branded on my forehead.'[14] Almost all the newspapers and magazines joined in the vilification and when a single editor tried to defend him Lady Byron's father called at his office to remonstrate with him.

Byron's reputation was destroyed by accusations of a crime whose nature is still unknown and always will be. Hobhouse's verdict was that Lady Byron's supporters kept silent on the nature of the crime because they knew that conjecture and curiosity would destroy Byron. Hobhouse questioned them about every possible crime a human being could commit and they replied that it was none of these.

The ruin of Byron's reputation for all time was finally achieved by the destruction (with the connivance of Lady Byron) of his *Memoirs*.

The decision of some of Byron's friends, including Hobhouse, Moore and Augusta, to agree to the destruction of his memoirs unread, soon after his death, was more damaging to his reputation than anything perpetrated by his enemies. Witness to this is the conclusion of the *New Monthly Magazine*, October 1824, that the memoirs had not been expurgated because they must obviously be utterly unfit for publication. The opinon of those who had read the memoirs was directly opposed to this conclusion.

Not everyone was prepared to condemn Byron unheard. Many nineteenth century commentators pointed out that his almost universal condemnation was supported by evidence on Lady Byron's side alone. The matter never went to court so the evidence of Byron's friends and supporters never came before the public. A piece published in *Blackwoods* in 1869 sets out the anomalies in Byron's condemnation by the righteous on the sole grounds of Lady Byron's secret testimony:

> She lives with her husband for more than a year without communicating to her own parents or to anyone else any cause for discomfort. She leaves him without the slightest indication of displeasure. She tries to prove him mad; failing that, she declares her determination never to return to him. Through her mother she lays before Dr Lushington a statement of her case. He (no doubt very wisely) advises a reconciliation. Failing with Dr Lushington as she had with Dr Baillie, she seeks a personal interview, and then, in the secrecy of his Chambers under the seal of a confidence stricter than that of the confessional, she imparts to him something which he is bound to assume on her sole assurance to be true – which he was, without investigation or inquiry, to accept as the basis of his opinion – which he was, under no circumstances whatever, without her express authority (an authority which death has now put it out of her power to give) to divulge, upon which she obtains his opinion that a reconciliation was impossible. What that something was we shall probably never know but, save in the case of the victims

who were sent to the guillotine on suspicion of being suspected, we know of no condemnation so monstrous, so revolting to every principle of justice and common sense as that which has been passed on Lord Byron.[15]

The occasion for publication of various defences of Byron in the mid-nineteenth century was the publication by Mrs Harriet Beecher Stowe in 1869 of a *Vindication of Lady Byron* based on confidences made to her by Lady Byron several years earlier. This book demonised Byron and canonised his wife on no evidence but the word of the injured wife. Nineteenth century editors were shocked and pointed to the lack of reliable evidence. They were much less credulous than present day writers, many of whom appear to accept the wildest unfounded allegations by writers on Byron as statements of fact.

Macmillan's magazine deplored the 'blasting of the reputation of one of the three or four most gifted men England has produced for centuries' and went on to ask, 'Did it never occur to Mrs Beecher Stowe that very strong language may be applied to people who, when reputation is at stake, are guilty of inaccuracy upon inaccuracy which moderate attention would prevent. There is an amount of negligence which English law holds tantamount to fraud.'[16]

In *Tinsley's Magazine*, 1869, a reviewer of Harriet Beecher Stowe wrote: 'At worst Lord Byron's detractors can only array probabilities against him and his defenders may comfort themselves that as imposing an array can be made on his side.'[17] In the *Vindication of Lord Byron* Alfred Austin used stronger terms, 'The uncharitable, the inexperienced and the prurient attributed to Lord Byron unutterable things, sensible men of the world came to the conclusion that there was nothing to solve, that what is called incompatibility, an imperfect fidelity on the part of the husband and an exacting jealousy on the part of the wife had conspired to put asunder a couple who ought never to have been joined together.' He adds a comment with which no sensible person could disagree – 'Great compassion was felt for the lady for no one could pretend that Lord Byron was likely to make an exemplary husband.'[18]

This last sentence is the key to a sensible attitude to the controversies about the marriage. Byron himself stated that he had no one to blame but himself. But for what happened during and after the separation some compassion must be spared for Byron.

Some years later Byron commented sadly on the loss of his daughter. In July 1821 he received a letter from a dying girl in England:

> ...[who] could not go out of the world without thanking me for the delight which my poesy for several years etc. ... [She begged] me to *burn* her *letter* which ... I can *not* do, as I look upon such a letter, in such circumstances, as better than a diploma from Gottingen. I had a similar tribute from Norway... These are the things which make one at times believe oneself a poet.[19]

Later in that year he commented:

> What a strange thing is life and man. If I were to present myself at the door of the house where my daughter now is – the door would be shut in my face ... and if I had gone ... to Drontheim, the furthest town in Norway ... I should have been received with open arms into the mansion of strangers and foreigners.[20]

20

THE SEPARATION POEMS

'All words are idle'.

In March 1816 Byron asked Murray to print 50 copies of the 'Farewell Verses' and of the 'Sketch' (on Mrs Clermont) for private distribution. Byron's poem on Mrs Clermont was inspired by the anger Byron felt when he discovered the part she had played during the marriage and separation. Hobhouse, in his account of the separation, relates that Hanson decided to test the strength of Byron's case by trying to induce the servants at 13 Piccadilly Terrace to reveal facts which might be unfavourable to Byron. All of them replied, 'What! Is my Lady not coming back? Is anything the matter?' and Hobhouse emphasises that Mrs Milward, who was the wife of Sir Ralph Noel's butler, an old family retainer of the Milbankes, agreed with the servants that it was all caused by Mrs Clermont. Mrs Milward remained with Byron until his last day in London. Dr le Mann expressed his belief that Mrs Clermont was introduced into Byron's household to watch him. Byron himself wrote of her to Lady Byron:

> Of the woman alluded to – you recollect that she came into this house uninvited by me – that she was neither relative – nor domestic – nor had any business here – except what appears to have been the business of her life. – But she was *your* guest – & as such treated by me with every attention and proper consideration – she was *your* stranger – and I made her our inmate – she came as a guest – she remained as a spy – she departed as an informer – & reappeared as an evidence – if false – she belied – if true – she betrayed me – the worst of treacheries – a 'bread and suet Traitress' she ate & drank and slept and awoke to sting me – the curse of my Soul light upon her and hers forever![1]

This was the frame of mind in which he wrote 'The Sketch', which was much praised as a skilful satire but deplored as a violent attack on a female servant.

FROM A SKETCH

'Honest – honest Iago!
If that thou be'st a devil, I cannot kill thee.'
SHAKESPEARE

BORN in the garret, in the kitchen bred,
Promoted thence to deck her mistress' head;
Next – for some gracious service unexpressed,
And from its wages only to be guessed –
Raised from the toilet to the table, – where
Her wondering betters wait behind her chair.
With eye unmoved, and forehead unabashed,
She dines from off the plate she lately washed.
Quick with the tale, and ready with the lie,
The genial confidante, and general spy –
Who could, ye gods! her next employment guess –
An only infant's earliest governess!
She taught the child to read, and taught so well,
That she herself, by teaching, learned to spell,
An adept next in penmanship she grows,
As many a nameless slander deftly shows:
What she had made the pupil of her art,
None know – but that high Soul secured the heart,
And panted for the truth it could not hear,
With longing breast and undeluded ear.
Foiled was perversion by that youthful mind,
Which Flattery fooled not, Baseness could not blind,
Deceit infect not, nor Contagion soil,
Indulgence weaken, nor Example spoil,
Nor mastered Science tempt her to look down
On humbler talents with a pitying frown,
Nor Genius swell, nor Beauty render vain,
Nor Envy ruffle to retaliate pain,
Nor Fortune change, Pride raise, nor Passion bow,
Nor Virtue teach austerity – till now.
Serenely purest of her sex that live,
But wanting one sweet weakness – to forgive; . . .[2]

It was only when Annabella had left him that Byron was moved to write about her in verse. The verses he composed for her are of a different order from the passionate poems addressed to Augusta:

> Dearest Bell – I send you the first verses that ever I attempted to write upon you, and perhaps the last that I may ever write at all. This at such a moment may look like affectation, but it is not so. The language of all nations nearest to a state of nature is said to be Poetry. I know not how this may be; but this I know.
>
> You know that the lover, the lunatic, and the poet are 'of imagination all compact.' I am afraid you have hitherto seen me only as the two first, but I would fain hope there is nothing in the last to add to any grievances you may have against the former.

FARE thee well! and if for ever,
  Still for ever, fare *thee well:*
Even though unforgiving, never
  'Gainst thee shall my heart rebel.
Would that breast were bared before thee
  Where thy head so oft hath lain,
While that placid sleep came o'er thee
  Which thou ne'er canst know again:
Would that breast, by thee glanced over,
  Every inmost thought could show!
Then, thou would'st at last discover
  'Twas not well to spurn it so.
Though the world for this commend thee –
  Though it smile upon the blow,
Even its praises must offend thee,
  Founded on another's woe:
Though my many faults defaced me,
  Could no other arm be found,
Than the one which once embraced me,
  To inflict a cureless wound?
Yet, oh, yet, thyself deceive not –
  Love may sink by slow decay,
But by sudden wrench, believe not,
  Hearts can thus be torn away;
Still thine own its life retaineth –
  Still must mine – though bleeding – beat;
And the undying thought which paineth
  Is – that we no more may meet.
These are words of deeper sorrow
  Than the wail above the dead;
Both shall live – but every morrow
  Wake us from a widowed bed.

And when thou would'st solace gather –
  When our child's first accents flow –
Wilt thou teach her to say 'Father!'
  Though his care she must forego?
When her little hands shall press thee –
  When her lip to thine is pressed –
Think of him whose prayer shall bless thee –
  Think of him thy love *had* blessed!
Should her lineaments resemble
  Those thou never more may'st see,
Then thy heart will softly tremble
  With a pulse yet true to me.
All my faults perchance thou knowest –
  All my madness – none can know;
All my hopes – where'er thou goest –
  Wither – yet with *thee* they go.
Every feeling hath been shaken;
  Pride – which not a world could bow –
Bows to thee – by thee forsaken,
  Even my soul forsakes me now.
But 'tis done – all words are idle –
  Words from me are vainer still;
But the thoughts we cannot bridle
  Force their way without the will.
Fare thee well! thus disunited –
  Torn from every nearer tie –
Seared in heart – and lone – and blighted –
  More than this I scarce can die.[3]

Jerome Christensen writes of the farewell verses and 'The Sketch': 'Lord Byron never goes to court but his impulse to vindication is acted upon in the greatly wicked poems of farewell.'[4] This is a surprising judgement.

We shall see why Byron reluctantly refrained from going to court. In any case, it seems clear that the rumours and accusations already circulating had so ruined his reputation that he had nothing to lose by an appeal to the courts. In view of the vilification he was experiencing he was entitled to appeal to Lady Byron in the 'Fare Thee Well' poem. The worst he does in these verses is to call her 'unforgiving'. He tries to convince his wife that she should not lightly deprive their child of a father. Since his wife had slept with him and enjoyed full conjugal relations up to the very day on which she set off for Kirkby Mallory on the understanding that he was soon to join her there, it was perfectly reasonable to ask her not to spurn the breast on which she had laid her head. The 'Fare Thee Well' verse may not be a very good poem – it is over-sentimental – but it is not wicked.

Christensen describes what he sees as Byron's motives for writing 'The Sketch'. They seem perfectly reasonable. Indeed, I am not sure that Christensen is not being too charitable in his reading of Byron's motives:

> Byron works himself up into a frenzy of antithesis as he attempts to divide Lady Byron from her bad angel, Mrs Clermont, and to retrieve his influence, if not her love.[5]

As for Mrs Clermont, she was clearly a bad angel to both of them in the build-up to the separation. He was not being wicked in trying to drive a wedge between the mischief-maker and the girl he still regarded as an innocent.

The verses met with a mixed reception. Wordsworth wrote of them that they were disgusting in sentiment and contemptible in execution. Pushkin cannot have agreed with Wordsworth for he placed the first two lines of 'Fare Thee Well' at the beginning of Book Seven of *Eugen Onegin.* Thomas Moore discussed the poem with Byron:

> It was about the middle of April that his two celebrated copies of verses, 'Fare thee well,' and 'A Sketch,' made their appearance in the newspapers: – and while the latter poem was generally and, it must be owned, justly condemned, as a sort of literary assault on an obscure female, whose situation ought to have placed her as much *beneath* his satire as the undignified mode of his attack certainly raised her *above* it, with regard to the other poem, opinions were a good deal more divided. To many it appeared a strain of true conjugal tenderness, a kind of appeal, which no woman with a heart could resist: while by others, on the contrary, it was considered to be a mere showy effusion of sentiment, as difficult for real feeling to have produced as it was easy for fancy and art, and altogether unworthy of the deep interests involved in the subject. To this latter opinion, I confess my own to have, at first, strongly inclined; and suspicious as I could not help regarding the sentiment that could, at such a moment, indulge in such verses, the taste that prompted or sanctioned their publication appeared to me even still more questionable. On reading, however, his own account of all the circumstances in the Memoranda, I found that on both points I had, in common with a large portion of the public, done

> him injustice. He there described, and in a manner whose sincerity there was no doubting the swell of tender recollections under the influence of which, as he sat one night musing in his study, these stanzas were produced – the tears, as he said, falling fast over the paper as he wrote them. Neither, from that account, did it appear to have been from any wish or intention of his own, but through the injudicious zeal of a friend whom he had suffered to take a copy, that the verses met the public eye.[6]

Moore was mistaken. The agent who made sure the poems met the public eye was no friend of Byron. The man was Brougham who persuaded his friend, John Scott, editor of *The Champion*, to publish the 'Fare Thee Well' and 'A Sketch' although Bryon had printed only a limited number of copies intended for private circulation only. Brougham, as one of Lady Byron's legal advisers, dined with her the day before publication '... obtaining her approval of the publication only when it was rather too late for her to interfere if she had wished to.'[7]

The writer (David Erdman of the Carl H. Pforzheimer Library in *Shelley and his Circle*), goes on:

> The well-kept secret of Brougham's connection with *The Champion* had only recently been discovered by biographers of Byron, and it has not been perfectly assimilated, since it conflicts with the traditional attribution of *The Champion's* attack to Tory politics. Journalistic necessity led to the swift and extensive reprinting of both poems in the rest of the London papers, and it is true that, (except for fair treatment in the Tory *Courier*) vituperation accompanies them in the Tory papers and defensive comment in the Whig *Morning Chronicle* and *Sunday News* and in the independent *Examiner.*[8]

The publication of the verses in *The Champion* was accompanied by an editorial piece accusing Byron of using the poems to 'turn the whole current of public reproach and displeasure against his wife' and attacking him violently on the same lines as earlier attacks in *The Champion* on 'The Prince or Poet who plays the ruffian with his wife or the rogue with his neighbours'.[9]

Later the editor of *The Champion* admitted that 'extraordinary means' had been used to induce him to publish the campaign against Byron. Brougham's malice against Byron was not satisfied by these means. He was heard maligning Byron for his deformity at Brook's Club and he told Perry, editor of the *Chronicle* that

Byron had cheated the Duchess of Devonshire out of £500 by failing to pay the rent of 13 Piccadilly Terrace.

Years later Teresa Guiccioli scolded Byron for 'Fare Thee Well' which she told him was not worthy of him.

Not long after leaving England he wrote a poem about his wife which describes the tragic consequences of their parting for both of them, but particularly for her:

LINES ON HEARING THAT LADY BYRON WAS ILL

AND thou wert sad – yet I was not with thee;
  And thou wert sick, and yet I was not near;
Methought that Joy and Health alone could be
  Where I was *not* – and pain and sorrow here!
And is it thus? – it is as I foretold,
  And shall be more so; for the mind recoils
Upon itself, and the wrecked heart lies cold,
  While Heaviness collects the shattered spoils.
It is not in the storm nor in the strife
  We feel benumbed and wish to be no more,
  But in the after-silence on the shore,
When all is lost, except a little life...

Mercy is for the merciful! – if thou
Hast been of such, 'twill be accorded now.
Thy nights are banished from the realms of sleep: –
  Yes! they may flatter thee, but thou shalt feel
  A hollow agony which will not heal,
For thou art pillowed on a curse too deep;
Thou hast sown in my sorrow, and must reap
  The bitter harvest in a woe as real!
I have had many foes, but none like thee;
  For 'gainst the rest myself I could defend,
  And be avenged, or turn them into friend;
But thou in safe implacability
Hadst nought to dread – in thy own weakness shielded,
And in my love, which hath but too much yielded,
  And spared, for thy sake, some I should not spare;
And thus upon the world – trust in thy truth
And the wild fame of my ungoverned youth –
  On things that were not, and on things that are –
Even upon such a basis hast thou built
A monument, whose cement hath been guilt!
  The moral Clytemnestra of thy lord,

And hewed down, with an unsuspected sword,
Fame, peace, and hope – and all the better life
Which, but for this cold treason of thy heart,
Might still have risen from out the grave of strife,
And found a nobler duty than to part.[10]

In 1818 Lady Byron went to Newstead. Byron had never taken her there because he knew that it must be sold and feared she might become attached to the place. The account of the visit in Annabella's Journal shows that Byron's words in 'Lines on Hearing that Lady Byron was Ill' were prophetic.

Annabella describes the hall at Newstead where she saw Byron's fencing sword and single sticks. Nothing seemed to have changed and she felt as if he might have walked in. Before leaving she spent some time gossiping with the housekeeper.

It is remarkable that Judith Milbanke failed to teach her daughter such elementary rules of honourable behaviour at the time as the absolute embargo on discussing with servants the private affairs of their employers. If Byron had known that Lady Byron had gone uninvited to his old home, had allowed one of his former servants to talk about his relationship with Augusta Leigh and to make comments about the amounts he gave to charity, he would probably have said what he had written to Augusta when he discovered that Lady Byron had secretly opened his letter trunks before she left Town: 'Upon such conduct I am utterly at a loss to make a single comment – beyond every expression of astonishment. I am past indignation.'[11]

Some lines from Canto IV of *Childe Harold's Pilgrimage* may refer to Byron's sadness and disillusion over the marriage and the separation:

CXX

Alas! our young affections run to waste,
Or water but the desert; whence arise
But weeds of dark luxuriance, tares of haste,
Rank at the core, though tempting to the eyes,
Flowers whose wild odours breathe but agonies,
And trees whose gums are poison; such the plants
Which spring beneath her steps as Passion flies
O'er the World's wilderness, and vainly pants
For some celestial fruit forbidden to our wants.

CXXI

Oh. Love! no habitant of earth thou art –
An unseen Seraph, we believe in thee,
A faith whose martyrs are the broken heart, –
But never yet hath seen, nor e'er shall see
The naked eye, thy form, as it should be;
The mind hath made thee, as it peopled heaven,
Even with its own desiring phantasy,
And to a thought such shape and image given,
As haunts the unquench'd soul – parched,
wearied, wrung – and riven.

CXXV

Few – none – find what they love or could have loved
Though accident, blind contact, and the strong
Necessity of loving, have removed
Antipathies – but to recur, ere long,
Envenomed with irrevocable wrong;[12]

After Annabella's departure Augusta's presence was necessary for Byron's welfare and Annabella – having invited her to join them at 13 Piccadilly Terrace with Georgiana for an open-ended visit and then repented of it – found herself obliged to ask Augusta to stay on and to send her daily bulletins about Byron's health. This was not easy for Augusta. George Leigh wanted her to come home. Her children needed her. The Duchess of Leeds wrote to her that she must leave at once for the sake of her reputation. These considerations were set aside. Byron needed her and Annabella had asked for her help.

Peter Gunn gives Augusta unstinting praise:

> On the morning Annabella left Piccadilly Terrace for Kirkby, Augusta accompanied by George Byron [who, it will be remembered, had been invited to join the household to help deal with Byron's wild moods] paid a visit to the solicitor, Hanson. That afternoon she began a series of almost daily bulletins that kept Annabella in touch with all that was going on in London. Never once did she falter in her absolute loyalty to both Byron and Annabella. It is in these intimate, truthful, amazingly perceptive and tactful letters, at times revealing her despair, at all times her perfect naturalness and balance – written at intervals of running the household, ordering Byron nourishing meals, seeing that he moderated his drinking and followed his medical regimen, interviewing doctors and solicitors, attending to his correspondence as well as her own, and

> looking after Georgiana – that we see the full measure of the woman, and understand something of the reason why she was Byron's unfailing love.[13]

At first Augusta was influenced by Lady Byron's resentment against Hobhouse who tended to drink heavily with Byron when Augusta was trying to keep him on a healthy and moderate regime. But it was not long before she began to appreciate what a faithful friend he was, and when Byron was at his lowest ebb she wrote poignantly to Hobhouse:

> Do not forsake your most unfortunate friend – if you do he is lost – he has so few *sincere* friends and well judging ones. I can never express what I feel about him, but believe me, I am grateful from my heart for your friendship and friendly forbearance towards his infirmities, of whatever kind they may be. His *mind* makes him the most unhappy of human beings. Let us hope it may not always be so. God bless you. I thank you for all your kindness.[14]

She had always been on the best of terms with Francis Hodgson and often wrote to consult him about Byron's welfare – thus remaining a friend to the group of loyal friends of Byron named 'The Piccadilly crew of blackguards' by Lady Byron.

Before he left England Byron gave Augusta some verses meant only for her eyes:

FROM STANZAS TO AUGUSTA

WHEN all around grew drear and dark,
And reason half withheld her ray –
And Hope but shed a dying spark
Which more misled my lonely way;
In that deep midnight of the mind,
And that internal strife of heart,
When dreading to be deemed too kind,
The weak despair – the cold depart;
When Fortune changed – and Love fled far,
And Hatred's shafts flew thick and fast,
Thou wert the solitary star
Which rose and set not to the last.
Oh! blest be thine unbroken light!
That watched me as a Seraph's eye,
And stood between me and the night,

For ever shining sweetly nigh.
And when the cloud upon us came,
Which strove to blacken o'er thy ray –
Then purer spread its gentle flame
And dashed the darkness all away.[15]

Note

'Parisina' was published during the separation crises and did nothing to calm speculation about Byron's iniquities. Jerome McGann's commentary to the *Complete Poetical Works* explains its application to current affairs at the time of publication:

> Byron used *Parisina* to treat current social and political affairs in a veiled way – Byron habitually used older historical situations – and especially people and events from the Italian Renaissance – to highlight analogous circumstances in the contemporary English and European political scene. *Parisina* exposes the moral conflict involved in the 'justice' of Niccolo III of Ferrara (1393–1441) towards his wife and son. Byron's generic terms for such acts was 'cant'. The crux of the tale hangs on the character of Niccolo whose personal life was notoriously profligate, … Byron probably imagined the work personally in terms of his own life on the one hand and the social world of the Regency on the other, which he saw as badly corrupt though full of a canting morality.[1]

21

LAST DAYS IN LONDON

'I have now been compared to Nero, Apicius, Heliogobalus, Epicurus, Caligula, Henry VIII and the Devil. Were I to be beaten down by the world and its inheritors I would have succumbed long ago.'[1]

After the departure of Annabella and Ada, Augusta wrote almost daily to her 'Dear Sis', keeping her informed about events at Piccadilly Terrace and trying to awaken in her some feeling for Byron's distress, and concern for his illness.

The squint and prominence of the left eye, together with the painful headaches described by Augusta may indicate some type of neurological disease. There is, however, no record of Byron's experiencing double vision at the time and, so far as we know, there was no recurrence of the severe headaches, fits of irritation and intolerable thirst described by Byron himself and Augusta, until many years later. It is possible that the stress caused by the trials of the preceding months, the brandy and laudanum resorted to either for relief or oblivion, together with the severe anxiety caused by the sudden (and, to him, inexplicable) demand for a separation, may have brought on the symptoms described. Byron seems to have been free of them once he decided on action and began planning for his future life abroad – 'There is a world elsewhere.'[2]

In January Augusta wrote to Annabella with wry amusement covering deep concern:

> B returned between 12 and 1 this Mng with Hobhouse – both drunk – sent me and George to bed & call'd for Brandy! Fletcher says H drank none but B. replied to his declarations to that effect 'So much the better

> – there will be more for me' – and drank two glasses – would not take his Calomel & in short so far so bad! One comfort is H looks really dying – God forgive me, I hope he will take him to a better world – but however B. frown'd to such a degree at me to go away that this dear friend (I mean fiend) either was or pretended to be quite shock'd – said he w'd go – & when B pursued me out of the room to apologise for his frowns (when by the bye he tumbled flat on his face up the staircase) H said to George all sorts of *tendresses* of course to be repeated to me – I was *all the Angels* in ye world and fortunate for him I was married! Fletcher has just informed me he left the house door open at 3 o'clock in ye morn'g and 'lucky we had not all our throats cut!'[3]

This letter cannot have pleased Annabella – Augusta usurping her own preferred role of angel. Augusta may have been exaggerating her dislike of Hobhouse in sympathy with Annabella for she soon became convinced of his true worth as a loyal friend both to herself and to her brother. To her dismay Byron continued to dine out and visit the theatre, all his friends rallying round him, anxious about the rumours and puzzled about the abrupt departure of Annabella.

Byron's friends, like George Leigh, completely discounted the suggestion that he had committed incest with Augusta.

It was perhaps with a feeling of relief that Byron continued with his London avocations, business and pleasure, though the rumour that the beautiful actress, Mrs Mardyn, had been his mistress, obliged him to stay away from Drury Lane to protect her reputation. The unfortunate woman had been hissed off the stage though she had met Byron only once and there had been no impropriety between them.

On 20 January he had written to Samuel Rogers about a plan suggested by Sir James Mackintosh. Byron was still refusing to accept payment for his poems and had rejected a cheque for over £1000 from John Murray for *The Siege of Corinth* and *Parisina*. Mackintosh suggested that Byron might donate the money to William Godwin, the philosopher, who was in great financial difficulties. Byron stipulated that the matter should be handled with tact (which was unnecessary since Godwin felt no shame whatsoever about sponging on the young Shelley, or anyone else) and wrote to Rogers, 'I shall feel very glad if it can be of any use to Godwin – only don't let him be plagued – nor think himself obliged and all that – which makes people hate one another.'[4] Murray refused to produce the money for such a purpose, thereby infuriating his most lucrative author who angrily demanded the return of the manuscripts before relenting and allowing them to be published. He wrote of Murray to Leigh Hunt:

> ...he is really a very good fellow – and his faults are merely the leaven of his 'trade' ... I feel sure that he will give your work a fair or a fairer chance in every way than your late publishers.[5]

In February Leigh Hunt's *Rimini* came out with a fulsome and over-familiar dedication to Byron who wrote to him:

> Your prefatory letter to 'Rimini' I accepted as it was meant as a public compliment and a private kindness – I am only sorry that it may perhaps operate against you – as an inducement and with some a pretext – for attack – on the part of the political and personal enemies of both.[6]

He answered a kind letter from Thomas Moore:

> I don't know that in the course of a hair-breadth existence I was ever, at home or abroad, in a situation so completely uprooting of present pleasure, or rational hope for the future, as this same ... But I shall not sink under it ... By the way, however, you must not believe all you hear on the subject; and don't attempt to defend me ... Leigh Hunt's poem is a devilish good one – quaint, here and there, but with the substratum of originality, and with poetry about it, that will stand the test ... I have not the most distant idea what I am going to do myself ... I had, a few weeks ago, some things to say, that would have made you laugh; but they tell me now that I must not laugh.[7]
>
> (To Thomas Moore, 29 February 1816)

There was little to make him laugh in the failure of all attempts to placate Annabella and her parents. He had written to Lord Holland, 'They think to drive me by menacing with legal measures – let them go into court – they shall be met there – After what has been already said – they cannot be more anxious for investigation than myself ...' but he added, 'I can attach no blame to *her*.'[8] (To Lord Holland, 23 February 1816)

He tried to persuade Annabella to consent to an interview but she remained adamant. When he received no immediate reply to Lord Holland's attempt at mediation he wrote, 'I will now not only sign no separation – but agree to none – not even to a verbal permission for Lady Byron's absence.'[9] (To Lord Holland, 2 March 1816)

Annabella decided to offer Byron a bribe of half her inheritance when her mother died and all but £200 a year from the income payable as part of the marriage settlement. Byron saw this offer as the greatest insult he had received from Annabella's family:

> If you or yours conceive that I am actuated by mercenary motives – I appeal to the tenor of my past life in such respects – I appeal to my conduct with regard to settlements previous to our marriage – I appeal to all who know me – or who ever will know –.[10]
>
> (Byron to Lady Byron, 4 March 1816)

In early March Byron and Hobhouse discussed with Hanson the possibility of prosecuting the Milbankes for conspiracy or detainer. But now the situation changed. Annabella and her advisers had threatened legal measures in order to induce Byron to agree to a private arrangement. Once they realised that Byron was prepared to meet them in court they changed tack and accused Byron of cruelty in insisting on dragging Lady Byron through the courts. She wrote to him and reminded him that he had promised to agree to a separation if convinced that she was acting of her own accord and not under the influence of her parents. She went to see Augusta and convinced her that she would never go back to Byron. In consequence of this appeal from Annabella Byron consented in principle to a separation. He suggested turning over the entire income of the marriage settlement to her but stipulated that he would not be bound by any agreement over the Wentworth inheritance but would act justly on the matter when it came in.

Hobhouse had suggested that Byron should demand a disavowal of the rumours by Lady Byron. This was not to be a part of the agreement as it would seem as if it was being demanded in return for the settlement. Much argument ensued over this disavowal and its text, Lady Byron at first declaring that she would never sign it. In the end Annabella herself drafted a disavowal which was torn up when the negotiations fell through. Byron's cousin, Robert Wilmot (husband of the girl who 'walked in beauty like the night') had been chosen to mediate the agreement. It was an unfortunate choice since both he and George Byron were to go over to Lady Byron. After some discussion Wilmot was under the impression that Byron had agreed on a formula for the agreement and took offence when Byron told him he was mistaken. He had agreed it only as a basis for negotiation. The matter came close to causing a duel between the cousins.

Byron now heard that Lady Byron had complained that he was abusing her to his friends. He went to great trouble to produce letters from Lord Holland, Samuel Rogers and others stating that he had never said a word against her in their presence.

Byron's advisers were in disarray, arguing among themselves. In the end Byron agreed to accept legal arbitration over the Wentworth inheritance and the separation papers were finally signed on 21 April. Lady Byron was now asked to reinstate her disavowal and produced a document which avowed that she and her friends had nothing to do with the rumours but carefully refrained from stating that they were untrue.

Byron's friends were so horrified by the general rumours that they had advised him not to come to a private arrangement '... which might compromise his character, by the supposition that he was *afraid* of the disclosures of a public court of law.'[11] By mid-January Caroline Lamb's accusations of incest had been spread abroad. Incest was a shocking, but not a criminal, offence and was a theme prominent in the literature of the day. By the end of February Caroline had added hints of homosexuality to her campaign. This was an even more serious allegation. In 1808 the Earl of Leicester had won his case in court when accused of homosexual acts but the scandal forced him to leave the country. When Byron and Hobhouse were in Greece a military man and the drummer boy with whom he had been discovered *in flagrante delicto* were both executed.

Byron was the victim not only of Caroline Lamb's revelations but of political machinations which built on these accusations. In 1816 John Wilson Croker wrote, 'Party is in England stronger than love, avarice or ambition.'[12] Byron had angered both the Tory and the Whig parties. He had praised Napoleon and was regarded as unpatriotic. His fame and success, together with his support for Whig policies, had alienated the Tories; the allegations against him were alienating the Whigs and everyone else. Now that the scandal had destroyed his reputation his political opponents gathered to bring about his downfall. Enemies like Brougham fanned the flames.

There was little his friends could do. He would neither conform nor apologise. He made no attempt to conceal his contempt for many of the politicians. He kept company openly with the Princess of Wales, who was anathema in both court and government circles. The Princess was delighted with him:

> He was all 'couleur de rose' last evening ... he sat beside me at supper and we were very merry. I always tell him there are two Lord Byrons and when I invite him I say I ask the agreeable Lord, not the disagreeable one. He takes my *plaisanterie* all in good part.[13]

A bond between them may have been their dislike of Brougham, whom she had misguidedly chosen as her advocate against the Prince Regent. She wrote, 'If my head ends up on Temple Bar Brougham will be to blame.'[14]

When Byron went to the House of Lords most of the peers shunned him. Lord Holland kept an open mind but while the rumours circulated and the outcome was uncertain the Hollands felt it prudent to distance themselves from him for the time being, without going to the length of cutting him. Lord Holland did what he could to offer mediation between the parties over the separation.

On 19 March Brougham spoke in the Commons on the repeal of the income tax, which was regarded generally as an iniquitous imposition, acceptable only in time of war and which should have been repealed immediately once the peace was signed. The Whigs won the day with a huge majority and expected to form a new ministry forthwith. (It was said that the roads were blocked with coaches from all over the country bringing petitions against the income tax and the Commons was stuffed to the ceiling with parchment.) The Tory ministry was reeling and in need of whatever help it could get. According to the account of Teresa Guiccioli (written in 1869) '... an influential person, not belonging to the peerage, came to visit him [Byron] and told him that if he wished to see how far the folly of men went, he had only to give orders for having it shown that nothing said against him was true, but that he must change politics and come over to the Tory party.'

David Erdman speculates that this influential Tory might have been Canning, who had joined the 'shaky Liverpool – Castlereagh government' a few days before 19 March. 'The Tories were fighting for dear life ... Canning might well have proposed something to

Byron when the Whigs began to desert him; as for changing the tune of the government papers, Canning was accustomed to use such tactics.' Guiccioli relates that Byron rejected the proposal and was told that '... he must suffer the consequences, which would be heavy, since his [Byron's] colleagues were determined on his ruin, out of party spirit and political hatred.'[15]

The Tories were rescued when Brougham, two days later, made an attack on the Prince Regent in the Commons so intemperate that the Whig majority crumbled away. From being the much-fêted saviour of his party Brougham became the villain of the piece. His disappointment and anger may have put him in a mood to take the extreme measures he initiated in April for destroying Byron's reputation.

Byron was not sick of politics but he *was* sick of this sort of politics. Going abroad would lead him into utterly different political paths.

At the end of March he received a letter from a young woman who was unknown to him, asking for an interview. Claire Clairmont was an eighteen-year-old girl whose step-sister, Mary Godwin, daughter of Godwin and his first wife, Mary Wollstonecraft, had run away with the poet, Shelley. Hoping to catch for herself a more famous poet than her sister, Claire offered herself to Byron, suggesting that they should travel about ten miles outside London and spend the night together. Byron disliked this sort of behaviour intensely but in the end he succumbed. It was a brief distraction from his troubles but he was to regret it. Claire made a point of preaching about the views of her family on the degradation of marriage and the beauty of free love, believing that this would please Byron. She was wrong.

Claire Clairmont sang so beautifully that Shelley wrote a poem about her called 'To Constantia Singing.' These 'Stanzas for Music' were thought to have been addressed to Claire but it is hard to imagine Byron writing in such romantic terms of 'that odd-headed girl'[16]:

STANZAS FOR MUSIC

1

THERE be none of Beauty's daughters
  With a magic like thee;
And like music on the waters
  Is thy sweet voice to me:

When, as if its sound were causing
The charmed Ocean's pausing
The waves lie still and gleaming,
And the lulled winds seem dreaming;

2

And the midnight moon is weaving
  Her bright chain o'er the deep;
Whose breast is gently heaving,
  As an infant's asleep:
So the spirit bows before thee,
To listen and adore thee;
With a full but soft emotion,
Like the swell of Summer's ocean.[17]

He once wrote that he had heard one of Lord Grey's daughters play upon the harp so modestly that she '*looked* music'.[18] Of Claire his opinion was different. She had blatantly pursued him and he gave in reluctantly to her importunities. She wrote to him humbly: 'I shall ever remember the gentleness of your manners and the wild originality of your countenance.'[19] She brought her sister Mary to meet him and hinted that they should all three meet again. She was planning to persuade Mary and Shelley to travel with her to Switzerland, there to await the arrival of Byron when he left England.

To understand why Byron could not tolerate the company of Claire Clairmont it is only necessary to read such entries in her journal as the 'Caricatures for Albé', one of which is described in the entry for 8 November, Florence, 1820:

> Another to be called Lord Byron's receipt for writing pathetic Poetry. He sitting drinking spirits playing with his white mustachios. His mistress the Fornara opposite him Drinking coffee. Fumes coming from her mouth, over which is written garlich; these curling direct themselves towards his English footman who is knocked backward – Lord Byron is writing he says, Imprimis to be a great pathetic poet. 1st Prepare a small colony, then dispatch the mother by worrying and cruelty to her grave afterwards to neglect and ill treat the children – to have as many and as dirty mistresses as can be found: ... from their embraces to catch horrible diseases.[20]

Hobhouse was now a constant visitor at 13 Piccadilly Terrace.

When he felt he was needed he came up from the country to join Scrope Davies in his lodgings. One day he found Augusta in tears, because she must leave for Six Mile Bottom. She had stayed long enough to discredit the rumours and ought to return to her husband and children. Hobhouse promised to move in with Byron if it proved necessary (and he did in fact do so on 13 April). Augusta's return home was delayed by her appointment as lady-in-waiting to the Queen, which necessitated a move into rooms in St James's Palace. This place she never lost and it was assumed that the court discredited the rumours too. The small salary from this appointment and the grace and favour apartments later granted to the Leighs at St James's were to save them from complete financial ruin.

On 8 April Augusta had bravely accompanied Byron and Hobhouse to a party at Lady Jersey's. When they came into the room many of those present left and Mrs George Lamb gave Augusta the cut direct. Byron never forgot the kindness of Lady Jersey and of the heiress, Mercer Elphinstone – with whom he had once had a brief flirtation.

Byron was determined to go abroad as soon as the separation papers were signed. He had been longing for blue skies and seas at intervals ever since his return from Greece. More important, he was still being dunned by creditors and he knew that everything at 13 Piccadilly Terrace would soon be commandeered by the bailiffs. As the time of his departure grew near his friends gathered about him. He himself alternated between light-hearted moments and moods of deep depression. Sir Walter Scott wrote of a happy occasion when they had joined friends for an early dinner at Long's in September 1815: 'I never saw Byron so full of fun, frolic and wit and whim. He was as playful as a kitten. Well, I never saw him again.'[21]

During the years of exile Byron missed Scott. 'Wonderful man! I long to get drunk with him.'[22] He wrote to him from Italy 'The gods be with your dreams'.[23]

Samuel Rogers wrote to Thomas Moore describing Byron in a sadder mood shortly before he left England:

> He goes to Italy in a few days. I see him now as he looked when I was leaving him one day and he cried out after me with a gay face and a melancholy accent 'Moore is coming and you and he will be together and I shall not be with you.' It went to my heart for he loves you dearly.[24]

Byron wrote to Moore from Venice: 'Remember me in your "smiles and wine".'[25]

He was planning for his departure and had ordered a large Napoleonic carriage for the journey. He appointed a young doctor, John Polidori, as his personal physician. John Murray offered this young man a substantial sum for any diary he might keep during his travels with Byron.

On 14 April Byron wrote to Samuel Rogers excusing himself from a planned meeting with Sheridan: 'My sister is now with me and leaves town tomorrow; we shall not meet again for some time, at all events – if ever.'[26] He then wrote to Lady Byron:

> I have just parted from Augusta – almost the last being you had left me to part with – and the only unshattered tie of my existence – wherever I may go – and I am going far – you and I can never meet again – let this content and atone. – If any accident occurs to me – be kind to *her*. – if she is then nothing – to her children. – some time ago – I informed you that with the knowledge that any child of ours was already provided for by other and better means – I had made my will in favour of her and her children – as prior to my marriage: this was not done in prejudice to you for we had not then differed – & even this is useless during your life by the settlements ... she has ever been your friend ... She is gone – I need hardly add that of this request she knows nothing.[27]
>
> (Byron to Lady Byron, Sunday, [14] April 1816)

On 15 April he wrote to Augusta:

> I trust you got home *safe* – and are well – I am sadly without you – but I won't complain ... ever thine – dearest A
>
> Most truly
>
> B
>
> turn over –
>
> P.S. – I can't bear to send you a short letter – & my heart is too full for a long one – don't think me unkind or ungrateful – dearest A – & tell me how is Georgey & *Do* – and you and *tip* – and all the *tips* on four *legs* or *two* – ever and again – and for ever thine
>
> P.P. Clerk of this parish[28]
>
> (Byron to Augusta Leigh, 15 April 1816)

On the 16th he wrote to James Wedderburn Webster, husband of Lady Frances, reminding him of the loan he had made three years earlier. Hearing that his friend was buying lands and tenements he thought he might be able to settle, but added '... if inconvenient to you – I will say no more on the subject.'[29]

On 22 April Byron gave all his papers up to Hobhouse. Mr and Mrs Kinnaird called that night with a cake and two bottles of champagne.

On the 23rd Polidori and Hobhouse set off at 9.30 in the morning in Scrope Davies's chaise, Byron and Scrope in the Napoleonic carriage. 'There was a crowd about the door ... Arrived at Dover by half past 8 – dined at the Ship.'[30]

On the 24th Byron wrote to Hanson from Dover:

> Dear Sir – Denen has distrained on the effects left at the house in Piccadilly Terrace for the half year's rent: ... there is one trunk of wood with papers – letters etc – also some *shoes* ... I could wish redeemed from the wreck – They have seized all the *servants' things*, Fletcher's and his wife's etc – I hope you will see to these poor creatures having *their* property secured – as for *mine* it must be sold ... I sail tonight for Ostend ... I wish you for yourself and family every possible good.[31]
>
> (Byron to John Hanson, Dover, 24 April 1816)

On the same day he sent some news to Augusta for passing on to Lord Carlisle, whose youngest son had been killed at Waterloo:

> I met last night with an old school fellow (Wildman by name) a Waterloo aide de camp of Lord Uxbridge's. He tells me poor Fred Howard was *not* mangled, nor in the hands of the French; he was shot through the body charging a party of infantry and died (*not* on the field) half an hour afterwards at some house not far off, and in no great pain. I thought this might make his friends easier as they had heard he was a sufferer by falling into the enemy's hands.[32]
>
> (Byron to Augusta Leigh, 24 April 1816)

In his last letter to Hanson before departure Byron had reminded him '... to seize an early opportunity of bringing Rochdale and Newstead to the hammer – or private contract.'[33] Wildman was the man who bought Newstead Abbey in 1818.

On the 24th the winds were contrary. That evening they walked to the church to see Churchill's tomb. 'Byron lay down on his grave and gave the man a crown to fresh turf it.'[34]

On the 25 April Hobhouse wrote:

> Up at 8. breakfasted, all on board except the company. The Captain said he could not wait, and B could not get up a moment sooner –

even the serenity of Scrope was perturbed. – however after some bustle out comes Byron and, taking my arm, walked down to the quay ... the bustle kept B in spirits, – but he looked affected when the packet glided off.[35]

Note

During the first summer of his exile Byron wrote a most extraordinary poem about his visit to the grave of Churchill, the eighteenth century satirist. In a note he explained that he is attempting 'a serious imitation in the style of a great poet – its beauties and its defects.'[1] The great poet was Wordsworth.

Byron's attitude to Wordsworth here is somewhat equivocal and one cannot imagine that the older poet regarded the poem as anything other than an insult. David Woodhouse points out some biographical references. The description of Churchill as 'him who blazed/The Comet of a season' could be applied to Byron's own 'sudden change of fortunes.'[2]

CHURCHILL'S GRAVE

A FACT LITERALLY RENDERED

I stood beside the grave of him who blazed
   The Comet of a season, and I saw
The humblest of all sepulchres, and gazed
   With not the less of sorrow and of awe
On that neglected turf and quiet stone,
With name no clearer than the names unknown,
Which lay unread around it; and I asked
   The Gardener of that ground, why it might be
That for this plant strangers his memory tasked,
   Through the thick deaths of half a century;
And thus he answered – 'Well, I do not know
Why frequent travellers turn to pilgrims so;
He died before my day of Sextonship,
   And I had not the digging of this grave.'
And is this all? I thought, – and do we rip
   The veil of Immortality? and crave
I know not what of honour and of light
Through unborn ages, to endure this blight?
So soon, and so successless? As I said,
The Architect of all on which we tread,
For Earth is but a tombstone, did essay
To extricate remembrance from the clay,
Whose minglings might confuse a Newton's thought
   Were it not that all life must end in one,

Of which we are but dreamers; – as he caught
   As 'twere the twilight of a former Sun,
Thus spoke he, – 'I believe the man of whom
You wot, who lies in this selected tomb,
Was a most famous writer in his day,
And therefore travellers stop from out their way
To pay him honour, – and myself whate'er
   Your honour pleases:' – then most pleased I shook
   From out my pocket's avaricious nook
Some certain coins of silver, which as 'twere
Perforce I gave this man, though I could spare
So much but inconveniently; – Ye smile,
I see ye, ye profane ones! all the while,
Because my homely phrase the truth would tell.
You are the fools, not I – for I did dwell
With a deep thought, and with a softened eye,
On that Old Sexton's natural homily,
In which there was Obscurity and Fame, –
The Glory and the Nothing of a Name.[3]

David Woodhouse points out that:

> ... the graveside musings on 'The Glory and Nothing of a Name' (line 42) place more emphasis on the 'Nothing' than the 'Glory', as if Byron were laying his own good name to rest on the eve of his departure from England.[4]

22

POET INTO EXILE

'There is a world beyond Rome'.

When Byron embarked on the Lisbon packet in 1809 he was a comparatively insouciant and unknown young man. He embarked at Dover in 1816 a famous literary figure. Wherever he went he was recognized. Society women dressed up as chambermaids to watch him walk from the Ship Inn at Dover to the quayside. When he reached Switzerland and moved into the Villa Diodati near Geneva, English tourists would spy on him with telescopes from the other side of Lac Léman. The fame was derived from his poetry. Yet most of his finest work was yet to come.

Goethe had already written of him in 1815, 'I have taken cognisance of the English poet Lord Byron who deserves to interest us. His strange nature shines out in his poems which find much favour because of his wild yet controlled talent.'[1] The 'wild yet controlled talent' was to develop though suffering into something much deeper. Michael Cooke writes of '. . . the austere sense of responsibility to be principled and humane in action, to acknowledge without collapse the normal complexities and corruptions of existence, to profit and be honoured by the opportunity of confronting the self and the universe through suffering.'[2]

G. Wilson Knight calls Byron '. . . a great tragic poet directing us to a sense of (1) human magnificence, (2) its inevitable tragedy; and (3) a supervening acceptance.'[3]

These are the aims of the highest philosophy and these were the directions in which the poet was heading as he embarked, 'Once more upon the waters! yet once more!'[4]

It has been suggested that it is only by reading the lives and letters of his astonished contemporaries that you are able to form some estimate of the powers of Byron. A better way to estimate his powers would be to read his poetry. But this remark demonstrates the extraordinary fame of the young man who was now to oblige his readers with a third and fourth canto of *Childe Harold.*

It was as a great poet that he was known in Europe, not, as in England, an object of scandal. But, strongly as he felt at this time that England was not fit for him, in little more than a year he was to write, with affectionate amusement: 'England! with all thy faults I love thee still.'[5]

Working men in England did not join in the general vilification. They even hoped that Byron would return to England and lead a revolution. As late as 1872 Charles Harney, the Chartist, spoke of Byron's poetry as an inspiration, and its influence was already at work soon after he left England:

> He was being toasted, along with Burns and Shelley, at secret Tom Paine dinners around 1820, and his works, like Shelley's, were much reprinted in cheap (mostly pirated) editions. Louis James notes twenty five such editions for working class readers before 1844.[6]

The very reasons which made Byron popular with the poor ensured that he would not be loved by the English Establishment. Sydney Smith describes the hatred felt for a reformer in early nineteenth century England:

> ...he was sure to be assailed with all the Billingsgate of the French Revolution. Jacobin, leveller, atheist, Socinian, incendiary, regicide, were the gentlest of appellations used, and anyone who breathed a syllable against the senseless bigotry of the two Georges, or hinted at the abominable tyranny and persecution against Catholic Ireland, was shunned as unfit for the relations of social life. To say a word against ... the delays of the Court of Chancery, or the cruel punishments of the Game-laws [or, one might add, the death penalty for the framebreakers] or against any abuse which a rich man inflicted and a poor man suffered, was treason against the plutocracy, and was bitterly and steadily resented.[7]

Byron had made himself a target for all this hatred by his outspokenness against all such evils. Some of the English came to regard the poet himself as the embodiment of evil. In February 1822 the Reverend John Styles preached in Holland Chapel, Kensington, describing Byron as 'A denaturalised human being who, having drained the cup of sin to its bitterest dregs, is resolved to show that he is no longer human, even in his frailties, but a cool, unconcerned fiend.'[8]

His European contemporaries were to take a different view.

PROMETHEUS

I

TITAN! to whose immortal eyes
    The sufferings of mortality,
    Seen in their sad reality,
Were not as things that gods despise;
What was thy pity's recompense?
A silent suffering, and intense;
The rock, the vulture, and the chain,
All that the proud can feel of pain,
The agony they do not show,
The suffocating sense of woe,
    Which speaks but in its loneliness,
And then is jealous lest the sky
Should have a listener, nor will sigh
    Until its voice is echoless.

II

Titan! to thee the strife was given
    Between the suffering and the will,
    Which torture where they cannot kill;
And the inexorable Heaven,
And the deaf tyranny of Fate,
The ruling principle of Hate,
Which for its pleasure doth create
The things it may annihilate,
Refused thee even the boon to die:
The wretched gift Eternity
Was thine – and thou hast borne it well.
All that the Thunderer wrung from thee
Was but the menace which flung back
On him the torments of thy rack;
The fate thou didst so well foresee,
But would not to appease him tell;
And in thy Silence was his Sentence,
And in his Soul a vain repentence,
And evil dread so ill dissembled,
That in his hand the lightnings trembled.

III

Thy Godlike crime was to be kind,
   To render with thy precepts less
   The sum of human wretchedness,
And strengthen Man with his own mind;
But baffled as thou wert from high,
Still in thy patient energy,
In the endurance, and repulse
   Of thine impenetrable Spirit,
Which Earth and Heaven could not convulse,
   A mighty lesson we inherit;
Thou art a symbol and a sign
   To Mortals of their fate and force;
Like thee, Man is in part divine,
   A troubled stream from a pure source;
And Man in portions can foresee
His own funereal destiny;
His wretchedness, and his resistance,
And his sad unallied existence:
To which his Spirit may oppose
Itself – and equal to all woes –
   And a firm will, and a deep sense,
Which even in torture can descry
   Its own concentered recompense,
Triumphant where it dares defy,
And making Death a Victory.[9]

APPENDIX

Lady Byron and Harriet Beecher Stowe

The account of her marriage given to Mrs Harriet Beecher Stowe in 1857 produced the melodramatic *Vindication of Lady Byron* published by Mrs Stowe in 1869. The influence of this version is to be found at second or third hand in many modern accounts of the marriage.

Mrs Stowe had met Lady Byron only briefly and had never set eyes on Lord Byron. She knew nothing of the background to the events of the separation and accepted everything Annabella told her. She relates that Byron's debts were paid off by Lady Byron with her own money when they came in – that she had 'thrown a princely fortune at his feet' when she married him and that Byron kept this money when she left him. Lady Byron is even described as having a keener reason than her husband.

Extracts from the *Vindication of Lady Byron*

The result of Byron's intimacy with Miss Milbanke and the enkindling of his nobler feelings was an offer of marriage, which she, though at the time deeply interested in him, declined with many expressions of friendship and interest. In fact, she already loved him, but had that doubt of her power to be to him all that a wife should be which would be likely to arise in a mind so sensitively constituted and so unworldly. They, however, continued a correspondence as friends; on her part, the interest continually increased; on his, the transient rise of better feelings was choked and overgrown by the thorns of base unworthy passions.

From the height at which he might have been happy as the husband of a noble woman, he fell into the depths of a secret adulterous intrigue with a blood relation, so near in consanguinity, that discovery must have been utter ruin and expulsion from civilised society.

From henceforth, this damning guilty secret became the ruling force in his life; holding him with a morbid fascination, yet filling him with remorse and anguish, and insane dread of detection. Two years after his refusal by Miss Milbanke, his various friends, seeing that for some cause he was wretched, pressed marriage upon him...

Her answer was a frank, outspoken avowal of her love for him, giving herself to him heart and hand. The good in Lord Byron was not so utterly obliterated that he could receive such a letter without emotion, or practise such unfairness on a loving, trusting heart without pangs of remorse. He had sent the letter in mere recklessness; he had not seriously expected to be accepted; and the discovery of the treasure of affection which he had secured was like a vision of lost heaven to a soul in hell.

But, nevertheless, in his letters written about the engagement, there are sufficient evidences that his self-love was flattered at the preference accorded him by so superior a woman, and one who had been so much sought. He mentions with an air of complacency that she has employed the last two years in refusing five or six of his acquaintance; that he had no idea she loved him, admitting that it was an old attachment on his part. He dwells on her virtues with a sort of pride of ownership. There is a sort of childish levity about the frankness of these letters, very characteristic of the man who skimmed over the deepest abysses with the lightest jests. Before the world, and to his intimates, he was acting the part of the successful *fiancé*, conscious all the while of his deadly secret that lay cold at the bottom of his heart.

When he went to visit Miss Milbanke's parents as her accepted lover, she was struck with his manner and appearance: she saw him moody and gloomy, evidently wrestling with dark and desperate thoughts, and anything but what a happy and accepted lover should be. She sought an interview with him alone, and told him that she had observed that he was not happy in the engagement; and magnanimously added, that, if on review, he found he had been mistaken in the nature of his feelings, she would immediately release him, and they should remain only friends.

Overcome with the conflict of his feelings, Lord Byron fainted away. Miss Milbanke was convinced that his heart must really be deeply involved in an attachment with reference to which he showed such strength of emotion, and she spoke no more of a dissolution of the engagement...

The moment the carriage-doors were shut upon the bridegroom and the bride, the paroxysm of remorse and despair – unrepentant remorse and angry despair – broke forth upon her gentle head:

'You might have saved me from this, madam! You had all in your own power when I offered myself to you first. Then you might have made me what you pleased; but now you will find that you have married a *devil*!'

In Miss Martineau's Sketches, recently published, is an account of the termination of this wedding-journey, which brought them to one of Lady Byron's ancestral country seats, where they were to spend the honeymoon.

Miss Martineau says, –

'At the altar she did not know that she was a sacrifice; but before sunset of that winter day she knew it, if a judgment may be formed from her face, and attitude of despair, when she alighted from the carriage on the afternoon of her marriage-day. It was not the traces of tears which won the sympathy of the old butler who stood at the open door. The bridegroom jumped out of the carriage and walked away. The bride alighted, and came up the steps alone, with a countenance and frame agonized and listless with evident horror and despair. The old servant longed to offer his arm to the young, lonely creature, as an assurance of sympathy and protection. From this shock she certainly rallied, and soon. The pecuniary difficulties of her new home were exactly what a devoted spirit like hers was fitted to encounter. Her husband bore testimony, after the catastrophe, that a brighter being, a more sympathising and agreeable companion, never blessed any man's home. When he afterwards called her cold and mathematical, and over-pious, and so forth, it was when public opinion had gone against him, and when he had discovered that her fidelity and mercy, her silence and magnanimity, might be relied on, so that he was at full liberty to make his part good, as far as she was concerned.

'Silent she was even to her own parents, whose feelings she magnanimously spared. She did not act rashly in leaving him, though she had been most rash in marrying him.'

Not all at once did the full knowledge of the dreadful reality into which she had entered come upon the young wife. She knew vaguely, from the wild avowals of the first hours of their marriage, that there was a dreadful secret of guilt; that Byron's soul was torn with agonies of remorse, and that he had no love to give to her in return for a love which was ready to do and dare all for him. Yet bravely she addressed herself to the task of soothing and pleasing and calming the man whom she had taken 'for better or for worse.'

Young and gifted; with a peculiar air of refined and spiritual beauty; graceful in every movement; possessed of exquisite taste; a perfect companion to his mind in all the higher walks of literary culture; and with that infinite pliability to all his varying, capricious moods which true love alone can give; bearing in her hand a princely fortune, which, with a woman's uncalculating generosity, was thrown at his feet, – there is no wonder that she might feel for a while as if she could enter the lists with the very Devil himself, and fight with a woman's weapons for the heart of her husband....

But there came an hour of revelation, – an hour when, in a manner which left no kind of room for doubt, Lady Byron saw the full depth of the abyss of infamy which her marriage was expected to cover, and understood that she was expected to be the cloak and the accomplice of this infamy.

Many women would have been utterly crushed by such a disclosure; some would have fled from him immediately, and exposed and denounced the crime. Lady Byron did neither. When all the hope of womanhood died out of her heart, there arose within her, stronger, purer, and brighter, that immortal kind of love such as God feels for the sinner, – the love of which Jesus spoke, and which holds the one wanderer of more account than the ninety and nine that went not astray. She would neither leave her husband nor betray him, nor yet would she for one moment justify his sin; and hence came two years [*sic*] of convulsive struggle, in which sometimes, for a while, the good angel seemed to gain ground, and then the evil one returned with sevenfold vehemence.

Lord Byron argued his case with himself and with her with all the sophistries of his powerful mind. He repudiated Christianity as authority; asserted the right of every human being to follow out what he called 'the impulse of nature.' Subsequently he introduced into one of his dramas the reasoning by which he justified himself in incest...

Lady Byron, though slight and almost infantine in her bodily presence, had the soul, not only of an angelic woman, but of a strong reasoning man. It was the writer's lot to know her at a period when she formed the personal acquaintance of many of the very first minds of England; but, among all with whom this experience brought her in connection, there was none who impressed her so strongly as Lady Byron. There was an almost supernatural power of moral divination, a grasp of the very highest and most comprehensive things, that made her lightest opinions singularly impressive. No doubt, this result was wrought out in a great degree from the anguish and conflict of these two years, when, with no one to help or counsel her but Almighty God, she wrestled and struggled with fiends of darkness for the redemption of her husband's soul....

During this time, such was the disordered and desperate state of his worldly affairs, that there were ten executions for debt levied on their family establishment; and it was Lady Byron's fortune each time which settled the account.

Toward the last, she and her husband saw less and less of each other; and he came more and more decidedly under evil influences, and seemed to acquire a sort of hatred of her.

She followed him through all his sophistical reasonings with a keener reason. She besought and implored, in the name of his better nature, and by all the glorious things that he was capable of being and doing; and she had just power enough to convulse and shake and agonise, but not power enough to subdue....

When Lord Byron found that he had to do with one who would not yield, who knew him fully, who could not be blinded and could not be deceived, he determined to rid himself of her altogether.

It was when the state of affairs between herself and her husband seemed darkest and most hopeless, that the only child of this union was born. Lord Byron's treatment of his wife during the sensitive period that preceded the birth of this child, and during her confinement, was marked by paroxysms of unmanly brutality, for which the only possible charity on her part was the supposition of insanity. Moore sheds a significant light on this period, by telling us that, about this time, Byron was often drunk, day after day, with Sheridan. There had been insanity in the family; and this was the plea which Lady Byron's love put in for him. She regarded him as, if not insane, at least so nearly approaching the boundaries of insanity as to be a subject of forbearance and tender pity; and she loved him with that love resembling a mother's, which good wives often feel when they have lost all faith in their husband's principles, and all hopes of their affections. Still, she was in heart and soul his best friend; true to him with a truth which he himself could not shake.

In the verses addressed to his daughter, Lord Byron speaks of her as

> 'The child of love, though born in bitterness,
> And nurtured in convulsion.'

A day or two after the birth of this child, Lord Byron came suddenly into Lady Byron's room and told her that her mother was dead. It was an utter falsehood; but it was only one of the many nameless injuries and cruelties by which he expressed his hatred of her. A short time after her confinement, she was informed by him, in a note, that, as soon as she was able to travel, she must go; that he could not and would not longer have her about him; and, when her child was only five weeks old, he carried this threat of expulsion into effect....

The re-action of society against him at the time of the separation from his wife was something which he had not expected, and for which, it appears, he was entirely unprepared. It broke up the guilty intrigue and drove him from England. He had not courage to meet or endure it. The world, to be sure, was very far from suspecting what the truth was: but the time was setting against him with such vehemence as to make him tremble every hour lest the whole should be known; and henceforth, it became a warfare of desperation to make his story good, no matter at whose expense.

This account is deeply false and was judged to be so by many of the nineteenth century commentators cited in the chapter on Byron's Defence.

ABBREVIATIONS

PWB	*The Poetical Works of Lord Byron*, revised Edn, ed. Ernest Hartley Coleridge (London: John Murray, 1903), 7 volumes.
BLJ	*Byron's Letters and Journals*, ed. Leslie A. Marchand (London: John Murray, 1973–97), 13 volumes.
Prothero	*The Works of Lord Byron: The Letters and Journals*, ed. Rowland E. Prothero (London: John Murray, 1898), 6 volumes.
Moore	Moore, Thomas, *Letters and Journals of Lord Byron with Notices of His Life* (London: John Murray, 1832; repr. 1932).
Recollections Lord Broughton	*Recollections of a Long Life: Lord Broughton*, ed. Lady Dorchester [his daughter] (London: John Murray, 1902), 2 volumes.

REFERENCES

Epigraph

1. Byron's Letter to John Murray Esqre, 1821. Prothero Vol. V, p. 559.
2. *Byron the Poet* by M.K. Joseph, Victor Gollancz, London 1964, pp. 93–4. Reproduced by kind permission of the Orion Publishing Group.
3. *Byron the Erotic Liberal* by Jonathan David Gross, Rowman and Littlefield, 2001, p. 8. By kind permission of Rowman and Littlefield.

Introduction

1. *The Byron Journal* 2003, 'Byron in Our Time', by John Clubbe
2. *Gorky Park* by Martin Cruz Smith, William Collins, London, 1981
3. BLJ Vol. 9, p. 11

Preface

1. *Byron: Romantic Paradox* by William J. Calvert, Chapel Hill, The University of North Carolina Press, 1935, p. 67

Scotland

1. PWB Vol. VI, p. 405
2. Ibid., p. 405
3. BLJ Vol. 7, p. 212
4. BLJ Vol. 8, p. 73
5. BLJ Vol. 7, p. 204
6. Moore, p. 7
7. PWB Vol. VI, p. 382

8. BLJ Vol. 1, p. 136
9. Moore, p. 46
10. PWB Vol. VI, p. 51
11. Moore, p. 9
12. Moore, p. 9 n.1
13. Moore, p. 8
14. BLJ Vol. 2, p. 89
15. Ibid., p. 136
16. PWB Vol. VI, p. 401

Notes

1. *The Byron Journal*, 1989, 'The Temptations of a Biographer' by William St Clair
2. *Byron and Thomas Moore, A Literary Friendship* by Jeffery Vail, Johns Hopkins University Press, Baltimore & London, 2001, p. 81

Newstead Abbey

1. PWB Vol. VI, p. 498
2. Moore, p. 5
3. Ibid., p. 7
4. Ibid., p. 10
5. Ibid., p. 10
6. BLJ Vol. 1, p. 39
7. Moore, p. 23
8. PWB Vol. 1, p. 95
9. BLJ Vol. 9, p. 40

Harrow

1. BLJ Vol. 1, p. 42
2. Moore, p. 19
3. *The Byron Journal 1989*, 'Byron's Harrow' by C.J. Tyerman
4. BLJ Vol. 1, p. 42
5. 'Byron's Harrow', op. cit.
6. Moore, p. 19
7. 'Byron's Harrow', op. cit.
8. *Abbotsford and Newstead Abbey* by Washington Irving, George Bell & Sons, London, 1878, p. 88
9. Ibid., p. 89
10. BLJ Vol. 1, p. 46/7
11. Ibid., p. 43

12. Ibid., p. 43
13. BLJ Vol. 1, p. 54
14. *The Making of the Poets: Byron and Shelley in Their Time* by Ian Gilmour, Chatto and Windus, London, 2002, p. 88 (copyright © 2002 by Ian Gilmour)
15. PWB Vol. 1, pp 128/129
16. BLJ Vol. 7, p. 117
17. BLJ Vol. 10, p. 68
18. *Lord Byron at Harrow School, Speaking Out, Talking Back, Acting Up, Bowing Out* by Paul Elledge, Johns Hopkins University Press, Baltimore and London, 2000, p. 137
19. *Lord Byron's Strength: Romantic Writing and Commercial Society* by Jerome Christensen, Johns Hopkins University Press, Baltimore and London, 1993, p. 54
20. BLJ Vol. 1, p. 44
21. BLJ Vol. 10, p. 208
22. BLJ Vol. 1, p. 46
23. Ibid., p. 52
24. Ibid., p. 44
25. Ibid., p. 52
26. Ibid., p. 56
27. Ibid., p. 59
28. Ibid., p. 61
29. Ibid., p. 55
30. Ibid., p. 66
31. 'Byron's Harrow', op. cit.
32. Ibid.
33. PWB Vol. 1, p. 87
34. BLJ Vol. 1, p. 49
35. BLJ Vol. 3, p. 242
36. *The Wit and Wisdom of the Rev. Sydney Smith*, Longman's Green And Co., London, 1869, p. 2
37. BLJ Vol. 1, p. 53
38. PWB Vol. 1, p. 91 n.
39. PWB Vol. 1, p. 96
40. *Lord Byron: The Complete Miscellaneous Prose*, edited by Andrew Nicholson, Oxford University Press, 1991, p. 6

Southwell and Cambridge

1. BLJ Vol. 1, p. 95
2. Prothero Vol. 1, p. 110
3. Ibid., p. 109 n.
4. BLJ Vol. 1, p. 80

5. Ibid., p. 81
6. BLJ Vol. 1, p. 89
7. *Lord Byron at Harrow School*, op. cit., pp. 136/7
8. BLJ Vol. 1, p. 113
9. BLJ Vol. 3, p. 44
10. BLJ Vol. 2, p. 47
11. BLJ Vol. 1, pp. 117/18
12. BLJ Vol. 8, p. 24
13. *Byron and Shakespeare* by G. Wilson Knight, Barnes & Noble Inc, New York, 1966, p. 28
14. *Lord Byron's Strength*, op. cit., p. 61
15. PWB Vol. 111, p. 33 'To Thyrza'
16. *Lord Byron at Harrow School*, op. cit., p. 204
17. *Byron the Erotic Liberal* by Jonathan David Gross, Rowman and Littlefield, Lanham, Boulder, New York, Oxford, 2001, p. 3
18. BLJ Vol. 1, p. 123
19. Ibid., p. 124
20. PWB Vol. 1, pp. 213/216
21. BLJ Vol. 1, pp. 130/131
22. Ibid., p. 105

Notes

1. *Byron and the Limits of Fiction*, edited by Bernard Beatty and Vincent Newey, Liverpool University Press, 1988, 'Lyric Presence in Byron from the Tales to *Don Juan*' by Brian Nellist, p. 44
2. *The Blind Man Traces the Circle. On the Patterns and Philosophy of Byron's Poetry* by Michael G. Cooke, Princeton University Press, Princeton, 1969, pp. 11/12/13

The Newly Published Poet

1. PWB Vol. 1, p. 300
2. BLJ Vol. 7, p. 50
3. *The Spirit of the Age or Contemporary Portraits* by William Hazlitt, Oxford University Press, 1935, p. 187 (first published 1825)
4. *The Letters of Sydney Smith*, edited by Nowell C. Smith, Oxford at the Clarendon Press, 1953, Vol. 1, p. 152
5. *The Antiquarian Review and Magazine*, December 1807
6. *The Monthly Monitor*, January 1808
7. BLJ Vol. 1, p. 26
8. Ibid., p. 162
9. *The Eclectic Review*, February 1808
10. Prothero, Vol. 1, p. 183 n.1

11. Moore, p. 80
12. PWB Vol. 1, p. 341
13. Ibid., p. 320
14. Ibid., p. 328
15. Ibid., p. 315
16. Ibid., p. 338
17. Ibid., p. 335
18. Ibid., p. 352
19. Ibid., p. 354
20. Moore, p. 81
21. BLJ Vol. 3, p. 224
22. BLJ Vol. 4, p. 68
23. Ibid., p. 74
24. *Spirit of the Age*, op. cit., p. 100
25. PWB Vol. VII, p. 46

Return to Newstead

1. PWB Vol. 1, p. 124
2. BLJ Vol. 1, p. 135
3. Ibid., p. 158
4. Ibid., p. 127
5. PWB Vol. 1, p. 263
6. Prothero Vol. 1, p. 154 n.
7. *Byron the Erotic Liberal*, op. cit., p. 10
8. BLJ Vol. 8, p. 146
9. *Abbotsford and Newstead*, op. cit., p. 78
10. *Recollections Lord Broughton*, op. cit., Vol. II, p. 231
11. BLJ Vol. 1, p. 174
12. Ibid., p. 176
13. *A Publisher and his Friends, Memoir and Correspondence of the late John Murray*, Samuel Smiles, John Murray, London, 1891, Vol. 1, pp. 353/354

The Pilgrimage

1. BLJ Vol. 4, p. 152
2. BLJ Vol. 1, p. 203
3. Ibid., p. 206
4. BLJ Vol. 2, p. 259
5. *The Making of the Poets*, op. cit., p. 179
6. BLJ Vol. 1, p. 207
7. *Byron the Erotic Liberal*, op. cit., p. 137

8. BLJ Vol. 1, p. 208
9. Ibid., p. 210
10. Ibid., pp. 215/216
11. Ibid., pp. 219/222
12. PWB Vol. II, p. 118
13. Moore, p. 84
14. BLJ Vol. 2, p. 243
15. PWB Vol. II, pp. XXI/XXIV
16. BLJ Vol. 1, p. 225
17. Ibid., pp. 226/229
18. Prothero Vol. 1, p. 269 n.
19. BLJ Vol. 1, p. 234
20. Ibid., p. 237/239
21. BLJ Vol. 4, p. 152
22. BLJ Vol. 1, p. 256
23. BLJ Vol. 2, p. 8
24. Ibid., p. 28
25. BLJ Vol. 1, p. 241
26. PWB Vol. II, p. 121
27. Ibid., p. 18
28. BLJ Vol. 2, p. 49
29. PWB Vol. III, p. 15
30. BLJ Vol. 2, p. 35
31. *Byron and Goethe: Analysis of a Passion* by E.M. Butler, Bowes and Bowes, London, 1956, p. 40
32. Ibid., p. 14
33. BLJ Vol. 2, p. 29
34. Ibid., p. 31
35. BLJ Vol. 2, p. 46
36. BLJ Vol. 1, p. 232
37. Ibid., p. 243
38. BLJ Vol. 2, p. 25
39. Ibid., p. 34
40. Ibid., p. 57
41. Ibid., p. 66
42. Ibid., p. 51
43. Ibid., p. 68
44. Ibid., p. 81
45. *Byron the Erotic Liberal*, op. cit., pp. 133/134
46. BLJ Vol. 2, p. 93
47. Ibid., p. 68

Note

1. BLJ Vol. 4, p. 152

The Maiden Speech

1. *The Making of the Poets*, op. cit., p. 261
2. BLJ Vol. 2, p. 86
3. Ibid., p. 159
4. John Mortimer's Introduction to *Bright Darkness* by Anne Fleming, Nottingham Court Press, London, 1984
5. BLJ Vol. 2, p. 165
6. Prothero Vol. II, p. 430
7. John Mortimer, op. cit.
8. Prothero Vol. II, p. 428
9. BLJ Vol. 9, p. 16
10. Ibid., p. 17
11. PWB Vol. VII, pp. 13/14
12. *The Spirit of the Age*, Hazlitt, op. cit., p. 185
13. BLJ Vol. 2, p. 91
14. BLJ Vol. 3, p. 55
15. *The Spirit of the Age*, op. cit., p. 236
16. BLJ Vol. 9, p. 30
17. Ibid., p. 20
18. PWB Vol. IV, p. 557
19. Prothero, Vol. II, p. 432
20. Ibid., p. 435
21. Ibid., p. 400
22. Ibid., p. 441
23. Ibid., p. 441

Childe Harold's Pilgrimage

1. *Edinburgh Review*, May, 1812
2. *John Bull's Letter to Lord Byron* by J.G. Lockhart, edited by Alan Lang, University of Oklahoma Press, 1947, p. 93
3. PWB Vol. 1, pp. 380/381
4. BLJ Vol. 2, p. 91
5. Ibid., p. 75
6. Ibid., pp. 90/91
7. Ibid., p. 92
8. *The Spirit of the Age*, op. cit., p. 96
9. *The London Magazine*, January, 1821
10. PWB Vol. II, p. 151
11. Ibid., pp. 49/50
12. *Lord Byron's Strength*, op. cit., p. 71
13. PWB Vol. II, pp. 48/49
14. Ibid., p. 39

15. Ibid., p. 77
16. *Letters of Sydney Smith*, op. cit., p. 150
17. PWB Vol. II, pp. 109/110
18. Ibid., p. 191 (Byron's note)
19. *Journey through Albania*, Hobhouse, Vol. I, p. 347
20. BLJ Vol. 2, p. 66 n.6
21. PWB Vol. II, p. 26
22. Ibid., pp. 155/157
23. Ibid., p. 131
24. Ibid., pp. 126/127
25. Ibid., p. 159
26. Prothero Vol. II, p. 130 n.
27. PWB Vol. II, pp. 103/105

Notes

1. *Byron the Poet* by M.K. Joseph, Victor Gollancz, a division of the Orion Publishing Group, London, 1964, p. 27
2. PWB Vol. II, pp. 115–6
3. BLJ Vol. 4, p. 167
4. *The Letters of William and Dorothy Wordsworth, Vol. III, The Middle Years*, edited by Ernest de Selincourt, Oxford at the Clarendon Press, 1970, p. 579
5. *The Byron Journal*, 2003, 'Byron and Wordsworth' by Philip Shaw
6. *Fiery Dust, Byron's Poetical Development* by Jerome J. McGann, University of Chicago Press, Chicago and London, 1968, p. 65. © 1968 by the University of Chicago. All rights reserved.
7. BLJ Vol. 3, p. 58
8. *Lord Elgin and the Marbles* by William St Clair, Oxford University Press, 1967, paperback edition 1983, p. 194 n.

Whig Ladies

1. PWB Vol. VI, p. 560
2. *The Reminiscences and Recollections of Captain Gronow*, Bodley Head, London, 1964, p. 114
3. *A Regency Chapter* by E. Colburn Mayne, Macmillan and Co., London, 1939, p. 238
4. *Letters of Harriet, Countess Granville*, edited by F. Leweson Gower, Longmans Green & Co, London, 1894, Vol. 1, p. 151
5. Ibid., p. 222
6. Ibid., pp. 15/16
7. Ibid., p. 16
8. Ibid., p. 87

9. Ibid., p. 21
10. Ibid., p. 17
11. Ibid., p. 199
12. Ibid., p. 169
13. Ibid., p. 192
14. Prothero Vol. II, p. 120
15. PWB Vol. VI, p. 473
16. *Byron's 'Corbeau Blanc' The Life and Letters of Lady Melbourne*, edited by Jonathan David Gross, Rice University Press, 1997, pp. 54, 3, 33, 35, 349
17. *The Young Melbourne* by David Cecil, Constable, London, 1939, p. 215
18. *Byron's 'Corbeau Blanc'*, op. cit., p. 26
19. BLJ Vol. 3, p. 240
20. PWB Vol. VI, p. 560
21. *Letters of Harriet Countess Granville*, op. cit., Vol. 1, p. 79
22. *The Spirit of the Age*, op. cit., pp. 253, 258
23. Moore, p. 163
24. Ward on Brougham
25. Letters of Countess Granville, op. cit., p. 200
26. Lord Holland's Rhyme
27. Gronow, op. cit., p. 43
28. *Studies in Literature* by Sir Arthur Quiller-Couch, Cambridge University Press, 1943, p. 12
29. PWB Vol. V, pp. 569/570
30. BLJ Vol. 3, p. 70
31. BLJ Vol. 9, p. 23
32. Gronow, op. cit., p. 255
33. *The Young Melbourne*, op. cit., p. 152
34. *Byron the Poet*, op. cit., p. 176
35. BLJ Vol. 6, p. 237
36. BLJ Vol. 2, p. 170
37. Ibid., p. 177
38. Ibid., p. 203
39. Ibid., p. 188
40. Ibid., p. 200
41. Ibid., p. 209
42. Ibid., p. 195
43. *Journal of the Conversations of Lord Byron during a Residence with His Lordship in Pisa in the Years 1821 and 1822* by Thomas Medwin, Galignani, Paris, 1824, Vol. 1, p. 32
44. PWB Vol. III, pp. 59/60
45. BLJ Vol. 2, p. 239
46. PWB Vol. II, pp. 12/13
47. BLJ Vol. 3, p. 36
48. BLJ Vol. 2, p. 198

49. Ibid., p. 242
50. PWB Vol. VII, p. 15
51. BLJ Vol. 3, p. 65

Love and Friendship

1. BLJ Vol. 3, p. 215
2. Ibid., p. 7
3. BLJ Vol. 4, p. 19
4. *Maria Edgeworth and her Circle, In the Days of Buonaparte and Bourbon* by Constance Hill, The Bodley Head, London, MCMX, pp. 128/129
5. BLJ Vol. 3, p. 244
6. Prothero Vol. 11, p. 384
7. *The Life and Letters of Anne Isabella, Lady Noel Byron*, Constable, London, 1929, p. 213
8. BLJ Vol. 3, p. 209
9. Ibid., p. 45
10. Ibid., p. 50
11. Ibid., p. 213
12. Ibid., p. 68
13. Ibid., p.87
14. *Life and Letters of Lady Byron*, op. cit., p. 165
15. BLJ Vol. 3, p. 72
16. *The Letters of Sydney Smith*, op. cit., Vol. 1, p. 238
17. BLJ Vol. 3, p. 76
18. Ibid., p. 77
19. *Journal of the Conversations of Lord Byron Noted During a Residence with His Lordship at Pisa in the years 1821 and 1822* by Thomas Medwin, A. and W. Galignani, Paris, 1824, Vol. 1, p. 33
20. BLJ Vol. 2, p. 243
21. BLJ Vol. 3, p. 120
22. Ibid., p. 124/125
23. Ibid., p. 128
24. Ibid., p. 135
25. Ibid., p. 135
26. Ibid., pp. 137/38
27. Ibid., p. 143
28. Ibid., pp. 146/147
29. Ibid., p. 151
30. Ibid., p. 155
31. PWB Vol. III, pp. 410/411
32. Moore, op. cit., p. 159
33. BLJ Vol. 3, p. 247
34. Moore, op. cit., p. 229, n.1

35. Ibid., op. cit., p. 74
36. BLJ Vol. 3, p. 109
37. Moore, op. cit., pp. 180/81
38. PWB Vol. III, pp. 435/436
39. BLJ Vol. 3, p. 173
40. Ibid., pp. 207/8
41. BLJ Vol. 9, p. 15
42. PWB Vol. IV, p. 73
43. BLJ Vol. 3, p. 233
44. BLJ Vol. 6, pp. 47/48
45. BLJ Vol. 3, p. 229
46. Ibid., p. 206
47. Ibid., p. 218
48. BLJ Vol. 4, p. 171

Byron, Moore and the Oriental Tales

1. PWB Vol. III, p. 137
2. Ibid., p. 73
3. Ibid., p. 225
4. Ibid., p. 90
5. *Lord Byron's Strength*, op. cit., p. 99
6. PWB Vol. III, pp. 88/89
7. BLJ Vol. 3, p. 141
8. BLJ Vol. 3, p. 230
9. BLJ Vol. 4, p. 28
10. *The Edinburgh Review*, July, 1813
11. *The British Review*, No. IX, pp. 132/35
12. *The Satirist*, July, 1813
13. *Painter of Passion. The Journal of Eugene Delacroix*, Phaidon Press Ltd for the Folio Society, London, 1995, p. 35
14. *The Spirit of the Age*, op. cit., p. 98
15. *The Critical Review*, 1814
16. *The Edinburgh Review*, April, 1814
17. *The British Critic*, March 1814
18. *A Publisher and his Friends*, op. cit., p. 357
19. BLJ Vol. 4, p. 77
20. Ibid., p. 77
21. *The Literary Relationship of Lord Byron and Thomas Moore*, Johns Hopkins University Press, Baltimore and London 2001, p. 194
22. BLJ Vol. 3, p. 245
23. *Letters of Countess Granville*, op. cit., 24 September, 1817
24. BLJ Vol. 2, p. 243
25. PWB Vol. III, pp. 234/5

26. Ibid., p. 270
27. BLJ Vol. 2, p. 181
28. BLJ Vol. 3, p. 208
29. The 'Opening Lines to Lara' do not appear in the early Coleridge edition of the Poetical Works. In my copy of Volume VII I found a newspaper cutting of this version of the lines printed in a letter to the Editor deploring their omission.
30. PWB Vol. III, p. 336
31. *The Literary Relationship of Lord Byron and Thomas Moore*, op. cit., p. 193
32. PWB Vol. VII, p. 46
33. *The Literary Relationship of Lord Byron and Thomas Moore*, op. cit., pp. 101/102

Notes

1. *Byron and the Dynamics of Metaphor* by W. Paul Elledge, Vanderbilt University Press, Nashville, Tennessee, 1968, p. 16
2. Ibid., p. 17, n.13
3. *Fiery Dust*, op. cit., p. 162
4. Ibid., p. 145
5. *Byron the Poet*, op. cit., p. 55
6. *Mapping Male Sexuality in Nineteenth Century England*, edited by Jay Losey and William D. Brewer, Associated University Presses, London 2000, p. 70
7. PWB Vol. III, pp. 91–2

Shock Tactics

1. Moore, p. 158
2. Prothero Vol. II, p. 429
3. BLJ Vol. 2, p. 260
4. BLJ Vol. 8, p. 27
5. Prothero Vol. II, p. 445
6. PWB Vol. VI, p. 478
7. *The Creevey Papers* by Thomas Creevey, edited by John Gore, BT Batsford Ltd, 1963, p. 51
8. Ibid., p. 28
9. Ibid., p. 90
10. PWB Vol. III, pp. 45/46
11. BLJ Vol. 4, p. 51
12. PWB Vol. IV, p. 548
13. BLJ Vol. 4, p. 53
14. BLJ Vol. 3, pp. 256/257
15. PWB Vol. III, pp. 305, 309, 314

16. BLJ Vol. 4, p. 298
17. *The Romantic Movement in English Poetry* by Arthur Symons, Constable, London, 1909, p. 256
18. *Letters of Sydney Smith*, op. cit., p. 244
19. *Wellington – The Years of the Sword* by Elizabeth Longford, Weidenfeld and Nicolson, a division of the Orion Publishing Group, London, 1969. One-volume edition, 1922, p. 225
20. *Byron the Erotic Liberal*, op. cit., p. 9
21. Ibid., p. 6
22. *A History of Western Philosophy* by Bertrand Russell, Routledge, London, 2000 (first published 1946), p. 718
23. *The Last Days of Lord Byron* by William Parry, Galignani, Paris, 1826, p. 7
24. BLJ Vol. 9, p. 41
25. BLJ Vol. 7, p. 80
26. *The Making of the English Working Class* by E.P. Thompson, Victor Gollancz, London, 1963, p. 5
27. BLJ Vol. 6, p. 226
28. BLJ Vol. 9, p. 49

Hebrew Melodies

1. PWB Vol. IV, pp. 95/96
2. *The Byron Journal*, 1999, 'Byron and Nathan: A Musical Collaboration' by Graham Pont
3. *Fugitive Pieces and Reminiscences of Lord Byron* by Isaac Nathan, London, 1829, p. 2
4. *The Byron Journal*, 1999, op. cit.
5. *Fugitive Pieces*, op. cit., p. viii
6. PWB Vol. III, pp. 381/382
7. Ibid., pp. 404/405
8. *Byron and Shakespeare* by G. Wilson Knight, Barnes and Noble, New York, 1960, pp. 14/15
9. PWB Vol. III, pp. 382/383
10. *The Blind Man Traces the Circle*, op. cit., p. 29 n.30
11. *Fugitive Pieces*, op. cit., p. 24
12. *The Literary Relationship of Lord Byron and Thomas Moore*, op. cit., p. 92
13. *Byron and Shakespeare*, op. cit., p. 207

Augusta

1. BLJ Vol. 10, p. 208
2. *Augusta Leigh* by Michael and Melissa Bakewell, Chatto and Windus, London, 2002, p. 77

3. BLJ Vol. 4, p. 112
4. *Augusta Leigh*, op. cit., p. 17
5. Ibid., p. 77
6. Ibid., p. 103
7. BLJ Vol. 4, p. 19
8. BLJ Vol. 4, p. 21
9. Diary of Frances Lady Shelley, edited by Richard Edgcumbe, John Murray, London, 1912, pp. 52/53
10. BLJ Vol. 4, p. 11
11. Ibid., p. 25
12. Ibid., p. 25
13. BLJ Vol. 4, p. 36
14. Ibid., p. 44
15. Ibid., p. 46
16. Ibid., p. 40
17. Ibid., p. 110
18. BLJ Vol. 4, p. 50
19. *Byron and Shakespeare*, op. cit., p. 235
20. PWB Vol. III, p. 413
21. BLJ Vol. 4, p. 49
22. Ibid., p. 54
23. Ibid., p. 69
24. Ibid., p. 56
25. Ibid., p. 57
26. Ibid., p. 84
27. Ibid., p. 53
28. Ibid., p. 61
29. Ibid., p. 75
30. Ibid., p. 101
31. Ibid., p. 101
32. Ibid., p. 130

Notes

1. BLJ Vol. 4, p. 104
2. *Augusta Leigh*, op. cit., p. 111

Childe Harold and the Princess of Parallelograms

1. BLJ Vol. 3, p. 227
2. BLJ Vol. 5, p. 44
3. BLJ Vol. 3, p. 108
4. Lady Tamworth to Judith Milbanke, 4 February 1812, *Lovelace Papers*, reproduced by kind permission of Pollinger Ltd and the Earl of Lytton

5. *The Life and Letters of Anne Isabella, Lady Noel Byron*, op. cit., p. 222
6. BLJ Vol. 3, p. 108
7. BLJ Vol. 2, p. 251
8. Ibid., p. 195
9. Ibid., p. 208
10. Annabella to Lady Gosford, 8 October 1814, *Lovelace Papers*, reproduced by kind permission of Pollinger Ltd and the Earl of Lytton
11. BLJ Vol. 4, p. 228
12. Ibid., p. 264
13. Ibid., p. 231
14. Ibid., p. 232
15. Ibid., p. 234
16. *Conversations of Lord Byron with the Countess of Blessington*, R. Bentley, for H. Colburn, 1834
17. BLJ Vol. 2, p. 195
18. *Recollections Lord Broughton*, op. cit., Vol. 1, p. 191
19. Ibid., p. 196

The Marriage

1. BLJ Vol. 4, p. 175
2. *Life and Letters of Lady Byron*, op. cit., p. 23
3. *Correspondence and Table Talk, Benjamin Robert Haydon*, Chatto and Windus, London, 1876, Vol. 2, p. 370

Annabella Through the Looking Glass

All letters from the *Lovelace Papers* are reproduced by kind permission of Pollinger Ltd and Lord Lytton.

1. *Annabella to her mother, March 1816, Lovelace Papers*
2. *Recollections Lord Broughton,* op. cit., Vol. II, p. 283
3. *Literary Life of William Harness*, L'Estrange, London, 1871, pp. 35/36
4. *Recollections Lord Broughton*, op. cit., Vol. II, p. 283
5. Ibid., pp. 278/279
6. Ibid., p. 265
7. Statement given by Annabella to her mother, 18 January 1816, *Lovelace Papers*
8. Ibid.
9. *Recollections Lord Broughton*, op. cit., Vol. II, pp. 252/253
10. BLJ Vol. 5, p. 63
11. *Recollections Lord Broughton*, op. cit., p. 260
12. Ibid., Vol. II, p. 207

13. *Lord Byron's Strength*, op. cit., p. 84
14. Annabella to her mother 21 January 1816, *Lovelace Papers*
15. BLJ Supplementary Volume, p. 79
16. Annabella to her mother, 4 March 1816, *Lovelace Papers*
17. Medwin, op. cit., p. 35
18. *Vindication of Lord Byron*, Alfred Austin, Chapman and Hall, London, 1869, p. 6
19. *Newcastle Daily Chronicle*, 1869
20. *Vindication of Lord Byron*, op. cit., pp. 5/6
21. *Recollections Lord Broughton*, Vol. 11, p. 280
22. Ibid., p. 280
23. Ibid., p. 263
24. PWB Vol. IV, pp. 64/65
25. *Pall Mall Gazette*, 1869, letter from John Robertson
26. Annabella to her mother, 8 September 1815, *Lovelace Papers*
27. BLJ Vol. 6, p. 181
28. Annabella to Byron, 3 September 1813, *Lovelace Papers*
29. Annabella to Dr Lushington, 11 February 1816, *Lovelace Papers*
30. Annabella to her mother, 12 April 1816, *Lovelace Papers*
31. Annabella to F.W. Robertson, 12 April 1851, *Lovelace Papers*
32. Augusta to Hodgson, 5 March 1816, *Lovelace Papers*

Byron for his Own Defence

1. BLJ Supplementary Volume, p. 79
2. BLJ Vol. 5, p. 22
3. BLJ Vol. 6, p. 150
4. BLJ Vol. 5, p. 26/27
5. *Recollections Lord Broughton* Vol. 11, p. 277
6. BLJ Vol. 5, p. 256
7. *Recollections Lord Broughton* Vol. 11, p. 280
8. BLJ Vol. 5, p. 25
9. BLJ Vol. 3, p. 249
10. BLJ Vol. 5, p. 223
11. Ibid., p. 225
12. *The Two Duchesses* by Vere Foster (Blackie 1898)
13. Ibid., p. 413
14. BLJ Vol. 5, p. 54
15. *Blackwoods*, July, 1869
16. *Macmillan's Magazine*, September, 1869
17. *Tinsley's Magazine*, October, 1869
18. *Vindication of Lord Byron*, op. cit., p. 13
19. BLJ Vol. 8, p. 146
20. BLJ Vol. 9, p. 24

The Separation Poems

1. BLJ Vol. 5, p. 63
2. PWB Vol. III, pp. 540/542
3. Ibid., pp. 537/540
4. *Lord Byron's Strength*, op. cit., p. 87
5. Ibid., p. 152
6. Moore, p. 302
7. *Shelley and his Circle*, 'Byron's Last Days in England' by David Erdman, Pforzheimer Library, New York, p. 645
8. Ibid., p. 645
9. *The Champion*, April 1816
10. PWB Vol. III, p. 63/65
11. BLJ Vol. 5, p. 93
12. PWB Vol. II, pp. 419/421
13. *My Dearest Augusta* by Peter Gunn, Bodley Head, London, 1969, p. 149
14. *Recollections Lord Broughton*, Vol. II, Appendix p. 352. The Hon. Mrs Leigh to Mr Hobhouse, St James's Palace, 3 January, 1816
15. PWB Vol. III, pp. 544/546

Notes

1. *The Complete Poetical Works of Byron* edited by Jerome J. McGann, Oxford University Press, 1980, Vol. III, Commentary, p. 490.

Last Days in London

1. BLJ Vol. 5, p. 29
2. Ibid., p. 25
3. Augusta Leigh to Lady Byron, 18 January 1860, *The Lovelace Papers*, reproduced by kind permission of Pollinger Ltd & the Earl of Lytton
4. BLJ Vol. 5, p. 16
5. Ibid., p. 19
6. Ibid., p. 32
7. Ibid., pp. 35/36
8. Ibid., p. 31
9. Ibid., p. 39
10. Ibid., p. 40
11. *Recollections Lord Broughton*, Vol. II, p. 269
12. *Croker Papers 1805–57*, J. Wilson Croker, edited by Bernard Pool, Batsford, London, 1967, p. 56
13. *Diary of a Lady in Waiting* by Lady Charlotte Bury, edited by A. Francis Steuart, London, John Lane, The Bodley Head, MCMVIII Vol. II, p. 280

14. Ibid.
15. *Shelley and his Circle*, Carl H. Pforzheimer Library 'Byron's Last Days in England' by David Erdman, p. 643
16. BLJ Vol. 5, p. 162
17. PWB Vol. III, pp. 17/19
18. BLJ Vol. 8, p. 28
19. *The Clairmont Correspondence* Vol. 1, 1808–1834, edited by Marion Kingston Stocking, Johns Hopkins University Press, Baltimore and London, 1995, p. 36
20. *Journals of Claire Clairmont*, edited by Marion Kingston Stocking, Harvard University Press, Cambridge, Massachusetts, 1968, Vol. 1, p. 183
21. The Journal of Sir Walter Scott, edited by W.E.K. Anderson, Canongate, 1988, p. 53
22. BLJ Vol. 8, p. 13
23. BLJ Vol. 9, p. 87
24. *The Literary Relationship of Lord Byron and Thomas Moore*, op. cit., pp. 101/102
25. BLJ Vol. II, p. 85
26. BLJ Vol. 5, p. 67
27. Ibid., p. 66
28. Ibid., p. 67
29. Ibid., p. 68
30. *Recollections Lord Broughton*, Vol. II, p. 334
31. BLJ Vol. 5, p. 70
32. BLJ Vol. 4, p. 302
33. BLJ Vol. 5, p. 70
34. *Recollections Lord Broughton*, Vol. 1, p. 335
35. Ibid., Vol. 1, pp. 335/336

Notes

1. PWB Vol. IV, pp. 46, 47
2. *The Byron Journal*, 1998, '"Churchill's Grave": A Line of Separation' by David Woodhouse
3. PWB Vol. IV, pp. 45, 48
4. *The Byron Journal*, 1998, op. cit.

Poet into Exile

1. *Byron and Goethe. Analysis of a Passion* by E.M. Butler, Bowes and Bowes, London, 1956, p. 14
2. *The Blind Man Traces the Circle*, op. cit., p. 182
3. *Byron and Shakespeare*, op. cit., p. 15
4. PWB Vol. II, p. 216

5. PWB Vol. IV, p. 174
6. *Nottingham Byron Lecture*, 1969, Professor Philip Collins. By kind permission of Professor Collins
7. *The Wit and Wisdom of Sydney Smith*, op. cit., p. 2
8. 'Lord Byron's Works Viewed in Connection with Christianity and the Obligations of Social Life'. A sermon preached in Holland Chapel, Kennington by the Revd. John Styles. Prothero Vol. VI, p. 9
9. PWB Vol. IV, pp. 48/51

BIBLIOGRAPHY

Byron: Works

The Works of Lord Byron: The Letters and Journals, Ed. Rowland E. Prothero (London: John Murray, 1898), 6 volumes

The Poetical Works of Lord Byron, revised Edn., Ed. Ernest Hartley Coleridge (London: John Murray, 1903), 7 volumes

Byron's Letters and Journals, Ed. Leslie A. Marchand (London: John Murray, 1973–97), 13 volumes

Lord Byron, The Complete Poetical Works, Ed. Jerome J. McGann (Oxford: Clarendon Press, 1980–93), 7 volumes

Lord Byron, The Complete Miscellaneous Prose, Ed. Andrew Nicholson (Oxford: Clarendon Press, 1991)

Byron, Life

Nathan, Isaac, *Fugitive Pieces and Reminiscences of Lord Byron* (London: Whittaker, Treacher & Co., 1829)

Moore, Thomas, *Letters and Journals of Lord Byron with Notices of His Life* (London: John Murray, 1832; repr. 1932)

Conversations of Lord Byron with the Countess of Blessington (London: Richard Bentley for Henry Colburn, 1834)

Austin, Alfred, *The Vindication of Lord Byron* (London: Chapman & Hall, 1869)

Guiccioli, Teresa, *My Recollections of Lord Byron* (London: Richard Bentley, 1869), 2 volumes

Stowe, Harriet Beecher, *The Vindication of Lady Byron* (London: 1869)

Irving, Washington, *Abbotsford and Newstead* (London: George Bell & Sons, 1878)

To Lord Byron. Feminine Profiles, Ed. George Parton and Peter Quennell (London: John Murray, 1939)

Origo, Iris, *The Last Attachment* (London: Jonathan Cape & John Murray, 1949)
His Very Self and Voice. Collected Conversations of Lord Byron, Ed. Ernest J. Lovell Jr (New York: Macmillan Co., 1954)
Marchand, Leslie A., *Byron: A Biography* (New York: Knopf, 1957), 3 volumes
Moore, Doris Langley, *The Late Lord Byron* (London: John Murray, 1961)
Moore, Doris Langley, *Lord Byron. Accounts Rendered* (London: John Murray, 1974)
Chapman, John S., *Byron and the Honourable Augusta Leigh* (New Haven & London: Yale University Press, 1975)
Marchand, Leslie A., *Byron: A Portrait* (London: John Murray, 1971)
Crompton, Louis, *Byron and Greek Love* (London: Faber and Faber, 1985)
Foot, Michael, *The Politics of Paradise. A Vindication of Byron* (London: Collins, 1988)
Elledge, W. Paul, *Lord Byron at Harrow School, Speaking Out, Talking Back, Acting Up, Bowing Out* (Baltimore & London: Johns Hopkins University Press, 1993)
Beckett, John, with Aley, Sheila, *Byron and Newstead: The Aristocrat and the Abbey* (Newark: University of Delaware Press, & London: Associated University Presses, 2001)
Gilmour, Ian, *The Making of the Poets: Byron and Shelley in their Time* (London: Chatto & Windus, 2002)
Guiccioli, Teresa, *Vie de Lord Byron en Italie*, Trans. Michael Rees as *Lord Byron's Life in Italy*, Ed. Peter Cochran (Newark: University of Delaware Press, 2005)

Byron in Greece

Gamba, Pietro, *A Narrative of Lord Byron's Last Journey to Greece* (Paris: A. & W. Galignani, 1825)
Parry, William, *The Last Days of Lord Byron* (Paris: A. & W. Galignani, 1826)
Kennedy, James, *Conversations on Religion with Lord Byron and Others Held in Cephalonia* (London: John Murray, 1830)
Finlay, George, *History of the Greek Revolution* (London: Zeno Publishers, 1971) [A reprint of vols. VI & VII of the author's *History of Greece* (Edinburgh: W. Blackwood, 1851).]
St Clair, William, *That Greece Might Still Be Free. The Philhellenes in the War of Independence* (London & New York: Oxford University Press, 1972)
Minta, Stephen, *On a Voiceless Shore: Byron in Greece* (New York: Harold Holt & Co., 1998)
Brewer, David, *The Flame of Freedom: The Greek War of Independence 1821–33*, (London: John Murray, 2001)

Letters

Letters of Harriet, Countess Granville, Ed. F. Leweson-Gower (London: Longmans, Green & Co., 1894)

Letters of Sydney Smith, Ed. Nowell C. Smith (Oxford: Clarendon Press, 1953)

Journals of Claire Clairmont, Ed. Marion Kingston Stocking (Cambridge, Massachusetts: Harvard University Press, 1968)

Letters of Percy Bysshe Shelley, Vol. II, Ed. F.L. Jones (Oxford: Clarendon Press, 1964)

Letters of William and Dorothy Wordsworth, Vol. III, The Middle Years, Ed. Ernest de Selincourt (Oxford: Clarendon Press, 1970)

Byron's Bulldog. Letters of John Cam Hobhouse to Lord Byron, Ed. Peter W. Graham (Columbus: Ohio State University Press, 1984)

Byron's Corbeau Blanc: The Life and Letters of Lady Melbourne, Ed. Jonathan David Gross (Houston, Texas: Rice University Press, 1997)

Clairmont Correspondence, Vol. I, 1808–1834, Ed. Marion Kingston Stocking (Baltimore & London: Johns Hopkins University Press, 1995)

Biographies

Anderson, W.E.K., Ed., *The Journal of Sir Walter Scott* (Canongate, 1988)

Smiles, Samuel, *A Publisher and his Friends: A Memoir and Correspondence of the late John Murray* (London: John Murray, 1891), 2 volumes

The Two Duchesses: Georgiana, Duchess of Devonshire, Elizabeth, Duchess of Devonshire. Family correspondence, 1777–1859, Ed. Vere Foster (London: Blackie & Son, 1898)

Recollections of a Long Life. Lord Broughton, Ed. Lady Dorchester [his daughter] (London: John Murray, 1902), 2 volumes

Mayne, Ethel Colburn, *The Life and Letters of Anne Isabella, Lady Noel Byron* (London: Constable, 1929)

Sadleir, Michael, *Blessington-D'Orsay: A Biography of Marguerite, Countess of Blessington and Alfred Count d'Orsay, A Masquerade* (London: Constable, 1933)

Cecil, David, *The Young Melbourne* (London: Constable, 1939)

Lady Bessborough and Her Family Circle, Ed. the Earl of Bessborough, in collaboration with A. Aspinall (London: John Murray, 1940)

Butler, E.M., *Byron and Goethe: The Analysis of a Passion* (London: Bowes & Bowes, 1956)

Herold, Christopher J., *Mistress to an Age: Madame de Staël* (London: Hamish Hamilton, 1959)

Elwin, Malcolm, *Lord Byron's Wife* (London: Macdonald, 1962)

Gunn, Peter, *My Dearest Augusta* (London: The Bodley Head, 1968)

Reid, Loren H., *Charles James Fox: A Man for the People* (London & Harlow: Longmans, 1969)
Holmes, Richard, *Shelley: The Pursuit* (London: Weidenfeld & Nicolson, 1974)
Burnett, T.A.J., *The Rise and Fall of a Regency Dandy: The Life and Times of Scrope Berdmore Davies* (London: John Murray, 1981)
Hinde, Wendy, *Castlereagh* (London: Collins, 1981)
Boyes, Megan, *Queen of a Fantastic Realm* [A Biography of Mary Ann Chaworth, 1785–1832] (Derby: M. Boyes, 1986)
Boyes, Megan, *Love Without Wings: the story of the unique relationship between Elizabeth Bridget Pigot of Southwell and the young poet, Lord Byron* (Derby: M. Boyes, 1988)
Holmes, Richard, *Coleridge: Early Visions* (London: Hodder & Stoughton, 1989)
St Clair, William, *The Godwins and the Shelleys: The Biography of a Family* (London: Faber & Faber, 1989)
Boyes, Megan, *My Amiable Mama: The Biography of Mrs Catherine Byron, the mother of the poet George Gordon, 6th Lord Byron* (Derby: M. Boyes, 1991)
Storey, Mark, *Robert Southey: A Life* (Oxford: Oxford University Press, 1997)
Foreman, Amanda, *Georgiana, Duchess of Devonshire* (London: HarperCollins, 1998)
Holmes, Richard, *Coleridge: Darker Reflections* (London: HarperCollins, 1998)
Bakewell, Michael and Melissa, *Augusta Leigh* (London: Chatto & Windus, 2000)
Normington, Susan, *Lady Caroline Lamb* (London: House of Stratus, 2001)
Douglas, Paul, *Lady Caroline Lamb* (Basingstoke: Palgrave Macmillan, 2004)
Hill, Constance, *Maria Edgeworth and Her Circle in the Days of Buonapate and Bourbon* (London: The Bodley Head, 1910)

Literary Background

Hazlitt, William, *The Spirit of the Age: or, Contemporary Portraits* (London: Henry Colburn, 1825) [also in 'The World's Classics' series, Oxford University Press, 1935]
Symons, Arthur, *The Romantic Movement in English Poetry* (London: Constable, 1909)
Quiller-Couch, Sir Arthur, *Studies in Literature, Second Series* (Cambridge: Cambridge University Press, 1943)
Praz, Mario, *The Romantic Agony*, 2nd Edn, Trans. Angus Davidson (London: Oxford University Press, 1951)
Byron: The Critical Heritage, Ed. Andrew Rutherford (London: Routledge & Kegan Paul, 1970)

Redpath, Theodore, *The Young Romantics and Critical Opinion, 1807–1824* (London: Harrap, 1973)
English Romantic Poets: Modern Essays in Criticism, 2nd Edn, Ed. M.H. Abrams (London: Oxford University Press, 1975)
Christiansen, Rupert, *Romantic Affinities: Portraits from an Age, 1780–1830* (London: The Bodley Head, 1988)
Schock, Peter A., *Romantic Satanism: Myth and the Historical Moment in Blake, Shelley and Byron* (Basingstoke: Palgrave Macmillan, 2003)
Cavaliero, Roderick, *Italia Romantica: English Romantics and Italian Freedom* (London & New York: I.B. Tauris, 2005)

Political and Social Background

Haydon, Benjamin Robert, *Correspondence and Table Talk* (London: Chatto & Windus, 1876)
In Whig Society: 1775–1818 ... the hitherto unpublished correspondence of Elizabeth, Viscountess Melbourne, and Emily Lamb, Countess Cowper, afterwards Viscountess Palmerston, compiled Mabell, Countess Airlie (London: Hodder & Stoughton, 1921)
Mayne, Ethel Colburn, *A Regency Chapter: Lady Bessborough and her Friendships* (London: Macmillan & Co., 1939)
The Mind of Napoleon: A Selection from his Written and Spoken Words, Ed. & trans. J. Christopher Herold (New York: Columbia University Press, 1955)
Briggs, Asa, *The Age of Improvement* (London: Longman, 1959)
Nicolson, Harold, *The Congress of Vienna* (London: Methuen, 1961)
The Creevey Papers, Revised Edn, Ed. John Gore (London: Batsford, 1963)
Gronow, R.H., *The Reminiscences and Recollections of Captain Gronow*, abridged, John Raymond (London: The Bodley Head, 1964)
Ayling, S.E., *The Georgian Century: 1714–1837* (London: Harrap, 1966)
The Croker Papers, 1808–1857, new & abridged Edn, Ed. Bernard Pool (London: Batsford, 1967)
Longford, Elizabeth, *Wellington, Vol. I: The Years of the Sword* (London: Weidenfeld & Nicolson, 1969)
Mitchell, L.G., *Charles James Fox and the Disintegration of the Whig Party, 1782–1794* (London: Oxford University Press, 1971)
Wardroper, John, *Kings, Lords and Wicked Libellers: Satire and Protest, 1760–1837* (London: John Murray, 1973)
Emsley, Clive, *British Society and the French Wars, 1793–1815* (London: Macmillan, 1979)
Gash, Norman, *Aristocracy and People, Britain 1815–1865* (London: Edward Arnold, 1979)
Butler, Marilyn, *Romantics, Rebels and Reactionaries: English Literature and its Background, 1760–1830* (Oxford: Oxford University Press, 1981)

Byron's Political and Cultural Influence in Nineteenth Century Europe: A Symposium, Ed. Paul Graham Trueblood (London: Macmillan, 1981)
Christie, Ian, *Wars and Revolutions: Britain 1760–1815* (London: Edward Arnold, 1982)
Porter, Roy, *English Society in the Eighteenth Century* (London: Allen Lane, 1982)
Mapping Male Sexuality: Nineteenth Century England, Ed. Jay Losey and William D. Brewer (London: Associated University Presses, 2000)

Miscellaneous

Blessington, Marguerite, Countess of, *The Idler in Italy* (London: Henry Colburn, 1839–40), 3 volumes
Russell, Bertrand, *History of Western Philosophy* (London: George Allen & Unwin, 1946)
Thompson, E.P., *The Making of the English Working Class* (London: Victor Gollancz, 1963)
Fermor, Patrick Leigh, *Roumeli: Travels in Northern Greece* (London: John Murray, 1966)
Anderson, William, *Dante the Maker* (London: Routledge & Kegan Paul, 1980)
Howell, Margaret J., *Byron Tonight: A Poet's Plays on the Nineteenth Century Stage* (Windlesham, Surrey: Springwood Books, 1982)
The Journal of Eugene Delacroix, 3rd Edn, Selected and Ed. Hubert Wellington, Trans. Lucy Norton (London: Phaidon Press, 1995)
Mapping Lives: The Uses of Biography, Ed. Peter France and William St Clair [British Academy Centenary Monograph] (Oxford: Oxford University Press, 2002)
Cheeke, Stephen, *Byron and Place: History, Translation, Nostalgia* (Basingstoke: Palgrave Macmillan, 2003)
St Clair, William, *The Reading Nation in the Romantic Period* (Cambridge: Cambridge University Press, 2004)
Liberty and Poetic Licence: New Essays on Byron, Ed. Bernard Beatty and Charles Robinson (Liverpool: Liverpool University Press, 2005)
Beevers, Robert, *The Byronic Image: The Poet Portrayed* (Abingdon: Olivia Press, 2005)

Criticism

Trueblood, Paul G., *The Flowering of Byron's Genius: Studies in Byron's Don Juan* (New York: Russell & Russell, 1962)
Chew, Samuel C., *The Dramas of Lord Byron: A Critical Study* (New York: Russell & Russell, 1964)

Joseph, Michael K., *Byron the Poet* (London: Victor Gollancz, 1964)
Knight, G. Wilson, *Byron and Shakespeare* (New York: Barnes & Noble, 1966)
Elledge, W. Paul, *Byron and the Dynamics of Metaphor* (Nashville: Vanderbilt University Press, 1968)
McGann, Jerome J., *Fiery Dust: Byron's Poetic Development* (Chicago & London: University of Chicago Press, 1968)
Cooke, Michael G., *The Blind Man Traces the Circle: On the Patterns and Philosophy of Byron's Poetry* (Princeton, New Jersey: Princeton University Press, 1969)
McGann, Jerome J., *Don Juan in Context* (London: John Murray, 1976)
Vassallo, Peter, *Byron: The Italian Literary Influence* (London: Macmillan, 1984)
Beatty, Bernard, *Byron's Don Juan* (Totowa, New Jersey: Barnes & Noble, 1985)
Byron and the Limits of Fiction, Ed. Bernard Beatty and Vincent Newey [Liverpool English Texts and Studies] (Liverpool: Liverpool University Press, 1988)
Christensen, Jerome, *Lord Byron's Strength: Romantic Writing and Commercial Society* (Baltimore & London: Johns Hopkins University Press, 1988)
Graham, Peter W., *Don Juan and Regency England* (Charlottesville: University of Virginia Press, 1990)
Barton, Anne, *Byron's Don Juan* (Cambridge: Cambridge University Press, 1992)
Donelan, Charles, *Romanticism and Male Fantasy in Byron's Don Juan: A Marketable Vice* (Basingstoke: Palgrave Macmillan, 2000)
Gross, Jonathan David, *Byron the Erotic Liberal* (New York & Oxford: Rowman & Littlefield, 2001)
Stabler, Jane, *Byron, Poetics and History* [Cambridge Studies in Romanticism] (Cambridge, England & New York: Cambridge University Press, 2002)
Vail, Jeffery, *The Literary Relationship of Lord Byron and Thomas Moore* (Baltimore and London: Johns Hopkins University Press, 2001)

From: *The Byron Journal*

1977 Jump, John D., 'A Comparison of *Marino Faliero* and Otway's *Venice Preserv'd*'
1979 William St Clair, 'Bamming and Humming'
1987 Graham, Peter, 'The Venetian Climate of *Don Juan*'
1989 C.J. Tyerman, 'Byron's Harrow'
1991 Clubbe, John, 'The Tempest-toss'd Summer of 1816: Mary Shelley's *Frankenstein*'
1991 Giddey, Ernest, '1816: Switzerland and the Revival of the "Grand Tour"'

1996 Spence, Gordon, 'Byron's Polynesian Fantasy'
1998 Woodhouse, David, 'Churchill's Grave: A Line of Separation'
1999 Pont, Graham, 'Byron and Nathan: A Musical Collaboration'
2001 Spence, Gordon, 'Natural Law and the State in *The Two Foscari*'
2001 Casadio, Andrea, 'Two New Letters from Ravenna'
2002 Beatty, Bernard, 'And Thus the Peopled City Grieves'
2003 Gardner, John, 'Hobhouse, Cato Street and *Marino Faliero*'
2003 Shaw, Philip, 'Wordsworth and Byron'

ACKNOWLEDGEMENTS TO WRITERS AND PUBLISHERS

My apologies are due to Jerome McGann. Although I have been able to quote from his invaluable critical works, most notably in my second volume, circumstances have obliged me to change from his edition of the poems of Byron to the earlier Coleridge edition. However, I have made sure that every stanza quoted in the book is numbered for those who wish to consult the McGann edition.

Innumerable fine books on Byron, his life and his poetry have been published over the years by John Murray. All I have ever written on Byron is informed by the works of such writers as Professor Marchand and Mrs Langley Moore. In this volume I have used the Coleridge edition of the poetry and the Marchand edition of the Letters and Journals, both published by John Murray.

My thanks are due to the following for permission to quote:

Sir John Mortimer for allowing me to quote from his introduction to *Bright Darkness* by Anne Fleming, Nottingham Court Press, London 1984.

Professor Philip Collins for permission to quote from his Nottingham Byron Lecture, 1969.

Pollinger Ltd and the Earl of Lytton for brief extracts from letters to be found among the *Lovelace Papers*.

Liverpool University Press for extracts from *Byron and the Limits of Fiction*, 1968, edited by Bernard Beatty and Vincent Newey.

University of Chicago Press for quotations from *Fiery Dust: Byron's Poetical Development* by Jerome J. McGann © 1968 by the University of Chicago. All rights reserved.

Johns Hopkins University Press for extracts from Elledge, Paul, *Lord Byron at Harrow School: Speaking Out, Talking Back, Acting Up, Bowing Out*, pp. 28, 40, 44, 50. © 2000 The Johns Hopkins University Press. Reprinted with permission of the Johns Hopkins University Press.

Vail, Jeffery W., *The Literary Relationship of Lord Byron and Thomas Moore*, pp. 156, 160, 161, 162, 185. © The Johns Hopkins University Press. Reprinted with permission of The Johns Hopkins University Press.

Christensen, Jerome, *Lord Byron's Strength. Romantic Writing and Commercial Society*, pp. 28, 48, 44, 103, 153, 218, 238. © 1993 The Johns Hopkins University Press. Reprinted with permission of The Johns Hopkins University Press.

Stocking, Marion Kingston, ed., *The Clairmont Correspondence*, pp. 225, 164. © 1995 The Johns Hopkins University Press. Reprinted with permission of The Johns Hopkins University Press.

Oxford University Press for extracts from: *The Complete Poetical Works of Byron – Commentary (1980)*, edited by McGann, Jerome. By permission of Oxford University Press.

The Letters of William and Dorothy Wordsworth. The Middle Years (1970), edited by de Selincourt, Ernest de. By Permission of Oxford University Press.

The Letters of Sydney Smith (1953) by Smith, Sydney, edited by Smith, Nowell C. By permission of Oxford University Press.

The Spirit of the Age WC57 (1953) by Hazlitt, William. By permission of Oxford University Press.

The Orion Publishing Group Ltd for extracts from:

Byron the Poet by M.K. Joseph, Victor Gollancz, 1964, an imprint of the Orion Publishing Group.

Wellington: The Years of the Sword by Elizabeth Longford, Weidenfeld and Nicolson, 1969, a division of the Orion Publishing Group Ltd.

The Random House Group Ltd for extracts from:

The Making of the Poets: Byron and Shelley in Their Time by Ian Gilmour, published by Chatto and Windus. Reprinted by permission of The Random House Group Ltd and of Gillon Aitken Associates Ltd. Copyright © 2002 by Ian Gilmour.

Augusta Leigh by Michael and Melissa Bakewell, published by Chatto and Windus, 2000. Reprinted by permission of The Random House Group Ltd.

My Dearest Augusta by Peter Gunn, published by Bodley Head, 1969. Reprinted by permission of The Random House Group Ltd.

Taylor and Francis for extracts from:

Byron and Shakespeare by G. Wilson Knight, Barnes and Noble, New York, 1960, pp. 14/15, 235, 15.

A History of Western Philosophy by Bertrand Russell, Routledge, London, 2000, p. 718.

The Rowman and Littlefield Publishing Group, Lanham, Boulder, New York, Oxford for extracts from:

Byron the Erotic Liberal by Jonathan David Gross, 2001.

Vanderbilt University Press, Nashville, Tennessee, for extracts from:

Byron and the Dynamics of Metaphor by Paul Elledge, 1968.

Cambridge University Press for extracts from:

Studies in Literature by Sir Arthur Quiller-Couch, London, 1943.

Constable and Robinson for an extract from:

The Young Melbourne by Lord David Cecil, Constable, 1943.

Harvard University Press for an extract reprinted by permission of the publishers from *The Journals of Claire Clairmont*, edited by Marion Kingston Stocking, Cambridge, Mass., Harvard University Press. Copyright © 1968 by the President and Fellows of Harvard College.

BJ Batsford for extracts from:

The Creevey Papers by Thomas Creevey, edited by John Gore, 1963

The Croker Papers by J. Wilson Croker, edited by Bernard Pool, 1967

Every effort has been made to track down all holders of copyright material quoted in *Byron the Maker*. If there is anyone who has not been acknowledged here we would be pleased to hear from them so that we can rectify the omission in the forthcoming second volume.

INDEX